SOUND RECORDING

SOUND RECORDING

John Eargle

VNR **VAN NOSTRAND REINHOLD COMPANY**
NEW YORK   CINCINNATI   ATLANTA   DALLAS   SAN FRANCISCO
LONDON   TORONTO   MELBOURNE

Van Nostrand Reinhold Company Regional Offices:
New York Cincinnati Atlanta Dallas San Francisco

Van Nostrand Reinhold Company International Offices:
London Toronto Melbourne

Library of Congress Catalog Card Number: 76-4888
ISBN: 0-442-22221-1

Manufactured in the United States of America

Published by Van Nostrand Reinhold Company
450 West 33rd Street, New York. N.Y. 10001

Published simultaneously in Canada by Van Nostrand Reinhold Ltd.

15 14 13 12 11 10 9 8 7 6 5 4 3 2

Library of Congress Cataloging in Publication Data

Eargle, John.
  Sound Recording.

  Includes bibliographies and index.
  1. Sound—Recording and reproducing. I. Title.
TK7881.4.E17   621.389'32   76-4888
ISBN 0-442-22221-1

Preface

Sound recording is a fast-paced industry. In 15 years its master recording requirements have progressed from simple three- and four-track capability to complex 16- and 24-track systems. During the same period the ancillary equipment and techniques used in recording have been broadened to include advanced digital techniques, both in signal processing and in console automation.

Fifteen years ago recording was chiefly concerned with documenting musical events, and the record was ideally a substitute for the event. During the mid-sixties, however, the phonograph record market changed dramatically; classical record sales in the U.S. slipped to about 5 percent of the total as the youth-oriented pop-rock market, spawned by the Beatles, gained the largest share. Most of this "new music" was born in the recording studio, and most of its sounds had their first existence over loudspeakers.

Many of the instruments of the new art depend heavily upon electronics and signal processing, and it is no longer easy to draw a distinct line between the tools of performance and those of recording. Even the roles of producer, musician, and engineer have intermingled; it is not uncommon for a musician to take on the duties of producer and engineer. In earlier days these roles were clear and distinct, but the new music has brought them together as a common creative endeavor.

Engineers used to work their way into the recording field by long years of apprenticeship. Today, many engineers come from a music-related background, and they are often required to advance in the recording art at a quick pace. Too often, there may be a good understanding of how the tools and techniques of recording are used, but only a meager understanding of how they work. It is the author's intent to relate cause and effect wherever possible so that young engineers can be given a firm basis on which to further their own education and growth in the recording arts.

Recording institutes and seminar programs have become popular in this country, and their aim is to give young engineers practical experience with the tools and techniques of recording along with a general broadening of their knowledge in the field. Typically, these schools present courses running anywhere from four to twelve weeks; some are affiliated with degree-granting institutions and allow credit for these courses. This book is designed as a supplement to the courses offered by these institutes and will be of value as a continuing reference work for their graduates.

As the seventies have progressed, a number of universities and colleges have set up degree programs in various phases of communications and electronic media. To the extent that these courses are involved with the tools and techniques of audio production work, this book will be of great benefit.

The book is broadly divided into two sections; the first consists of chapters of a tutorial nature, while the second discusses the devices and techniques used in recording. Chapter 1 covers those fundamentals of physical acoustics with which the recording engineer should be familiar. It calls for some mathematical background and will require careful study. Wherever possible, mathematical descriptions have been paralleled by graphical examples with their inevitable intuitive appeal. The engineer or technician, commensurate with his background, will appreciate both approaches, while the liberal arts student will probably opt for the latter. Chapter 2 covers the aspects of psychoacoustics which are important in recording and reproduction of sound. Chapters 3 and 4 cover the principles of stereophonic and quadraphonic recording, respectively.

The remaining chapters deal with microphones and their characteristics, monitor loudspeakers, audio control systems, magnetic recording, signal processing, and disc recording. Here, the emphasis is on how the devices work and how they have evolved. The discussions of microphones and signal processing deal as well with numerous recording applications.

Ultimately the United States will convert to the metric system. In the meantime most professional pursuits in this country continue to use a mixture of metric and English units. It is the author's feeling that a book which is devoted to practice should be written in terms most useful and applicable by the reader. Consequently, this book will retain those units which are a part of general practice. For example, architectural measurements are expressed in English units; electrical quantities, of course, are already compatible with the metric system. It may appear contradictory to some that the gross measurements of record groove geometry (groove width and pitch) are expressed in mils and lines per inch, respectively, while considerations of stylus velocity and acceleration are given in metric units. These are the standard terms used by the industry, and it is worth noting that engineers were measuring groove widths and pitch in the days of acoustical recording, while measurements of stylus velocity and acceleration are the products of a more advanced discipline.

The author is indebted to many manufacturers in all segments of the recording industry for their contributions to this book. Thanks are particularly due to the following companies for their permission to use illustrative material: Allison Research, Altec, Ampex, Automated Processes, Audio-Technica, Bruel & Kjaer, Electro-Voice, Gotham Audio, James B. Lansing Sound, Minnesota Mining & Manufacturing, Georg Neumann, Ortofon, Quad-Eight, Shure Brothers, Victor Company of Japan, Westlake Audio, and Westrex.

JOHN EARGLE

Contents

SOUND RECORDING

1

Physical Aspects of Sound

INTRODUCTION

The dedicated recording engineer ultimately becomes his own best teacher. As a young apprentice he learns from observing experienced engineers and by associating certain solutions with certain problems. But his real growth in the art comes when he begins to grasp the fundamentals of cause and effect, when he learns how to solve new problems through analysis of their elements. At the very foundation of this growth is a knowledge of basic principles of acoustics, sound generation, and sound propagation.

Though some mathematical background is essential for a thorough understanding of this chapter, the serious student of recording technology who has a limited mathematical background should not be frightened away. We have chosen to parallel mathematical explanations with graphical ones with the hope that pictures will suffice where numbers may not. Most of the concepts are intuitively obvious to anyone who has ever listened analytically and wondered why things sound the way they do. Accordingly, we suggest that the student who may find Chapter 1 difficult at first reread its sections slowly, making extra effort to associate its discussions with his own observations of sound behavior.

CONCEPT OF VIBRATION: PERIODIC MOTION

A *sine wave* is the simplest kind of vibration; it is that natural motion of a weight as it bobs up and down on a spring or of a pendulum swinging at a moderate displacement. Its characteristic motion is shown in Figure 1-1,a, a to-and-fro motion about a reference line. The motion can also be described as the projection of a point on a circle as that point moves about the circle with uniform velocity. One cycle of the wave constitutes rotation through the complete 360 degrees of the circle, and the time required for one cycle of the wave is called its *period* (T). A related term is *frequency*, the number of periods in a given interval of time. For example, if a sine wave has a period of one-fourth second (T = .25 sec), then its frequency is $1/T$, or 4 cycles per second (Hz). (The term *Hertz* (Hz) is now universally used in place of the older cycles per second.)

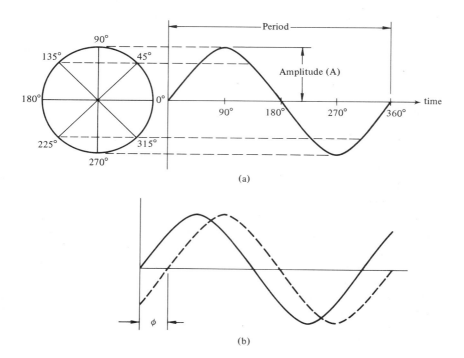

(a)

(b)

Figure 1-1. (a) Generation of a sine wave, showing amplitude and period. (b) Phase relationship between two sine waves of the same frequency.

EXAMPLE: Determine the frequency of a sine wave with a period of one-thousandth of a second.

$$\text{Frequency} = \frac{1}{T} = \frac{1}{.001} = 1000 \text{ Hz (or 1 kHz)}$$

(The term kHz, or kilohertz, means one thousand Hertz.)

Another characteristic of a sine wave is its *amplitude* (*A*), its displacement from the reference point. The displacement can be in distance, as in the case of a pendulum, or in a voltage or current if it is an electrical sine wave. The amplitude of a sound wave is customarily measured in pressure fluctuations above and below normal atmospheric pressure.

The concept of *phase* is important in describing sine waves. It refers to the relative displacement in time between sine waves of the same frequency. This is shown in Figure 1-1,b. Here, the dotted sine wave is displaced from the solid one by some distance ϕ, usually expressed in degrees, with one period of the wave representing 360 degrees.

As common as sine waves may be in electrical and mechanical engineering, they are rare in the world of sound for the reason that nearly all vibrating elements used in the generation of sound have a tendency to execute *complex* motions. If the motion is a sustained one, as in the case of a bowed string or a wind instrument, then the complex wave form can usually be expressed as an ensemble of sine waves, beginning with a *fundamental* wave and progressing upward through a set of harmonically related sine waves whose periods are related as 1, $\frac{1}{2}$, $\frac{1}{3}$, $\frac{1}{4}$, $\frac{1}{5}$, and so forth. This is shown in Figure 1-2, where four harmonically related waves are added together to produce a complex wave (Figure 1-2,c). The components of a complex wave are referred to as *harmonics*. At Figure 1-2,b and 1-2,d we have shown the frequency spectrum for each component as well as for the complex wave itself. By specifying the number of harmonics, their relative amplitudes, and phase relationships, we can generate practically any repetitive wave form.

APERIODIC MOTION: NOISE

Although we can describe as noise almost any unwanted sound, the term is usually reserved for wave forms of the kind shown in Figure 1-3,a. The wave has no period, and thus is called *aperiodic*. Just as a complex repetitive wave form can be shown to be made up of harmonically related sine waves, noise can be shown to be composed of a *continuous* band of an unbounded number of sine waves. If the array of frequencies present is as shown in Figure 1-3,b, the noise is re-

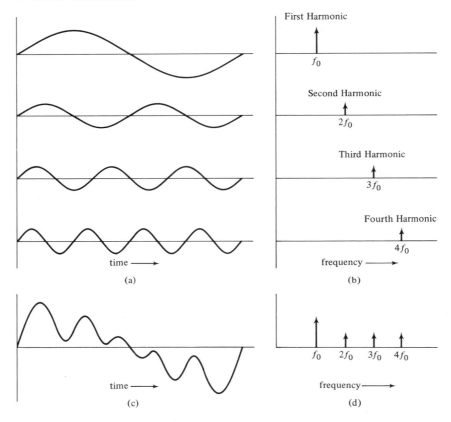

Figure 1-2. (a) Illustration of harmonically related sine waves. (b) Frequency spectra for sine waves shown in (a). (c) Generation of a complex wave by adding the sine wave components of (a). (d) Frequency spectrum for the complex wave shown in (c).

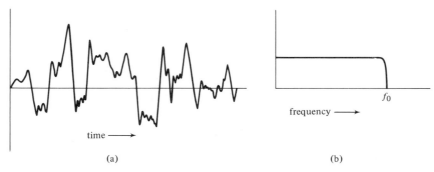

Figure 1-3. Wave form for a typical "white noise" signal (a) and its corresponding frequency spectrum (b).

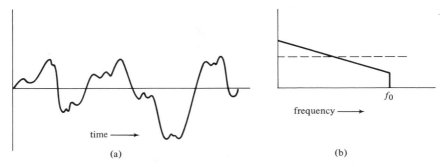

Figure 1-4. Wave form for a typical "pink noise" signal (a) and its corresponding frequency spectrum (b).

ferred to as "white noise" (similar to the interstation noise heard on FM sets). It is band-limited, containing frequency components up to some arbitrary f_0. The term white noise is by way of analogy with white light, which contains all components in the visible range equally. *Pink noise*, again by analogy with light, has less energy at higher frequencies; for each doubling of frequency, the energy present is halved. The waveform shown in Figure 1-4,a shows noticeably less high-frequency energy than the white noise waveform of Figure 1-3,a, and the corresponding frequency spectrum at Figure 1-3,b shows the characteristic roll-off at high frequencies.

White noise contains equal energy per cycle, or equal energy for each frequency present; pink noise contains equal energy per octave (or portion of an octave) and is useful, as we shall see in a later chapter, as a test signal for equalizing loudspeakers for desired response contours.

SOUND TRANSMISSION THROUGH AIR

If a vibrating object or surface is suitably large, then its vibrations impart energy to the air around it, and *sound* is produced. Generally, we can define sound as variations in pressure above and below the normal pressure of the atmosphere. The frequency range of *audible* sound is nominally 20 Hz to 20 kHz, and the velocity of sound through air is typically about 1130 feet per second. At elevated temperatures, the speed is greater, while at lower temperatures it is slower. Only in dealing with sound transmission over great distances out-of-doors will we ever be concerned with this velocity dependence on temperature. Figure 1-5 shows the range of frequencies produced by a variety of sound sources.

Let us assume a sound source of a frequency of 1130 Hz. At a velocity of 1130 feet per second, the period of the waveform begins anew every foot, and we now define wavelength as the distance between the beginning of successive

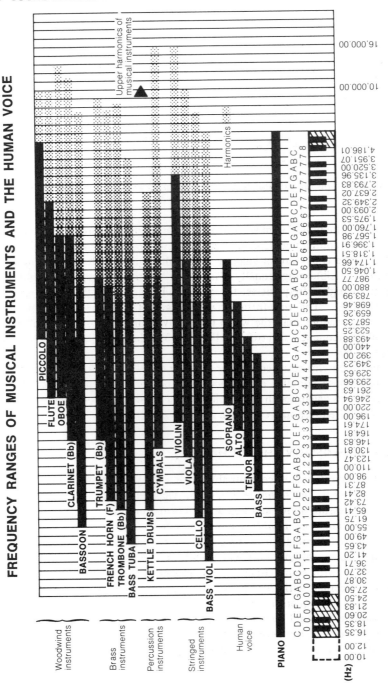

Figure 1-5. Range of frequencies for various sources of sound.

periods. In simple terms:

$$\text{Wavelength } (\lambda) = \frac{\text{speed of sound}}{\text{frequency}}$$

The Greek letter lambda, λ, is universally used to represent wavelength.

EXAMPLES: Determine the wavelength of a 10-kHz signal:

$$\lambda = \frac{1130}{10,000} = .113 \text{ feet, or about } 1\tfrac{1}{3}''$$

Determine the wavelength of a 50-Hz signal:

$$\lambda = \frac{1130}{50} = 22.6 \text{ feet}$$

Obviously, given any two of the three quantities, wave length (λ), frequency (f), or velocity (v), we can solve for the third:

$$\lambda = \frac{v}{f}, f = \frac{v}{\lambda}, \text{ and } v = f\lambda$$

The precise nature of radiation of sound through air or any other medium is extremely complex, and any further discussion of it would surely call for more mathematics than we have in mind for this book. However, two important observations on sound radiation can be made:

Efficient low-frequency radiation requires large radiators. A string bass and a piccolo are both the right size for their respective jobs.

Directional radiation requires large radiators. Although a string bass can produce fairly low frequencies, it radiates them in many directions. By contrast, a large array of low-frequency loudspeakers used at a rock concert for "aiming" sound in a given direction might have dimensions approaching that of the radiated wavelength itself.

THE DECIBEL

Fundamentally, the *Bel* is defined as the common logarithm* of a power ratio:

$$\text{Bel} = \log \frac{P_1}{P_0}$$

Let us assign a value of 1 watt for P_0 and 2 watts for P_1. Then we have:

$$\text{Bel} = \log \frac{2}{1} = .3$$

*See Appendix I.

Thus, the *ratio* of 2 watts to 1 watt is said to be .3 bel. More conveniently, we use the unit *decibel* (dB), which is equal to one-tenth of a Bel. Our 2-to-1 watt power ratio is then 3 decibels. In fact, any 2-to-1 power ratio is a 3 dB ratio, 20-to-10 watts, 60-to-30, 6000-to-3000, and so forth. We can state a ratio either of two ways: 1 watt is 3 dB *less* than 2 watts, or 2 watts is 3 dB *greater* than 1 watt.

Extending the notion, we refer to a 4-to-1 power ratio as 6 dB; 1-to-2 represents 3 dB, and 2-to-4 another 3 dB, making a total of 6.

Let us express a 10-to-1 power ratio in dB:

$$dB = 10 \log \left(\frac{10 \text{ watts}}{1 \text{ watt}} \right) = 10 \times 1 = 10 \text{ dB}$$

Any 10-to-1 power ratio is a 10 dB ratio: 50-to-5, 1-to-0.1, and so forth. Figure 1-6 presents a useful nomograph for determining by inspection the value of power ratios in dB. Simply locate the two levels and read the number of dB between them.

dB ABOVE AND BELOW A ONE WATT REFERENCE LEVEL

POWER IN WATTS

Figure 1-6. Nomograph for determining power ratios directly in dB.

EXAMPLE: Find the ratio in dB between 20 and 500 watts:
Above 20 watts read 13; above 500 watts read 27.

$$27 - 13 = 14 \text{ dB}$$

The chief value of decibel notation is that it allows us to deal with a large range of physical values with a relatively small range of numbers.

The watt is the unit of power, the rate at which work is done or energy expended. Electrically, power is the product of the voltage across a load and the current flowing through it:

Power (W) = Voltage (E) × Current (I)

In Figure 1-7,a we show a 1-volt battery connected in series with a load resistance of 1 ohm. One volt across a resistance of 1 ohm results in a current of 1 ampere, and the resulting power is 1 watt. In Figure 1-7,b the voltage

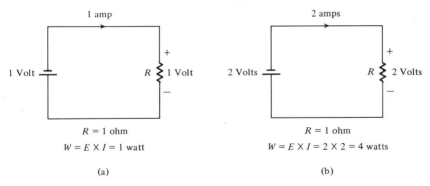

Figure 1-7. Power relationships in a simple DC circuit.

source has been increased to 2 volts, and by Ohm's law, the current has increased to 2 amperes:

$$\text{Ohm's Law: } I = \frac{E}{R} = \frac{2 \text{ volts}}{1 \text{ ohm}} = 2 \text{ amperes}$$

Accordingly, the power is:

$$W = E \times I = 2 \times 2 = 4 \text{ watts}$$

Assuming that we are dealing with a fixed load resistance, we can express power ratios in dB in terms of voltage or current ratios. Since increasing the voltage across a load by any degree causes the same degree of current increase, we can say that the power dissipated in the load is proportional to the square of the voltage or current. Stated another way:

$$W = \frac{E^2}{R} = I^2 R$$

Thus, by the elementary properties of logarithms (see Appendix I), the power ratio in dB is expressed:

$$dB = 20 \log \frac{E_1}{E_0} = 20 \log \frac{I_1}{I_0}$$

A 2-to-1 voltage or current ratio represents a 6-dB power ratio:

$$dB = 20 \log \frac{2}{1} = 20 \times .3 = 6 \text{ dB}$$

In a similar manner, a 10-to-1 voltage or current ratio is a 20-dB power ratio:

$$dB = 20 \log \frac{10}{1} = 20 \times 1 = 20 \text{ dB}$$

Figure 1-8. Nomograph for determining voltage or current ratios directly in dB.

A convenient nomograph which converts voltage or current ratios to power ratios in dB is given in Figure 1-8. It is used in the same manner as the nomograph of Figure 1-6. Only one restriction holds: the two voltage or current readings must relate to a fixed load.

EXAMPLE: Find the ratio in dB between 4 volts and 80 volts:
Above 4 volts read 12 dB; above 80 volts read 38 dB.

$$38 - 12 = 26 \text{ dB}$$

Sound pressure is analogous to voltage, and acoustical energy levels are proportional to the square of the sound pressure. Thus:

$$\text{Power ratio (dB)} = 20 \log \frac{P_1}{P_0}$$

The standard reference P_0, for sound pressure measurements is established as the pressure of .0002 dynes per square centimeter (dynes/cm^2), and most values of sound pressure are stated in dB above that value. The reference value is indeed quite small, and it is very close to the threshold of audibility in the 1-kHz to 3-kHz range for persons with normal hearing. This will be discussed in more detail in the chapter on psychoacoustics. A value of sound pressure stated in dB above the reference level is usually indicated as dB-SPL. Since zero is .0002 dynes/cm^2, a pressure level of .002 dynes/cm^2 is equivalent to 20 dB-SPL; a pressure of .02 dynes/cm^2 is equivalent to 40 dB-SPL, and so forth. Figure 1-9 shows values, both in pressure and in dB-SPL, for a variety of common sounds and noises.

THE MEASUREMENT OF SOUND PRESSURE

The standard tool for the measurement of sound pressure levels is the Sound Level Meter (SLM), a device which reads directly in dB-SPL. The desired characteristics of this instrument have been established by the American National Standards Institute, and any device bearing the designation of sound level meter is expected to conform to those standards. A typical sound level meter is shown in Figure 1-10.

Among the characteristics specified for an SLM are the ballistics, or dynamic behavior, of its meter movement, the accuracy of its weighting networks, and its absolute calibration accuracy. Standard SLM's have both fast and slow meter characteristics; the fast response is more appropriate for impulsive-type noise readings, while the slow response is more appropriate for determining more sustained noise or music levels.

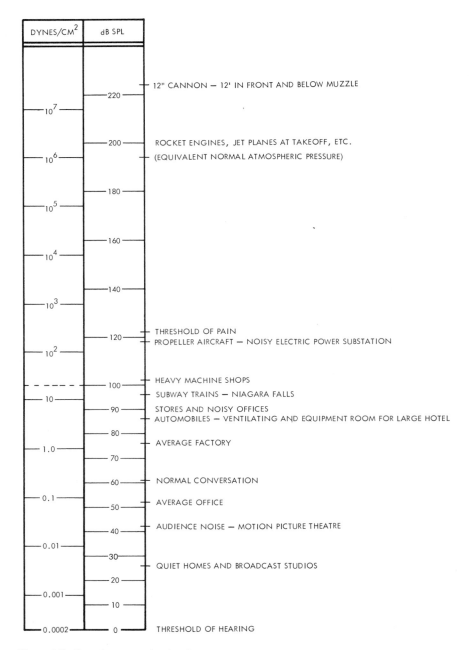

Figure 1-9. Sound pressure levels of common sound sources. Persons with normal hearing can detect sound over a range of 120 dB without enduring pain or physical damage; this is a million-to-one energy range. Although a 3-dB change represents a doubling of acoustical energy, estimates of relative loudness by most listeners indicate that an increase of 6 to 10 dB results in a sound which is "twice as loud."

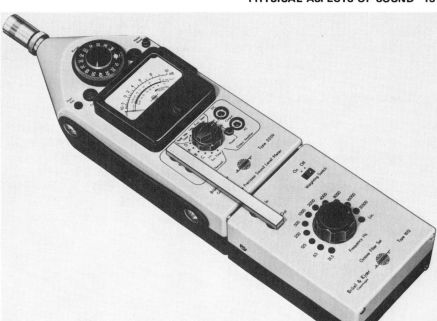

Figure 1-10. Illustration of a typical high-quality sound level meter. (*Courtesy B & K Instruments*)

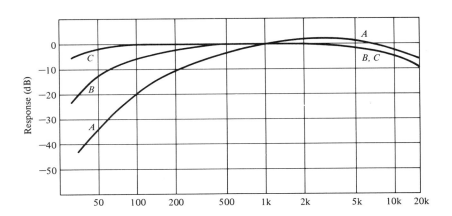

Figure 1-11. Weighting curves for a sound level meter.

Standard curves for the three weighting networks are shown in Figure 1-11. The weighting networks are important in determining the annoyance level of noise, and their characteristics will be dealt with in a later chapter.

SUMMING POWER LEVELS IN dB

If sound power levels of 1 watt and 2 watts are added together, then the resultant power level is 3 watts. However, if power levels are expressed in dB above some reference point, we cannot simply add those levels in dB to get the resultant level. Assume that two sound sources both produce SPL's of 97 dB. Then together, because both power levels are equal, we would expect an increase of *3 dB*. The sum is 97 + 3 = 100 dB; not 97 + 97 = 194 dB.

Figure 1-12 illustrates a graphical method for determining the resultant power level when two powers expressed in dB are added together.

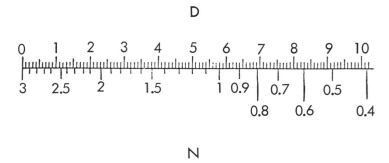

Figure 1-12. Nomograph for adding power levels expressed in dB. Summing sound level output of two sound sources where *D* is their output difference in dB-SPL, *N* is added to the higher level to derive total level.

EXAMPLE: Find the resultant SPL when SPL's of 90 and 96 are added together:
D = 96 − 90 = 6. Below 6 read 1.
Therefore: resultant level = 96 + 1 = 97 dB-SPL.

It is easy to see that if two levels differ by more than about 10 dB, their sum will be insignificant compared to the larger value alone. This is in accord with our normal observation of sound. A level of 75 dB-SPL, the level of normal speech at a distance of about 4 feet, will be nearly completely masked by a noise level of, say, 97 dB-SPL.

THE ATTENUATION OF SOUND OUTDOORS—INVERSE SQUARE LAW

If there are no obstructions near a sound source located outdoors, then the attenuation of sound we observe as we move away from the source can be described fairly simply. In Figure 1-13 we have constructed a number of spheres located at radii of 4, 8, and 16 feet around a sound source. Let us assume that the

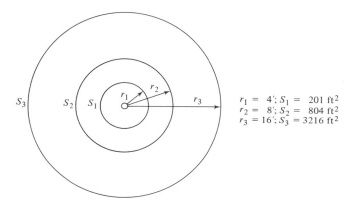

$$r_1 = 4'; S_1 = 201 \text{ ft}^2$$
$$r_2 = 8'; S_2 = 804 \text{ ft}^2$$
$$r_3 = 16'; S_3 = 3216 \text{ ft}^2$$

Figure 1-13. Sound behavior in a free field.

source produces a constant sound power level, say, 1 acoustical watt. Then, at a distance of 4 feet we have a power level of 1 watt passing through a sphere whose area is $4\pi(4)^2$, or 201 square feet. At twice this distance, 8 feet, we observe the same power of 1 watt passing through an area of $4\pi(8)^2$, or 804 square feet. Now, since the area of the sphere with radius 8 feet is four times that of the sphere with 4-foot radius, it follows that the power passing through 1 square foot at a distance of 8 feet will be only *one-fourth* that passing through 1 square foot at 4 feet. Thus, the sound pressure level at 8 feet will be 6 dB *lower* than at 4 feet. Moving on to a distance of 16 feet, the area is $4\pi(16)^2$, or 3216 square feet, and this is four times the area of the sphere with 8-foot radius. Again, the SPL is observed to be 6 dB lower at 16 feet than at 8 feet.

All of this discussion is related to experience; we have all observed that as we walk away from a sound source outdoors the sound pressure level falls off quickly at first, and then more slowly as we get farther away. Each time we double our distance from the source, the SPL drops about 6 dB, and this relationship is called *inverse square law*. Its equation is:

$$\text{Loss in dB} = 10 \log \left[\frac{r_1}{r_2}\right]^2$$

Figure 1-14. Nomograph for determining inverse square law relationship directly in dB.

This equation gives the relative loss in SPL as measured between any two values of r.

EXAMPLE: What is the inverse square loss observed between distances of 10 and 100 feet from a sound source?

Let r_1 be 10 feet and r_2 100 feet; then:

$$\text{Loss in SPL} = 10 \log \left[\frac{10}{100}\right]^2 = -20 \text{ dB}$$

As was also the case with dB measurements of electrical quantities earlier, we can express the equation as a simple nomograph (Figure 1-14).

EXAMPLE: Using the nomograph of Figure 1-14, find the attenuation of sound due to inverse square law between 10 feet and 100 feet:

Above 10 feet read -20 dB; above 100 feet read -40 dB.

Then, -40 - (-20) = -20 dB.

The sound field which exists out-of-doors is often called a *free field*, one which is substantially free of objects large enough to obstruct or reflect sound in any substantial way. Inverse square law generally holds, and there are two very simple rules to remember: When doubling (or halving) the distance away from a sound souce in a free field, the SPL decreases (or increases) by 6 dB. When increasing (or decreasing) the distance by a factor of 10, the SPL decreases (or increases) by 20 dB.

As a further observation of inverse square law, Figure 1-15 shows values of SPL measured at various distances from a speaker located on the stage of an open-air theater. Note that the measured SPL's only approximate inverse square law; they are usually within ±2 dB of the theoretical values, because of the presence of many nearby reflecting and absorbing surfaces.

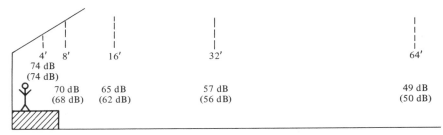

Figure 1-15. Departure from inverse square law observed in practice. Measured values of speech peaks are given in dB-SPL. Calculated values are indicated in parentheses.

DIFFRACTION AND REFRACTION OF SOUND

The reflection and absorption of sound are relatively easy to understand. Diffraction and refraction are somewhat more complex, and we shall only describe these phenomena in a very general way. In a free field, sound diffracts, or "bends around," large obstacles, as is shown in Figure 1-16. Thus, sound goes around corners and tends to spread out evenly even when it passes through a

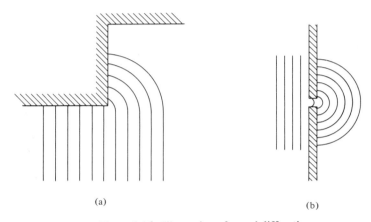

(a)   (b)

Figure 1-16. Illustration of sound diffraction.

narrow opening. Generally, longer wavelengths (lower frequencies) diffract more noticeably than shorter ones (higher frequencies).

Sound refracts, or changes direction, as it passes between zones of differing temperatures. The effect is usually noticed out-of-doors and is as shown in Figure 1-17.

Out-of-doors, wind often has an effect on sound propagation similar to differences in temperature. The speed of sound is equal to its velocity in still air *plus* the velocity of wind in a given direction. Moderate winds will have little

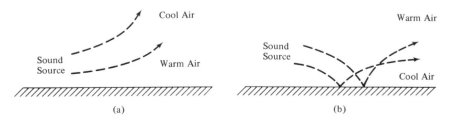

(a)   (b)

Figure 1-17. Illustration of sound refraction due to temperature gradients.

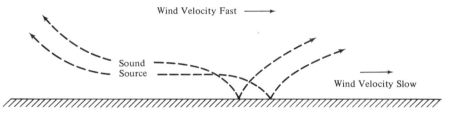

Figure 1-18. Effect of wind upon sound propagation.

effect, but strong winds can, over large distances, affect the distribution of sound. This effect is shown in Figure 1-18.

DIRECTIVITY OF SOUND SOURCES AND RECEIVERS

So far, we have assumed that our sound sources radiated uniformly in all directions. Normally this is not the case; various musical instruments have their characteristic radiation patterns, and loudspeakers as well as microphones are usually designed to have precise directional characteristics.

Directivity is of concern in many areas. For example, in broadcasting, a transmitter located on a coastline would be designed to direct its signal landward insofar as possible and not waste energy toward the ocean. It would also be wasteful to radiate energy skyward, at least as far as local reception is concerned, and antennas are carefully designed not to do this. Imagine illuminating a football stadium with lamps minus their reflectors; more than half the light energy would be wasted and the economic toll intolerable.

So it is with sound. The high-level reinforcement of an outdoor rock concert requires a careful choice of radiating devices so that sound levels are maximized in the audience area and minimized elsewhere. A recording engineer chooses microphones for much the same reasons *in reverse*; the aim is to *pick up* sound in a preferred direction rather than from all directions equally.

If a device radiates energy equally in all directions, its directivity factor (Q) is said to be unity. As a device becomes more directional its Q *increases*. Mathematically, Q is defined as the ratio of energy measured along a given axis at a fixed distance from a radiator to the energy level which would be measured at the same distance if the energy were being radiated omnidirectionally. The symbol R_θ is also used for directivity factor.

The determination of the Q of a loudspeaker is a rather complicated mathematical function, and it is normally based upon *polar response graphs* such as are shown in Figure 1-19. A polar response graph is a measure of the output of a radiator, as a function of direction, with a constant signal input. The measure-

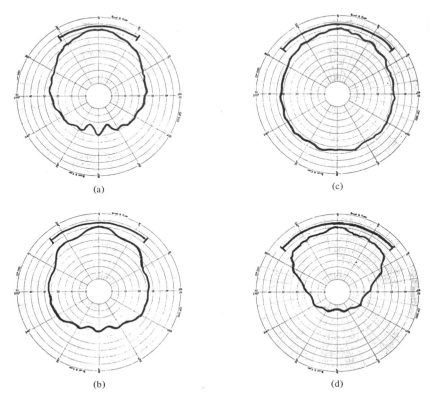

Figure 1-19. Typical polar response curves for loudspeakers. The factor Q and the effective coverage angle are not directly related. Polar responses shown at (a) and (b) both have $Q = 11$, but their effective coverage angles are respectively 68° and 85°. Polar responses shown at (c) and (d) both have coverage angles of 100°, but their Q's are, respectively, 4.8 and 11.4.

ments are normally made out-of-doors or in an *anechoic* chamber, a room substantially free of reflections.

The device to be measured is placed on a turntable, and a microphone is fixed some distance away from it. The loudspeaker is energized with a constant signal, normally a narrow band of noise, and the output of the microphone is plotted on a polar graph. The zero-degree reference point on a polar graph is usually taken in the direction of maximum output, and the Q calculations are generally made along that same major axis.

Microphones usually have well-defined polar response patterns, and three ideal types are shown in Figure 1-20. In a later chapter, the directional characteristics of microphones will be discussed in greater detail.

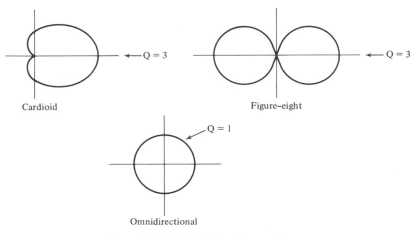

Figure 1-20. Typical microphone patterns.

Figure 1-21 lists the typical values of Q for a variety of sound sources. Note that certain types of sectoral horn loudspeakers and arrays exhibit fairly high values of Q. The factor Q is an important factor in sound reproduction and sound reinforcement, as we shall see later; but in many cases an estimate of its value is as good as a precise measurement.

Source	Directivity Factor (Q)
Talker	2.5
Coaxial Loudspeaker (in a flat baffle)	5
Cone Woofers	4–5
Multicelular Horns	5–15
Sectoral Horns	9–10
Stacked Horn Arrays	10–25

Figure 1-21. Typical values of Q for some common sources of sound.

THE NEAR AND FAR SOUND FIELDS

Earlier, we discussed inverse square law and stated that each time we halved our distance from a source in a free field the SPL increased 6 dB. If we are sufficiently far away from a source, then this is indeed the case; but it is intuitively clear that we cannot continue the process *ad infinitum*. Actually, as we move within a certain distance of a radiator, significant departures from inverse square law are observed. Figure 1-22 illustrates this for a 12-inch loudspeaker. Note

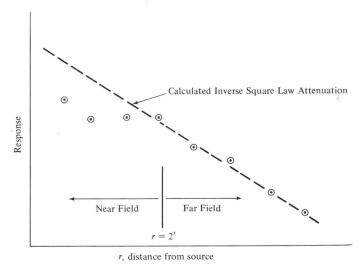

Figure 1-22. Illustration of near field and far field phenomena.

that when we move within a distance on the order of the dimensions of the radiator itself, the departure from inverse square law becomes evident. The *near field* is that part of the free field where inverse square law does not hold, and the *far field* is that part beyond it where inverse square law does hold.

Normally, we do not listen to loudspeakers at such close range as to be in their near field. However, microphones are very often used in their near fields, and this accounts in part for the rise in bass response we usually observe when microphones are placed close to a sound source.

THE ATTENUATION OF SOUND INDOORS

What happens to sound in a large room is indeed a complex thing, and we need to make a number of simplifying assumptions if we are to acquire an intuitive grasp of it. Let us assume that an impulsive sound is generated on the stage of an auditorium and that we are going to monitor what happens at some location in the audience area. What we would perceive might look something like Figure 1-23. The sound is generated at $t =$ zero and is perceived at some later time as a direct component. A bit later, single and multiple reflections begin to arrive at the monitoring position, few at first, but becoming more dense with time. After some time, these many echoes become so dense that they are perceived as a *continuous decay* of sound called *reverberation*. *Reverberation time* (T) is arbitrarily determined to be the length of time it takes for a sound to decay 60 dB after a source has been turned off. Subjectively, a room is said to be

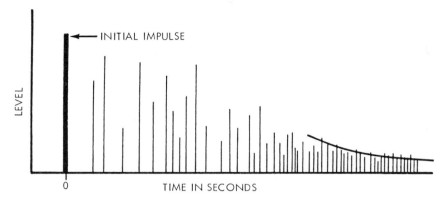

Figure 1-23. Ensemble of reflections of an impulsive sound indoors.

"live" if its T is long in relation to its volume, or "dead" if it is short in relation to its volume. Equations for T were arrived at empirically at first and were later derived mathematically.

If a room is fairly live, then its T is given fairly accurately by:

$$T = \frac{.05V}{S\bar{\alpha}}, \qquad \text{In metric units:} \quad T = \frac{.16V}{S\bar{\alpha}}.$$

where

V = Volume (ft^3),
S = Surface area (ft^2),
and $\bar{\alpha}$ = Average absorption coefficient.

Average absorption coefficient ($\bar{\alpha}$) is a new term; but let us first define what we mean by absorption coefficient.

The absorption coefficient (α) of a material determines how much sound is absorbed when sound strikes it. If E represents the energy in a sound wave striking a material with an absorption coefficient of α_1, then $E\alpha_1$ will be absorbed and $E(1 - \alpha_1)$ will be reflected. This is shown in Figure 1-24.

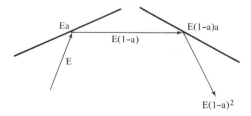

Figure 1-24. Illustration of losses of sound energy at successive reflections.

Perhaps now we can appreciate the complexity and apparent randomness of Figure 1-23. Sound impulses strike surfaces at various distances and with various values of α, and the early reflections clearly show this. Later, only after all surfaces have been brought into play, does an average absorption coefficient become apparent.

The calculation of $\bar{\alpha}$ is a tedious job, but it is a necessary calculation during the design phase of an auditorium. Mathematically it is given by:

$$\bar{\alpha} = \frac{S_1\alpha_1 + S_2\alpha_2 + \cdots + S_n\alpha_n}{S_1 + S_2 + \cdots + S_n}$$

where $S_{(1-n)}$ represent the areas of the individual boundary materials and $\alpha_{(1-n)}$ represent respectively their absorption coefficients. Typical values of α for common materials are given in Appendix II.

For more detailed calculations, we must include also the effects of atmospheric absorption as well as the effects of occupants in a room. These further considerations are thoroughly covered in references given in the bibliography.

Figure 1-25 gives recommended values of T as a function of volume for various kinds of rooms. Note that, in general, the larger the room, the larger the desired T. The reasons for this have to do largely with certain psychoacoustical observations which we will discuss in detail in a later chapter.

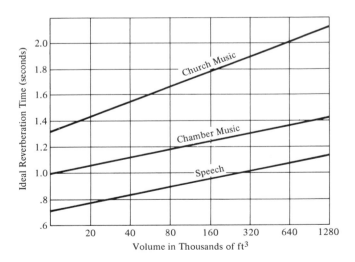

Figure 1-25. Optimum values of reverberation time vs. volume for several types of rooms.

THE REVERBERANT FIELD

As we have shown, the generation of reverberation involves an ensemble of reflections throughout a room, and this tends to establish a fairly uniform energy density in the room. We have all had the experience of listening to a sound source in a highly reverberant enclosure, perhaps a church or large public building. As we move away from the sound source, the attenuation seems to follow inverse square law at first, but then quickly reaches a level which remains fairly constant. We have shown this in Figure 1-26. Note that at the points where

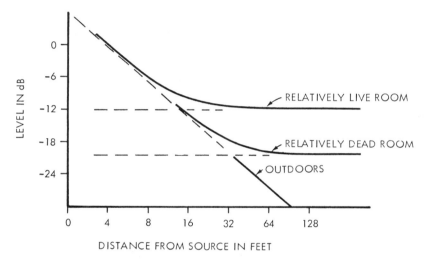

Figure 1-26. Illustration of sound attenuation indoors.

direct and reverberant fields are equal, the resultant sound pressure is 3 dB higher than either field, representing the summation of equal energy levels. The distance where the two fields are equal is referred to as *critical distance* (D_c), and it is a useful concept in sound reinforcement work. The equation which describes the indoor attenuation curve is:

$$\text{Loss in dB } (r) = 10 \log \left[\frac{Q}{4\pi r^2} + \frac{4}{R} \right]$$

The quantity R is known as *room constant* and is given by:

$$R = \frac{S\bar{\alpha}}{1 - \bar{\alpha}},$$

where S is the total boundary area and $\bar{\alpha}$ the average absorption coefficient. The term Q is the directivity factor for the radiator for the direction of observation, and r is the distance from the radiator.

The equation must be solved for two values of r, and it gives the difference in SPL between those two distances. The first term in the brackets is the inverse square law component, while the second term is the constant reverberant field component.

If we equate the two bracketed terms in the equation, we can solve for D_c, the distance at which the direct and reverberant fields are equal:

$$D_c = .14\sqrt{QR}$$

Note from Figure 1-26 that the attenuation of sound beyond D_c is minimal; it can only decrease an additional 3 dB.

The equation for attenuation with distance indoors is a rather cumbersome one to solve directly, and we have worked out a number of graphical solutions for it as shown in Figure 1-27. We have assumed a Q value of 5 for a sound source, typical for a normal loudspeaker array used for sound reinforcement.

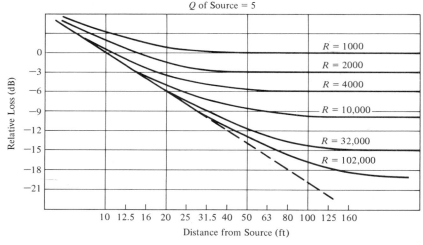

Figure 1-27. Indoor attenuation curves for a radiator with $Q = 5$ as a function of room constant.

A general estimate of room constant can be determined from the graph of Figure 1-28. Locate the reverberation time along the vertical axis and the room volume along the horizontal axis. They will intersect at one of the diagonal lines, indicating the approximate value of R. This graph is based upon what

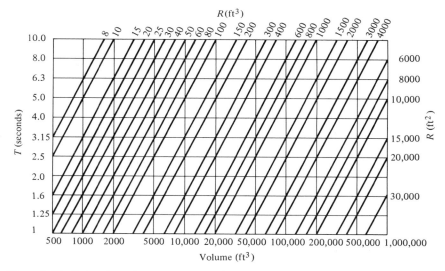

Figure 1-28. Estimation of room constant when volume and reverberation time are known.

might be called "normal" rooms, those whose length, width, and height dimensions do not exceed ratios of about 1.6.

EXAMPLE: In an auditorium with a volume of 500,000 cubic feet and a reverberation time of 2.5 seconds, find the sound attenuation between the distances of 15 feet and 60 feet along the major axis of a loudspeaker array with a directivity factor of 5.

ANSWER: Referring to Figure 1-28, locate the volume of 500,000 cubic feet along the bottom of the graph; then move upward until the horizontal line corresponding to 2.5 seconds of reverberation time is intersected. Note that this intersection takes place at the diagonal line representing a room constant of about 10,000 ft^2. Now, locate the curve in Figure 1-27 representing a room constant of 10,000 ft^2 and read directly the difference in dB between 15 and 60 feet. For 15 feet read −3 dB and for 60 feet read about −10 dB.

Then, 10 − 3 = 7 dB attenuation from 15 feet to 60 feet.

EXAMPLE: Using the graph of Figure 1-29, determine the value of D_c, that distance where the direct and reverberant sound fields are equal.

ANSWER: 31.5 feet.

The equations we have presented describing the attenuation of sound indoors are based upon theoretical models which assumed a highly diffuse reverberant

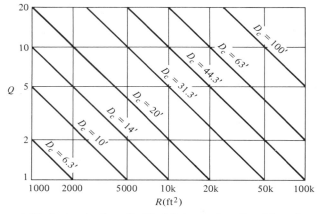

Figure 1-29. Determination of critical distance when Q and R are known.

sound field. They are fairly accurate in large reverberant churches and audi-
toriums, but tend to give erroneous results in small rooms or those with low
ceilings in relation to length and breadth. While the deviation from the theoretical curve may be only about ±2 dB in a large reverberant room, the errors noted
in rooms whose length and width are large with respect to ceiling height can be
significant, as shown in Figure 1-30.

Another significant departure from the equations presented earlier is the
variation in reverberant field level as a function of absorption coefficient of the
first reflecting surface. Workers in the field of sound reinforcement have long
observed that aiming directional loudspeakers at absorptive audience areas

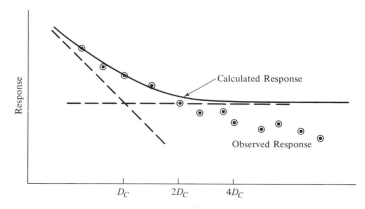

Figure 1-30. Departure from normal indoor attenuation curve often observed in large rooms
with low ceilings.

($\alpha = .6$ or greater) produced less reverberant energy in the room and gave values of D_c in excess of those given by the standard equation. Augspurger (1) has suggested that the equation for room constant be altered to take into account the absorption coefficient of the first reflective surface:

$$R' = \frac{S\bar{\alpha}}{1 - \alpha_1}$$

He suggests using R' instead of the more usual R. In this equation, $\bar{\alpha}$ is the average absorption coefficient and α_1 is the absorption coefficient of the first reflective surface. Figure 1-31 shows how sound attenuation can be influenced under these conditions.

THE NORRIS-EYRING REVERBERATION TIME EQUATION

The reverberation time equation presented earlier was arrived at empirically many years ago by Wallace Sabine, and it is quite accurate in most highly reverberant spaces. Another equation, which is due to Norris and Eyring, was arrived at mathematically and gives more accurate results than Sabine's equation in less reverberant rooms. It does assume, however, that diffuse conditions exist.

$$T = \frac{.05\,V}{-S \ln (1 - \bar{\alpha})} \qquad \text{In metric units:} \quad T = \frac{.16V}{-S \ln (1 - \bar{\alpha})}$$

THE BEHAVIOR OF SOUND IN SMALL ROOMS

It was easy to generalize about sound in large rooms and arrive at some fairly simple equations describing its statistical behavior. We assumed that, because of the great number of reflections, a generally diffuse condition existed. We further assumed that only the average absorption coefficient determined the behavior of sound as a function of frequency. In small rooms no such assumptions can be made; the dimensions of the room itself determine the room's behavior as a function of frequency.

All rooms, large or small, have *normal modes*, frequencies at which the room resonates; they are the room's "preferred" frequencies. For all but the simplest enclosures, calculation of normal modes is difficult. For a rectangular enclosure the equation determining normal modes is:

$$f = \frac{c}{2} \sqrt{\left(\frac{n_l}{l}\right)^2 + \left(\frac{n_w}{w}\right)^2 + \left(\frac{n_h}{h}\right)^2}$$

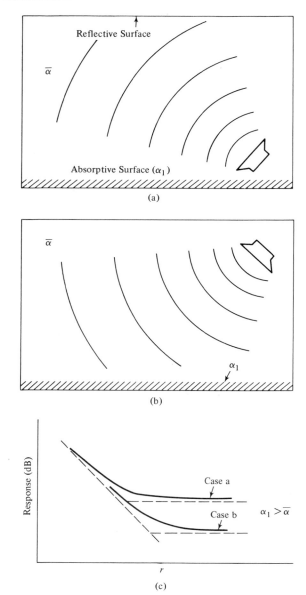

Figure 1-31. Attenuation of sound indoors as a function of absorption coefficient of the first reflective surface.

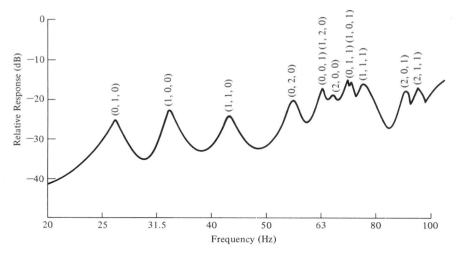

Figure 1-32. Illustration of normal modes in response of a room $17' \times 21' \times 9'$.

where c is the speed of sound in air, l, w, and h are the length, width, and height of the room, respectively, and n_l, n_w, and n_h are a set of integers (values $0, 1, 2, 3, \ldots$) taken in all possible combinations. We show some of these solutions for a typical room of dimensions $17' \times 21' \times 9'$ in Figure 1-32.

Here, we have shown for each of the lower modes the values of n_l, n_w, and n_h in parentheses. Note that beyond a frequency of 80–100 Hz the modes get closer together. Between 100 and 250 Hz the mode structure becomes increasingly dense, and beyond 250 Hz, not shown in this graph, the modes effectively overlap, resulting in a continuum of response. We can say that the room is a "small" one below a frequency of 250 Hz and a "large" one above that frequency.

In a typical control room with the largest dimension not exceeding 20 feet, the lowest normal mode would be about 28 Hz, and the overall room response would tend to be characterized by peaks and dips up to a frequency about 10 times that of the lowest mode. As stated before, the room would be small below that frequency and large above.

Consider a large rectangular church of dimensions $100' \times 75' \times 60'$. The lowest normal mode would be 5.5 Hz, well below the lower limit of audibility. At 10 times that frequency the normal modes would effectively overlap, and the room could be said to be a large one over the bulk of the audible frequency range.

Generally, the lowest normal mode of a room can be estimated by dividing 565 by the largest rectangular room dimension.

EXAMPLE: Find the lowest normal mode of a room $15' \times 25' \times 40'$:

$$565/40 = 14 \text{ Hz}$$

The effects of peaks and dips that are due to normal modes will be more pronounced in a room which has little acoustical absorption than in one which has a good deal of absorption. This fact explains why the most successful small control rooms and mix-down rooms are those which are liberally provided with low-frequency absorption. This consideration is often overlooked when existing premises are converted for critical listening. Too often, only high-frequency absorption is applied with little attention to the low-frequency problem. These considerations will be discussed in detail in a later chapter.

The existence of widely spaced normal modes at low frequencies in small rooms largely explains the differences observed in low-frequency response when the same recording is played in rooms of similar size but of different dimensions. Even at a given normal mode, the sound pressure will vary depending on the location in the room. Pressure maximums will be greater at room boundaries and generally less toward the middle of the room.

BIBLIOGRAPHY

1. G. Augspurger, "More Accurate Calculation of the Room Constant," *J. Audio Eng. Soc.*, vol. 23, no. 5 (1975).
2. L. Beranek, *Acoustics* (McGraw-Hill, New York, 1950).
3. V. Knudsen and C. Harris, *Acoustical Designing in Architecture* (John Wiley & Sons, New York, 1950).
4. H. Tremaine, *Audio Cyclopedia* (Howard W. Sams, Indianapolis, 1969).

2

Psychoacoustics

INTRODUCTION

The ear is a remarkable organ; people with normal hearing can perceive sound over a range of about 120 dB. At the lower limit, the threshold of hearing, the ear can detect air particle velocities of about 8×10^{-7} inches per second. At the upper limit, the threshold of feeling, the ear responds to air particle velocities on the order of 0.8 inches per second.

The ear and brain react to sound in a manner quite different from a simple microphone-amplifier-meter combination. The response of a typical measuring system is said to be *linear;* equal increments in input result in corresponding increments of output. A graph relating input and output will be a straight line, hence, linear. Though the input to the ear and brain combination is the same as that of the microphone-amplifier-meter combination, the "output" is quite different; it is essentially a mental judgment or comparison of acoustical events as influenced by:

1. The immediate past physical history of the listener.
2. The listener's prior training and acclimation.
3. Certain biases unique to the listener.

Because there is no simple way of relating a change in input, or stimulus, with the corresponding change in the listener's judgment, we refer to hearing as a *nonlinear* phenomenon.

Psychoacoustics is the interdisciplinary study which relates physical acoustical stimulus to psychological judgment. It is concerned with the subjective aspects of how we hear, among them: loudness, pitch, timbre (tone quality), annoyance levels of noise, and sound image localization. In this chapter we shall limit our study to loudness considerations, image localization and broadening phenomena, and those aspects of timbre that define source-to-listener distances in a reverberant field. These factors are the bases of many techniques used in sound recording which will be discussed in later chapters.

LOUDNESS

To an average listener, a 1-kHz tone at 100 dB-SPL is subjectively about as loud as a 100-Hz tone of the same level. However, a 1-kHz tone at 40 dB-SPL will be about 20 dB louder to an average listener than a 100-Hz tone of the same level. This seeming paradox points up all the more the essential nonlinearity of human hearing. No two people hear exactly the same way, and although an average listener might hear a 20-dB difference between 100 Hz and 1 kHz at a level of 40 dB-SPL, there will be some listeners who detect only a 10-dB difference, and very likely others who will hear a 25- or 30-dB difference.

Some years ago, Fletcher and Munson established average "equal loudness contours," based upon a study of a large group of people with normal hearing; those contours are shown in Fig. 2-1. The term *phon* is used to describe a contour, or

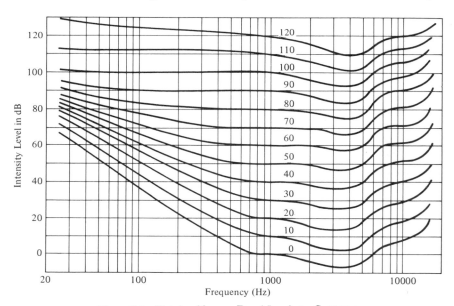

Figure 2-1. Fletcher-Munson Equal Loudness Contours.

curve, of equal loudness as a function of frequency. Note that at 1 kHz, subjective loudness levels in phons are equal to the actual values of SPL. The reason is that the 1-kHz loudness level was used as the reference in the Fletcher-Munson tests; listeners were asked to compare the subjective levels of other frequencies with the level of the 1-kHz tone, adjusting that level until it subjectively matched the 1-kHz reference. The differences were noted and averaged for the test group.

The most striking thing one observes about the Fletcher-Munson data is the relative insensitivity of the ear to low frequencies at low levels. We have all had the experience of hearing music played back over loudspeakers at a fairly high level and with apparently good musical balance between high and low frequencies. Upon lowering the playback level, the low frequencies seemed to be much weaker in proportion. If a good balance is established at peak levels of, say, 80 dB-SPL, and the volume then lowered 20 dB, program material in the 100-Hz region will subjectively be about 10 dB too low in level. We determine this by examining the differences between the 60- and 80-phon curves. At 1 kHz there is a 20-dB difference between them, but at 100 Hz the difference is only 10 dB. Thus, a level drop of 20 dB will leave us about 10 dB shy at 100 Hz. We stress again that these data are averages of the responses of many listeners; individual responses will depart from these averages in both directions.

Over the years, many consumer-type preamplifiers have incorporated loudness controls, switchable or continuously variable functions, which add a bass boost for low-level listening. The effect of a typical loudness control would be to add a 20-dB boost at 100 Hz relative to 1 kHz.

Loudness contours often call for adjustments in noise measurements made with sound level meters, and this is reason for the weighting curves shown in the previous chapter in our discussion of sound level meters (see Figure 1-11). The C scale is fairly flat and is the inverse of the curves for 100 phons and higher. The B scale is an inverse of the 70-phon curve and would be used for making noise measurements in that range. The A scale is the inverse of the 40-phon curve and would normally be used for making noise measurements in that range. (A very important exception is the use of the 40-phon or A scale in high-level noise measurements for determining potential hearing loss. It has been determined that moderately high sound pressure levels at low frequencies do not cause permanent hearing losses. Thus, the A scale is preferred for such measurements, since it is most sensitive in the 1–3 kHz region where prolonged exposure to noise can result in permanent hearing losses.)

BINAURAL HEARING AND LOCALIZATION

With only a single ear, a listener can determine pitch, loudness, timbre, and about every other attribute of sound except its direction, or localization. The addition of the second ear provides the cues necessary for localization, and a pair of normal ears through binaural hearing can easily localize a source to within a few degrees in the horizontal plane. Often, blind persons have localization acuity greater than the average because of their total dependence on the sense of hearing for all their localization efforts.

Figure 2-2 illustrates the two basic cues which are essential in localization, phase differences and amplitude differences existing at the ears. If a source S_1 is located directly ahead of a listener, then the amplitude and phase angles existing at the ears will be equal because of symmetry. Now, a source S_2 located at an angle θ away from center presents a different phase and amplitude at each ear; the phase angle at the right ear will *lead* that at the left ear, and if the frequency of the source is high enough, the amplitude at the right ear will be greater because of the shadowing effect of the head. Because of diffraction effects around the head, amplitudes at both ears are very much the same at frequencies up to about 700 or 1000 Hz, and phase relationships are felt to be the leading cue in

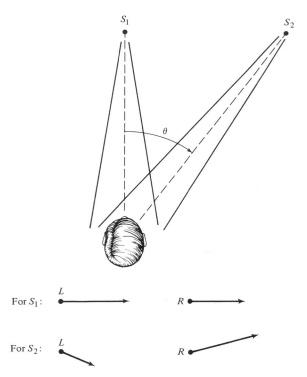

Figure 2-2. Phasors existing at the left and right ears for sounds in front of listener (S_1) and at front-right (S_2).

determining localization in the horizontal plane. There is a transition region, from 700 up to perhaps 2000 Hz, where both phase and amplitude cues are important. Finally, at the highest frequencies, the amplitude cues provided by shadowing around the head are most significant in determining localization.

Small side-to-side nodding movements of the head are useful in determining direction of sounds. Any listener will exhibit maximum localization acuity in the forward direction, and the nodding movements help him to "zero in," as it were, on the sound source. These same movements also help him to differentiate between fore and aft sound sources.

PHANTOM IMAGES

To a large extent a pair of loudspeakers located in front of a listener can simulate sound sources, phantom images, between the loudspeakers. This is shown in Figure 2-3. Here we have shown the relationship existing at each ear that is due to identical signals fed to each loudspeaker. The arrows are called "phasors"; their length indicates magnitude, and the relative angles between them represent phase relationships. When both loudspeakers are energized equally, the left ear receives components L_L and L_R, respectively, from the left and right loudspeakers. In just the same way, the right ear receives components R_L and R_R. Since both sets of components represent the same program material, we can add the phasors at each ear; these are represented as L_T and R_T. Since L_T and R_T both have the same magnitude and phase angle, the effect at the ears is the same as for a sound source located directly ahead of the listener.

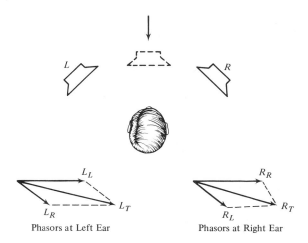

Figure 2-3. Simulation of phasors for a sound source in front of listener using a left-right pair of loudspeakers.

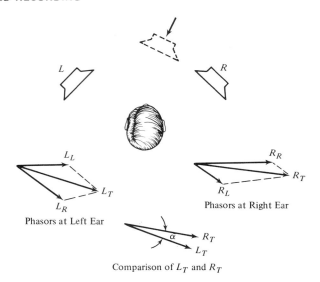

Figure 2-4. Simulation of phasors for a sound source located right of center using a left-right pair of loudspeakers.

Now, let us observe what happens when we energize the left loudspeaker at a somewhat lower level, as shown in Figure 2-4. In this case the net result of phasor addition produces resultant phasors, L_T and R_T, such that R_T is greater in magnitude than L_T and also leads it by some phase angle, α. The effect at the ears will be the same as for a source located somewhere between center and the right loudspeaker.

We can extend the examples further with very interesting results. Figure 2-5,a shows what happens when a signal exists only at the right loudspeaker. The only phasors present are due to the right loudspeaker; thus, $L_R = L_T$ and $R_R = R_T$, and localization is quite clearly at the right loudspeaker. Now, if we feed a small signal $180°$ out-of-phase to the left loudspeaker, note how the phasors behave (Figure 2-5,b). The magnitude of R_T is greater than L_T relative to Figure 2-5,a, and the phase relationship leads by an even greater angle. The effect, often a subtle one, is that of a sound source located *outside* the bounds of the loudspeaker array.

Phantom images are well named. As apparent sources located between loudspeakers, or beyond them, they are apt to wander and be ambiguous, depending on the exact position of the listener. Room acoustics play an important role as well. Our phasor analysis is based upon a listener in a forward attitude on a plane midway between the loudspeaker pair. If the listener moves even slightly to the left or right the phantom image will clearly shift in that same direction; even if the listener maintains the same location and simply moves his head to left

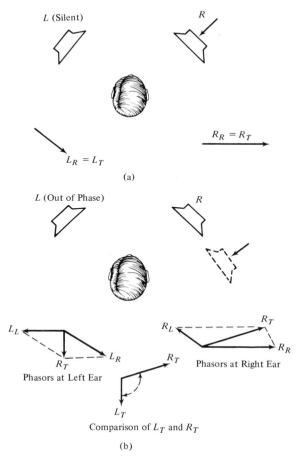

Figure 2-5. (a) Phasor conditions for right speaker only. (b) Simulation of phasors for a sound source located outside the bounds of the loudspeaker array.

or right, the phantom image will again shift accordingly. Stereophonic recording has long made use of phantom images between loudspeakers, but rarely those that occur outside the loudspeaker array.

Quadraphonic, or four-channel, recording poses some special problems. Phantom images between side pairs of loudspeakers are desirable, but unfortunately these images are never exact unless the listener turns to face either the right or left loudspeaker pair. In his normal front-oriented attitude, the listener cannot accurately localize a sound image at a point between a left or right loudspeaker pair, although he can clearly localize a source at either one of the pairs. Localization of phantom images between a *rear* pair of loudspeakers is also ambiguous; again, small movements of the head can result in large shifts of the apparent sound source. In a following chapter on quadraphonic sound we shall examine these problems in greater detail.

TIME DELAYS BETWEEN SOUND SOURCES—
THE PRECEDENCE EFFECT

Our phasor analysis of phantom source localization took into account only the relative intensities of sound coming from a front pair of loudspeakers. Just as important are the effects of small *time delays* between loudspeakers in determining localization.

In general, if two loudspeakers are symmetrically arranged in front of a listener, localization will be perceived between them if both are energized the same. However, if a small time delay is introduced in one loudspeaker transmission channel, localization will tend to be toward the earlier loudspeaker. This is

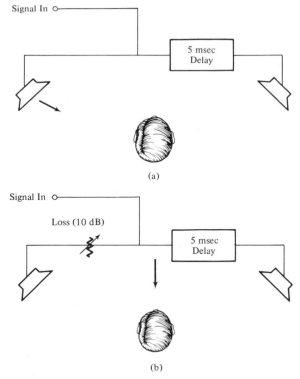

Figure 2-6. (a) Displacement of apparent sound source using time delay (precedence effect). (b) Effective cancellation of precedence effect by adjusting level of leading source.

known as the *precedence effect*, often called the *Haas effect*. The effect is a
very basic one and has been observed throughout years of architectural acoús-
tical design. Haas observed that the displacement of a sound source between
two loudspeakers due to slight time delays could be compensated for by intensity imbalances. In the example of Figure 2-6, a time delay of 5 milliseconds in
the left loudspeaker transmission channel results in localization at the left when
both channels are fed the same signal level. However, if the *leading* channel is
lowered in level some 10 dB, then the listener again perceives a phantom image
in the middle of the array. The trade-off between delay and intensity is a useful
one in sound recording and signal processing, and it is effective up to delays of
about 25–30 milliseconds, as shown in Figure 2-7. As this graph indicates, time
delays between frontal pairs of loudspeakers can be compensated by raising the
level of the delayed channel by the corresponding amount. Beyond 25–30 milliseconds, the ear begins to hear the delayed sound as a distinct echo, and the
trade-off is no longer effective in terms of restoring center localization.

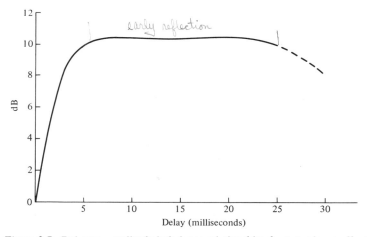

Figure 2-7. Delay vs. amplitude imbalance relationships for precedence effect.

IMAGE BROADENING DUE TO PHASE SHIFTS

We have seen how loudness and time-delay relationships between a frontal pair
of loudspeakers can determine localization for a listener located on the plane
of symmetry. A degree of image *broadening* can result from phase shifting of
one loudspeaker signal relative to the other. The networks which are used for
this effect produce constant phase *differences* with flat amplitude response over
a large portion of the audible spectrum, and the basic technique is shown in
Figure 2-8. The network in the left transmission channel produces a certain

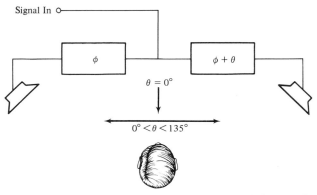

Figure 2-8. Image broadening due to all-pass phase shift networks.

phase shift, ϕ, with respect to frequency; the network in the right transmission channel produces the same shift plus an extra *phase lag*, θ, which is adjustable. When $\theta = 0°$, both loudspeakers receive the same signal, and localization for a listener on the plane of symmetry is a center phantom image. As θ is varied from zero up to about 135°, the image broadens; it is no longer perceived as a point source, but appears to come from a large area in front of the listener. As the phase angle is shifted beyond 135° the image begins to split apart; finally, at 180°, the familiar "out-of-phase" condition exists and localization is totally ambiguous.

As with the effects of time delay and amplitude differences between loudspeakers, the role of phase shifts depends largely upon listener orientation. If the listener is substantially off the axis of symmetry, then the effects as presented here are less distinct.

The ambiguity of localization for a frontal pair of loudspeakers fed equal but out-of-phase signals is startling. Again, we employ our familiar phasor analysis to see why this is so. In Figure 2-9, the resolution of phasors for L_T and R_T shows that the pair are of equal amplitude but in phase opposition. This condition corresponds to no set of cues for localization in any direction, and the ear-brain combination simply cannot make any sense out of it. The disorienting effect of equal out-of-phase signals has been used somewhat sparingly over the years in stereo recording for special effects; ordinarily, however, it is encountered only as the result of faulty signal processing. However, phase shifting at intermediate angles between 0° and 180° has been employed from time to time for special purposes, mainly in considerations of stereophonic-monophonic compatibility and those of two-channel matrix quadraphonic loudspeaker playback. We shall discuss these applications in later chapters.

The techniques for creating phantom images and diffused images which we have discussed so far in this chapter form the basis for many of the signal pro-

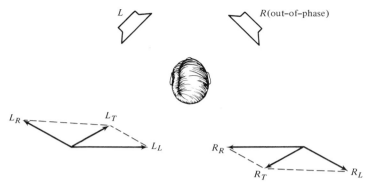

Figure 2-9. Phasor analysis of "out-of-phase" condition between two loudspeakers.

cessing techniques used in stereophonic and quadraphonic recording. With observations involving angular image displacement or image broadening, it is very difficult to attach numerical values to the phenomena; different listeners will hear the effect in different degree. In his excellent study of phasor analysis of stereophonic localization due to intensity cues, Bauer (1) suggests a "stereophonic law of sines" as an indicator of a precise degree of image shift as a result of intensity imbalances, but the observation is difficult to duplicate in typical listening environments.

A general study of image localization,fusion, and broadening has been given by Gardner (3) and is a useful supplement to the information given here.

SOME ASPECTS OF TIMBRE RELATING TO PERFORMANCE ENVIRONMENTS

Most of today's popular and rock music is recorded in relatively absoprtive, acoustically "dry," studios with close microphone placement. This method provides excellent separation on the multitrack master tape so that maximum flexibility in the mix-down process is assured. With the application of time delay and artificial reverberation techniques, it is possible to "process" these dry tracks for playback in either two-channel or four-channel formats with reasonable simulation of recordings made in natural performance environments. In order to understand these techniques thoroughly we first must appreciate the acoustical characteristics of such environments.

THE EARLY SOUND FIELD

The *early sound field* in a concert hall comprises the first few reflections of sound reaching the listener before the onset of a diffuse reverberant field. Much

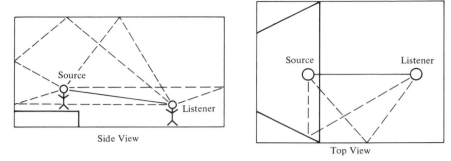

Figure 2-10. Direct and early reflected sound paths in an auditorium.

of the character of a concert hall is determined by the pattern of its early reflections, and much of the effort in modern architectural acoustical design is concerned with the optimization of these reflections, their density, and the avoidance of distinct echoes. Generally, the early sound field in a large room would last perhaps as long as 50 milliseconds; in smaller rooms it would be proportionally shorter. Figure 2-10 shows the nature of reflections reaching the listener from both a side wall and the ceiling after the direct sound has arrived. In good concert-hall design it is desirable for the initial time gap between the direct sound and the first reflections to be no greater than about 25 milliseconds, and this consideration often dictates the use of reflective, partially open, panels overhead in larger concert halls, as shown in Figure 2-11. The concert hall must be large enough to exhibit the desired reverberation time of 1.7–2.0 seconds, but such size in a simple structure often results in too great an initial time gap from side walls and ceiling, hence the use of "floating" reflectors to make the room effectively smaller for the optimization of early reflections. When proper attention has been given to control of the early reflections, the

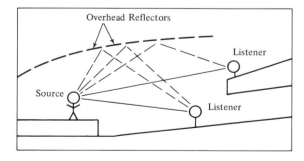

Figure 2-11. Use of reflectors to preserve desirable direct-to-early delays in an auditorium.

sound is often described as intimate and clear. In addition, the effect of reverberation time in the 1.7–2.0-second range will result in a degree of warmth and fullness. The early reflections reinforce the music, adding loudness to it without diminishing detail in the musical texture. However, a distinct echo or "slap" off a large wall or other surface in the hall could be very disturbing to a listener.

Fundamentally, the early sound field is the essential cue which tells a listener *how large* a room is. Consider the two environments, a large church or cathedral, and the typical medium-sized vestibule of a public building built in an earlier day. Both may have reverberation times very nearly the same at midfrequencies, but a blind-folded listener has no difficulty telling one from the other; the relatively longer initial time delay in the cathedral clearly establishes it as a much larger room. For relatively small source-to-listener distances, the direct-to-reverberant ratio will be greater in the large room than in the smaller, and music will be much clearer. For these reasons, small rooms designed to have reverberation times characteristic of larger ones are often not pleasing to either performer or listener. We can now refer again to Figure 1-25 in Chapter 1 with a better understanding of why optimum reverberation time increases with room volume. Small rooms demand less reverberation in order to ensure a proper direct-to-reverberant field ratio, while large rooms demand more reverbation in order to ensure adequate loudness of sound at the listener's location.

THE ROLES OF TIME DELAY AND ARTIFICIAL REVERBERATION IN RECORDING

To a large extent the recording engineer can manipulate his relatively dry tracks and simulate natural acoustical environments. The use of a reverberation device without time delay is only the first step in this monophonic simulation (Figure 2-12,a). Most reverberation sources are so small that they provide no early reflections in the 20–40-millisecond range, and their effect is often that of a small acoustical environment regardless of the decay rate. The addition of delay in the reverberation path is the next step in simulating a natural environment (Figure 2-12,b). In previous years it was customary to use tape recorders for the delay function; the delays so produced were fairly long, in the 50–100 millisecond range, and were suitable only for sustained program, vocals and string backgrounds, for example. The effect on percussion and rhythm tracks was usually an undesirable one. The introduction of high-quality digital delay devices in recent years has resulted in control of the delay function with gradations in the range of 2 to 5 milliseconds. As a result, both delay and reverberation can be applied with greater musical flexibility than before.

The next step in our attempt at simulating a natural acoustical environment is to process our single track into a stereo, or two-speaker, format as shown in Fig-

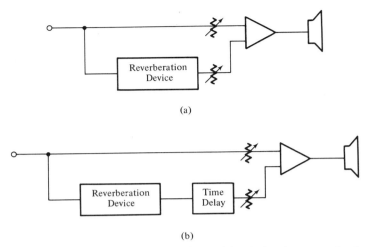

(a)

(b)

Figure 2-12. Application of reverberation and time-delay devices in a monophonic system.

ure 2-13. Here, our monophonic source has been fed to the left channel; delayed and reverberant components are then fed to both left and right channels. Component D_1 would be fairly short, say, in the range of 15 to 25 milliseconds, and D_2 would be in the range of 30 to 45 milliseconds. These delayed components would simulate early reflections from both the left and right of the stage, favoring the left side. Component D_3 would likely be in the range of 50 to 75 milliseconds, and the reverberation time itself would be selected to be in accord with the room dimensions implicit in the pattern of the delay time.

The final step, at least for the present, is the simulation via the four-speaker quadraphonic array of a sound field which surrounds the listener both front and rear. Let us again take a single channel source and locate it at one of our four loudspeakers, left-front. In a natural environment we would, of course, hear direct sound from the left-front, with early reflections coming from left-back and right-front. A later reflection should be heard from right-back. The pattern of the reverberant field would be structured to be weakest in the left-front direction, somewhat stronger in the flanking channels, and strongest in the right-back channel. The right-back reverberant information should also be delayed a bit more than the other three in order to create the impression of reverberant sound receding in a direction away from the source. The choice of delay times and reverberation time, as before, depends upon the nature of the music and the environment one wishes to simulate. Generally, the initial delays in both flanking and the opposite loudspeaker would not exceed 40 to 50 milliseconds, and

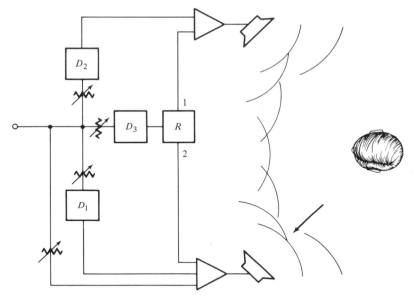

Figure 2-13. Application of reverberation and time-delay devices in a stereophonic system. The terms D_{1-2}, etc., represent different values of time delay, while R represents a reverberation device with two outputs, 1 and 2, which are randomly correlated.

the onset of the reverberated signals should be delayed another 20 milliseconds (see Figure 2-14).

The use of single simulated reflections prior to reverberation results in a surprisingly realistic simulation of a recording made in a natural environment. Somehow, a single reflection properly timed and balanced with relation to the direct impulse, suffices to take the place of the ensemble of early reflections which inevitably occur in any performance environment (see Figure 2-15). These techniques will be discussed in more detail in the following chapters on stereophonic and quadraphonic sound.

SUBJECTIVE ATTRIBUTES OF PERFORMANCE ENVIRONMENTS

It benefits the recording engineer to have an understanding of the subjective terms used by musicians and music critics when they talk about performing environments. Leo Beranek, in his book *Music, Acoustics, and Architecture* (2), has provided the basis of the following discussion. Where they are applicable, we have indicated those measures the recording engineer may employ in order to simulate these effects with his signal processing tools and devices.

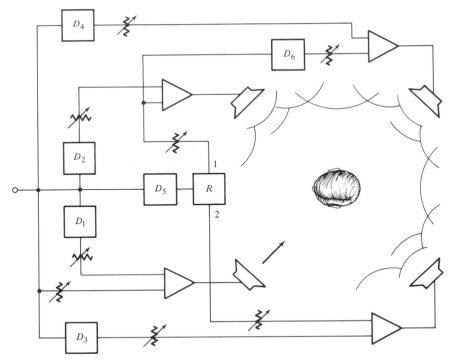

Figure 2-14. Application of reverberation and time-delay devices in a quadraphonic system.

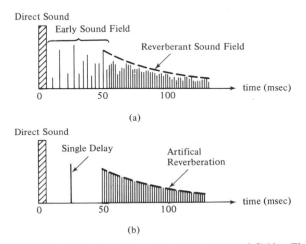

Figure 2-15. Simulation of direct, early, and reverberant sound fields. The response of a microphone to a sound impulse in an auditorium is shown at *a*. The effect at *b*, simulated through time delay and artificial reverberation, creates a similar effect to the listener.

Intimacy

Intimacy implies closeness of the listener to a performing group, and it results from an ensemble of early reflections which follow closely on the direct sound by no more than 15 or 20 milliseconds. The degree to which intimacy can be provided at distances up to 60 and 70 feet from the performers through the careful control of reflected sound is often surprising.

In recording, the engineer can simulate the effect of multiple reflections in both stereophonic and quadraphonic arrays through the proper application of digital time-delay devices, along with the appropriate degree of reverberation.

Liveness

Liveness implies a relatively high amount of reverberation in the mid-frequency range (0.5-2 kHz) along with initial delay patterns characteristic of not-too-large rooms. The effect is most often observed in old-style ballrooms where there is a good bit of high-frequency reflection because of mirrored surfaces and plaster finishing and substantial low-frequency absorption that is due to plywood and wallboard materials in the construction. Rooms of this sort are often excellent for recording, where an engineer can control the low-frequency content of a recording by electrical means. When they are used as performance environments, there is usually a disturbing lack of bass.

Liveness may be added to a recording by applying reverberation in the range of 1.5-2.0 seconds equalized to favor the 0.5-2-kHz part of the spectrum. Time delays should be kept on the short side since liveness is most often an attribute of moderate-sized rooms.

Warmth

Warmth is associated with high reverberation time at low frequencies (125-250 Hz) relative to mid-frequencies. It is an essential ingredient in any concert hall where music of the romantic period is to be performed. There is no other attribute more difficult to add to a recording by signal processing than this one. The problem is mainly the quality of reverberation devices; when boosted in the 125-250-Hz range they tend to exhibit unnatural coloration because of widely spaced natural modes. (Recall the last topic of Chapter 1.) Often, a moderate increase in low-frequency response and a slight reduction in high-frequency response may help, but generally a feeling of warmth, which is not already due to instrumental timbres or studio characteristics, is hard to create later electronically.

The recording engineer will have at his disposal many other signal processors in addition to time delay and artificial reverberation. Alteration of the recorded spectrum by means of equalizers and compression of the dynamic range will be of equal importance in arriving at many of the attributes associated with natural acoustical environments. These techniques, along with many others, will be the subject of a later chapter.

BIBLIOGRAPHY

1. B. Bauer, "Phasor Analysis of Some Stereophonic Phenomena," *J. Acoust. Soc. Am.*, vol. 33, no. 11 (1956).
2. L. Beranek, *Music, Acoustics and Architecture* (John Wiley & Sons, New York, 1962).
3. M. Gardner, "Some Single- and Multiple-Source Localization Effects," *J. Audio Eng. Soc.*, vol. 21, pp. 430–437 (July/August 1973).
4. H. Haas, "The Influence of A Single Echo on the Audibility of Speech," *J. Audio Eng. Soc.*, vol. 20, pp. 145–159 (March 1972).
5. J. Roederer, *Introduction to the Physics and Psychophysics of Music* (Springer-Verlag, New York, 1973).
6. F. Winckel, *Music, Sound and Sensation* (Dover Publications, Inc., New York, 1967).

3

Stereophonic Sound

A SHORT HISTORY

Stereophonic sound, or "stereo," as it is usually called, refers to a system of recording or sound transmission using multiple microphones and loudspeakers. Signals are picked up by the microphones and are fed to loudspeakers located in a geometrical array which corresponds to the microphone array; thus, many of the spatial aspects of the recording environment are preserved, and, by means of the principles discussed in Chapter 2, listeners are able to detect phantom images across the space occupied by the loudspeakers. Stereophonic transmission need not be limited to two channels; three- and five-channel systems have been used in the motion picture theater, but the term ordinarily implies two channels.

A distinction is made between *binaural* and stereophonic sound. In binaural sound transmission, two microphones are located at ear position in a dummy head, and their outputs are fed directly, or through a two-channel recording-playback system, to a pair of headphones worn by the listener. The aim is to transport the listener into the recording environment via the two-channel transmission. Each ear hears only what its corresponding microphone picked up (Figure 3-1), and side-to-side localization is extraordinarily realistic.

Experiments with binaural sound transmission date back to the late 1800s. Telephone receivers and transmitters were used, and the quality

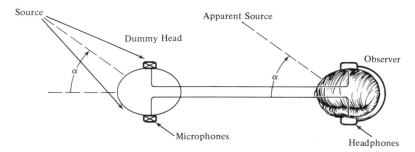

Figure 3-1. Principle of binaural sound transmission. Microphones located at ear position in a dummy head are fed to headphones worn by the listener. A sound source located at some angle α off center will arrive at the right microphone earlier than at the left; its high-frequency response at the left microphone will be somewhat shadowed. These two location cues give the listener the impression of a right-oriented source.

level was quite low. But the system did, however, convey a sense of space and ambience which seemed to transcend the physical limitations of fidelity and bandwidth. There appears to be only one drawback to binaural reproduction; the listener often has difficulty differentiating between sounds originating in front of and behind the dummy head. Apparently, the reason for this is that in the case of normal hearing the listener is free to move his head from side to side, thus providing the necessary time-delay cues between fore and aft sound sources. With headphones, there can be no such additional cues (since the sound source frame of reference moves with the head), and the listener is left with the fore-aft ambiguity.

Serious studies of stereo were carried out in the early 1930s by Bell Telephone Laboratories involving the transmission of three-channel symphonic music over high-quality telephone lines between Washington, D.C., and Philadelphia. These studies are noteworthy because of the vast research which went into the development of amplifiers, microphones, and loudspeakers, which were later to become the foundation of the recording and cinema sound arts. The Bell Laboratories studies also provided the basis for some of the earliest stereo psychoacoustical tests.

Although optical sound tracks offered multichannel capability from their beginning, it was not until the widespread application of magnetic recording during the years following World War II that stereo made a significant impression on the film and recording industries. As a commercial medium, stereo was first demonstrated in the motion picture theater in the late 1930s, but it did not become a standard for that medium until the 1950s. The first stereo product issued by the record industry was in 1954, in the two-track $7\frac{1}{2}$-ips quarter-inch tape format. The stereo disc was introduced in 1957 and pointed the way to rapid acceptance of stereo as the standard medium for home music entertainment.

STEREOPHONIC SYSTEMS

A number of approaches to stereo recording have evolved over the years; some have been better suited to preserving natural balances and perspectives in classical recording, while others have lent themselves more to the demands of popular recording. The techniques which have found favor in classical recording are the *coincident* microphone techniques (where two microphones are located as close together as possible), and the so-called *spaced-apart* technique (where two or three microphones are located some distance apart, usually arranged in a line, in front of a performing ensemble). Popular recording has favored a technique involving many microphones, closely placed to their sources to ensure good isolation, and subsequently assigned to a given loudspeaker or phantom-image position between the two stereo loudspeakers. We shall examine these techniques in detail.

Coincident Techniques

The term "M-S" (middle-side) refers to a coincident technique in which one microphone covers an ensemble along its major axis, emphasizing the *middle* of the group, and a figure-eight pattern at 90° emphasizes the *sides* of the group (see Figure 3-2). When the outputs are combined as shown, there are two resulting directional patterns, one oriented to the right and the other to the left, with an angular spread, 2θ, between their points of maximum pickup.

A signal located toward the center of the performing group is resolved equally by both patterns and will appear as a phantom center image in the stereo array. As sound sources move progressively to the right, there is more signal resolution by the right pattern and less by the left pattern, and the phantom images move accordingly. If the sound source is located at angle θ to the right, the left pattern will effectively resolve no signal, and the sound will be perceived at the right loudspeaker.

The M-S technique has the following characteristics:

1. It makes use only of intensity cues in determining position in the stereo array. There are no time delays between the microphones or between the resulting left and right pickup patterns.
2. It exhibits excellent monophonic (left-plus-right) compatibility. In the summation of the two channels, the figure-eight microphone output is canceled, and the monophonic output consists only of the cardioid microphone (see Figure 3-3).
3. Because proper angular coverage of large ensembles often requires that the M-S pair be located a considerable distance in front of the ensemble, the acoustical characteristics of the recording environment become critical.

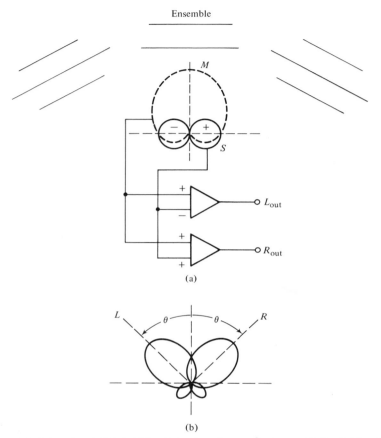

Figure 3-2. Principle of M-S (middle-side) microphone technique. (a) Cardioid and figure-eight microphones are located in front of a performing ensemble and connected electrically as shown. The respective electrical outputs are:

$$L = 1 + \sin \theta + \cos \theta = 1 + \sqrt{2} \cos (\theta - 45°)$$

$$R = 1 + \sin \theta - \cos \theta = 1 + \sqrt{2} \cos (\theta - 135°)$$

(b) The left and right outputs are directional patterns aimed, respectively, at left and right. Maximum response is at angles of $\pm \theta$.

Stated another way, for a given ensemble size, the engineer is locked into a fixed direct-to-reverberant relationship and a fixed distance from the ensemble (see Figure 3-4). Thus, more time must be spent in adjusting the relation between performers and microphones and in choosing an appropriate recording environment.

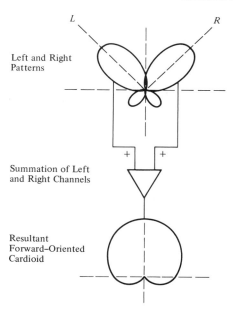

Left and Right
Patterns

Summation of Left
and Right Channels

Resultant
Forward–Oriented
Cardioid

Figure 3-3. Monophonic compatibility of the M-S technique. The M-S pair yields left and right directional patterns given by: $L = 1 + \sin \theta + \cos \theta$, and $R = 1 + \sin \theta - \cos \theta$. When these expressions are combined $(L + R)$, the cosine terms cancel, leaving only the forward-oriented cardioid pattern: $L + R = 2 (1 + \sin \theta)$.

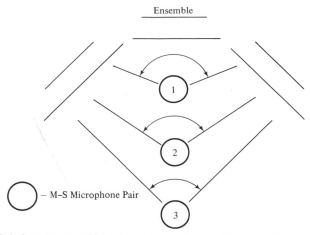

Figure 3-4. Relations between M-S microphone and ensemble perspectives. Three possible microphone locations are shown; only one of these is likely to convey the desired direct-to-reverberant relationship. Even though the angular coverage of the microphone pair can be adjusted electrically (see Figure 3-5), overall stereo separation is likely to suffer if acoustical conditions require rather distant placement of the microphones.

As the Blumlein experiments of the early thirties so aptly demonstrate, the search for the right environment is often worth the extra time and effort. A well done M-S recording often preserves an astonishing degree of realism, and this is due largely to the way the microphone pair responds to reverberant information. Because of their close spacing both microphones will pick up reverberant information of the same basic spectral energy distribution. However, because the microphones are oriented in different directions, the instantaneous phase and amplitude relationships at their outputs will be largely incoherent. The result is spread of reverberant sound between the loudspeakers, while direct sound sources will appear panned at some position between the loudspeakers. This effect seems to be maximized with the crossed figure-eight microphone arrangement shown in Figure 3-7, b, the approach favored by Blumlein.

M-S microphone pairs are often used with "width" and "position" controls, as shown in Figure 3-5. The width control varies the relative balance of cardioid and figure-eight components in the composite signals. If a narrower stereo spread

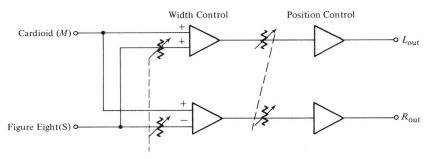

Figure 3-5. Width and position control of M-S microphones. The width control alters the amount of figure-eight or S component relative to the fixed cardioid or M component. The position control consists of a pair of attenuators connected differentially to act as a balance control.

is desired, the M component is increased, and this has the effect of increasing the common, or monophonic, component between the two channels. If a wider signal is desired, the S content is increased and has the effect of widening the array by introducing out-of-phase components into the left and right channels. The position control operates as a balance control between the channels and enables the stereo phantom images from a given pair of M-S microphones to be located anywhere in the stereo array. An example of the use of width and position controls is shown in Figure 3-6.

There are a number of variations on the M-S technique, and they are shown in Figure 3-7. The three-microphone arrangement shown in Figure 3-7,d is particularly interesting in that the outputs of the three microphones may be combined

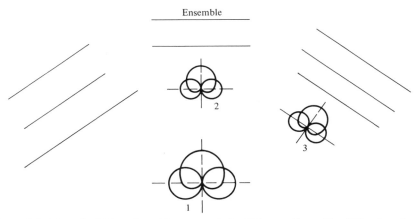

Figure 3-6. Use of width and position controls in M-S recording. The M-S microphone Pair 1 is for overall pickup; it would be adjusted for desired width and centered in the stereo loudspeaker array. Pairs 2 and 3 are for highlighting soloists and would be adjusted for narrower presentation. Pair 2 would be centered in the array, while Pair 3 would be located to the right.

to yield patterns which can be "steered" at any angle in the entire 360° array. The circuit of Figure 3-8 illustrates how this is done. Such a microphone array would be useful where it was desirable, or necessary, to fix the location of a set of microphones more or less permanently for a variety of recording applications.

As a rule, M-S techniques employ "stereo microphones," composite structures which include a pair of microphones whose patterns are individually adjustable and whose physical positions in the horizontal plane can be varied. The width and position functions are normally included as part of this composite system and operated at a point remote from the microphone pair.

Spaced-Apart Techniques

The "crossed-cardioid" arrangement shown in Figure 3-7,c, is the starting point for the spaced-apart approach. If the microphones, L and R, are moved apart, while maintaining the same angular relationship between them, then the resulting phantom images will be produced by both intensity and time-delay relationships as shown in Figure 3-9. When the inter-microphone distance exceeds eight or ten feet, there is a tendency for all sources of sound (except those almost exactly equidistant between the microphones) to pull toward one side or the other, resulting in what is called the "hole-in-the-middle." This happens because both intensity and time-delay cues are in effect adding together in the same direction; for an off-center source the leading channel is also the louder channel.

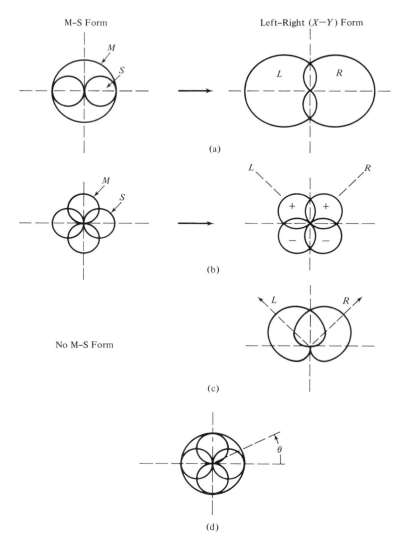

Figure 3-7. Variations on M-S techniques. (a) A figure-eight and omnidirectional micro-phone pair can be combined to yield back-to-back cardioid patterns as shown. This arrange-ment is useful only when performers can be located on opposite sides of the microphone pair. (b) A pair of M-S figure-eight microphones crossed at an angle of 90° yield another pair of figure-eights oriented left and right. This variation provides the most even distribu-tion of reverberant pickup of all the M-S techniques. (c) A pair of cardioid microphones may be crossed as shown for direct left and right pickup. The term X-Y is often used to describe this arrangement. (d) This arrangement of two figure-eight microphones and one omnidirectional microphone can be combined to yield a cardioid pattern which can be "steered" at any angle (see Figure 3-8).

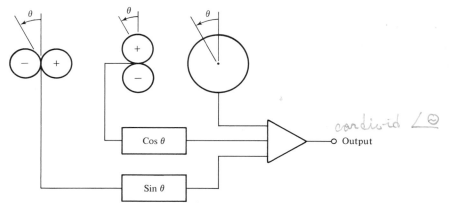

cardioid ∠☺

Figure 3-8. Steerable microphone array. The outputs of the figure-eight microphones are combined through potentiometers having cosine and sine attenuation characteristics and combined with the output of the omnidirectional microphone. The result is a cardioid pattern oriented at an angle θ.

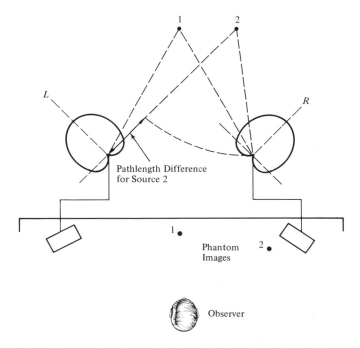

Figure 3-9. Spaced-apart microphones. Both amplitude and time delay differences provide cues for stereo localization.

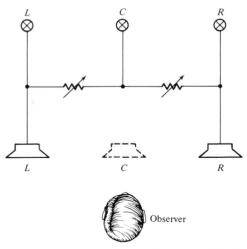

Figure 3-10. Center-placed microphone. The signal contributed by the center microphone creates a center phantom image in the stereo loudspeaker array.

The engineer may cure the hole-in-the-middle effect simply by adding a third microphone, as shown in Figure 3-10, and assigning its output equally between the left and right channels. The center phantom image which is produced stabilizes the entire stereo array and adds focus to any center-stage activity, such as a soloist.

The spaced-apart technique has been favored for classical recording in the United States because it seems to produce what may be described as a "warmer" sound. In addition to the early reflections present acoustically in the recording environment, the microphones generate, through the time delays between them, additional delayed signals which behave as early reflections. Through microphone placement these delays are in the hands of the engineer, and he can accordingly use them to his advantage. While the various coincident techniques produce superb recordings in the correct acoustical setting, the spaced-apart approach seems to offer the engineer greater flexibility in coping with less than ideal acoustical circumstances.

An additional technique often employed with the spaced-apart approach is the use of single microphones closely placed to individual sections or instrument of the orchestra to "highlight" or add presence to those instruments. Normally, the output of these microphones would be panned into the stereo array at roughly the position occupied by the instrument or section, and the signal from those microphones would be introduced only to the extent of adding the desired presence to the instrument—but no more. If the level is too great, then the signal from the highlighting microphone, because it is perhaps 20–30 milliseconds *ahead* of the main microphone signals, tends to stick out in front of the rest of the orchestra.

In classical recording, it is common to use highlighting microphones on the following instruments and sections: woodwinds, harp, tympani, softer percussion instruments, and first-chair strings. We have all heard classical recordings in which solo instruments have been exaggerated through excessive level of highlighting microphones, and a good bit of this problem is due to the anticipatory time aspect of the close-in microphones—the fact that they receive their input ahead of the main microphones. While nothing can counteract a heavy hand on the part of the engineer who is mixing a classical recording session, there is at least one measure available which will alleviate part of the problem. If a time delay is added to a highlighting microphone and is adjusted so the signal from that microphone does not anticipate the signal arrival at the main pair but rather arrives in step with it (or possibly 5–10 milliseconds later), then much of the problem with highlighting microphones disappears (see Figure 3-11). Only since the early seventies has high-quality time delay, adjustable in 2- to 5-millisecond increments, become available for such purposes. These devices will be discussed in detail in a following chapter on signal processing.

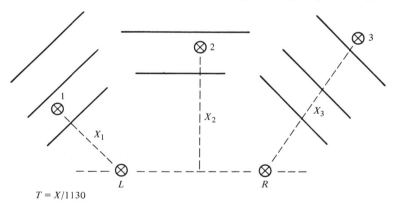

Figure 3-11. Use of time delay in adjusting arrival time differences between near and far microphones. The highlighting microphone should be delayed with respect to the main microphones by a value $T = X/1130$ seconds, where X is measured in feet.

The Evolution of Popular Stereo Recording

Beginning in the early fifties, popular recording in the studio developed along these lines:

1. The recordings were usually made in acoustically dry studios.

2. Small groups of instruments, or individual instruments, were assigned their own microphones, normally closely placed to maximize separation.
3. Because of the high degree of separation, both the recording engineer and the musicians themselves could alter musical balances.
4. Because the studio was acoustically inert, any semblance of natural room acoustics in the recording was produced almost entirely by signal processing devices, such as reverberation or time delay, under the control of the engineer.
5. Because of the highly detailed "up-front" nature of close microphone placement, engineers spent considerable time in the selection of microphones, their placement, and their relative balances in the final stereo array.

In the early years, up to about 1965, multichannel recording capability normally did not extend beyond three or four tracks, so most of the important musical balances had to be committed to the master tape at the time of the original recording. With the introduction of 8-, 16-, and even 24-track recording in the late sixties, it became possible to assign individual microphones to their own tracks on the master tape, thus deferring all important instrumental and sectional balances until a later *remix*, or *mix-down* session.

In the days of three- and four-track recording, instrumental and sectional placement in the stereo array was usually limited to a left, center, right presentation. Later, with more flexibility built into the multitrack master recording, it became possible to position individual instruments *via panpots* to any phantom position in the stereo array.

SIGNAL PROCESSING TECHNIQUES FOR STEREO

Panpots

As we discussed in Chapter 2, localization between a stereo pair of loudspeakers can be controlled by adjusting the relative balance of a common signal between the pair. For ease in handling signals in this way, panpots (a contraction of *pan*oramic *pot*entiometer) have been developed. A stereo panpot accepts a single input and provides two outputs for continuously variable positioning between a stereo pair of loudspeakers. Figure 3-12 shows the electrical schematic diagram of a panpot as well as its relative outputs as a function of position. Note that the two output levels are such that constant acoustical energy is maintained for all settings of the panpot. When the panpot is set at its center position, the resulting equal outputs are 3 dB down from either the full-left or full-right positions, and this condition ensures equal acoustical energy for left,

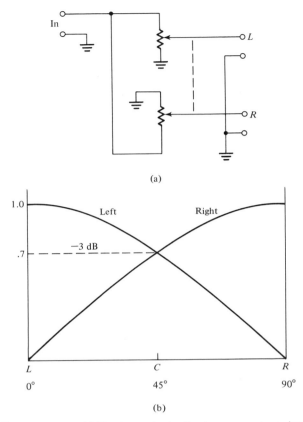

(a)

(b)

Figure 3-12. Stereo panpots. (a) The two outputs of a stereo panpot are given by:

$$L = (\cos \theta) \, \text{Input}$$

$$R = (\sin \theta) \, \text{Input}$$

where θ is the position of the panpot, $0°$ corresponding to full-left and $90°$ to full-right. (b) At center position, both outputs are -3 dB relative to either extreme. Acoustical output is proportional to the *square* of the left and right sound pressures, and since $\sin^2 \theta + \cos^2 \theta = 1$ for all values of θ, the acoustical output of a stereo panpot is constant for all panned positions.

center, and right positions. Constant acoustical energy is maintained similarly for all intermediate positions.

For three-channel stereo as used in motion picture recording, a panpot of the type shown in Figure 3-13 is used. As before, constant acoustical output is maintained for all settings of the panpot.

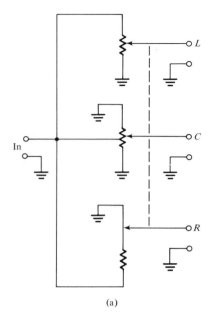

(a)

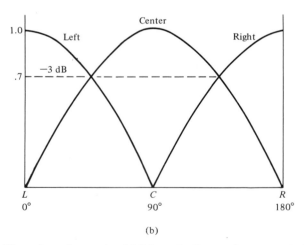

(b)

Figure 3-13. Three-channel panpots. (a) Schematic diagram for a panpot with left, center, and right outputs as used in motion picture sound. (b) Characteristics of the outputs of a three-channel panpot.

Techniques for Image Broadening

In the processing of signals for stereo, it is often desirable to broaden phantom images for certain musical purposes. In Chapter 2, we discussed image broadening by means of wide-band phase shift techniques. In this section we shall examine a number of other techniques.

1. *Broadening by Frequency Distribution.* If a monophonic source is fed to a stereo pair of channels with their frequency responses shaped as shown in Figure 3-14, the listener will hear a spread of sound between the speakers.

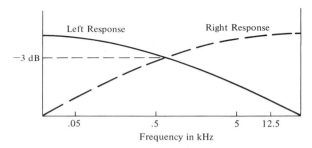

Figure 3-14. Image broadening by frequency distribution.

Actually, this technique is equivalent to panning each portion of the frequency spectrum individually from left to right. For maximum effectiveness, the frequency at which both signals are equal should be about 500 Hz.

2. *Broadening Due to Signal Incoherence.* If two microphones are located some distance apart in a reverberation chamber, their respective outputs will be largely *incoherent*; amplitude and phase relations between the two outputs will be randomly related, on a frequency-by-frequency basis, but the overall spectral distribution between them will be largely the same. The result when these two signals are reproduced over stereo loudspeakers will be a spread of sound between the loudspeakers, as shown in Figure 3-15.

3. *Broadening Due to Time Delays.* A related technique is shown in Figure 3-16. Here, the reverberation chamber has only one output. If this output were fed to both loudspeakers, there would be a single phantom center image with no impression of spread between the loudspeakers. If a suitable time delay is placed in one of the paths, the observer again will sense the incoherence between the loudspeakers, and the sound will be spread between them. Suitable delays for this effect are in the range of 40–60 milliseconds.

In our earlier discussion of the effect of time delays on localization, we observed that localization tended toward the earlier of the two signals. When the

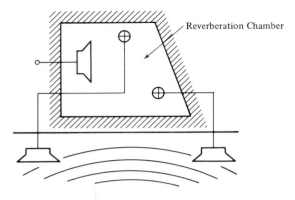

Figure 3-15. Incoherent signals from a single reverberation chamber using spaced-apart microphones.

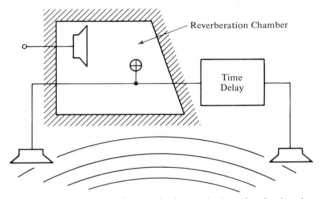

Figure 3-16. Incoherent signals from a single reverberant signal using time delay.

signal consists only of reverberation, however, this is not the case; reverberant signals are devoid of significant transient, or impulsive, sounds because of the relatively slow attack and decay of typical reverberation devices, and a delay as great as 60 milliseconds (even a greater delay when the reverberation time is longer) will not be noticed as such.

A variation of this technique is shown in Figure 3-17. A monophonic source, violins, for example, is given a desirable spread from left to just slightly left of center by panning a delayed signal to center. The level of the delayed signal is adjusted to yield the desired degree of spread.

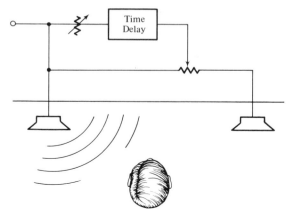

Figure 3-17. Image broadening by center panning of a delayed signal. For the effect shown here, time delays in the 15–30 msec range would be most effective.

PROBLEMS OF MONOPHONIC COMPATIBILITY

Until about 1968, the record industry produced both monophonic and stereo versions of the same record release. Where there was a concern for correct monophonic balances, as in AM radio broadcasting or jukebox play, a mono-phonic disc would be used. When monophonic discs were discontinued, the concern for stereo-to-monophonic mix-down performance became an important one. The problem, simply stated, is that in-phase signals will add in mono, and out-of-phase signals will cancel. The extent of the additions is to double the signal (an increase of 6 dB), and the cancellation can be nearly total. For signals which are normally panned between left and right, the total error in the stereo-to-monophonic mix-down is no greater than 3 dB, as shown in Figure 3-18.

A method for eliminating this error has been suggested by Holzer (U.S. Patent 3,646,574) and is shown in Figure 3-19. The all-pass phase shift of 90° in the Holzer device results in monophonic addition of equal stereo components which is 3 dB lower than the normal, non–phase-shifted components. The Holzer de-vice is located as the last signal-processing element in the stereo tape-to-disc transfer.

Perhaps the best overall approach to stereo-to-monophonic capability is simply an awareness that problems in combining can occur. The experienced engineer will, as a rule, avoid using out-of-phase components in his signal processing schemes if he is concerned about monophonic compatibility. Reverberation, in particular, can be a problem, inasmuch as it usually involves as much in-phase as

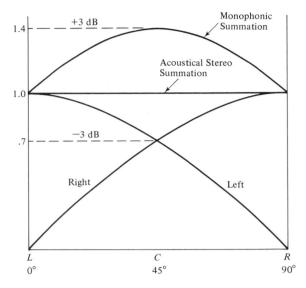

Figure 3-18. Illustration of center image build-up of 3 dB in monophonic playback of stereo program.

out-of-phase information. A good engineer will always alternately monitor his stereo program and its monophonic mix-down and not be satisfied until both requirements are met. In a later chapter on microphones we shall examine a number of microphone techniques which further reduce the monophonic compatibility problem.

Some engineers prefer to monitor certain aspects of stereo-monophonic compatibility by a device known as a *correlation meter*. The correlation meter indicates, over some time period (usually .5 to 1.0 second), the average *product* of the two stereo signals. If the two signals are totally separate and contain no common program, the average value will be zero. If there is in-phase program in the two channels, then the average product will be positive, and the meter will indicate a positive value. Should the common information between the two channels be out-of-phase, then the meter indication will be in a negative direction, indicating a stereo-to-monophonic compatibility problem. Details of the correlation meter are shown in Figure 3-20.

It should be stressed that the indication of the correlation meter means relatively little in terms of some of the esthetic considerations of stereo-to-monophonic compatibility; it only indicates the relative preponderance of in-phase or out-of-phase program content between the stereo pair of channels.

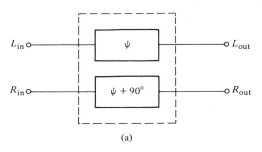

(a)

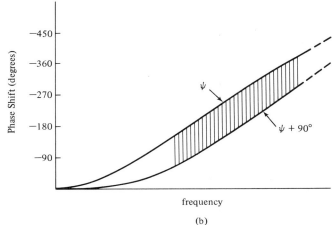

frequency

(b)

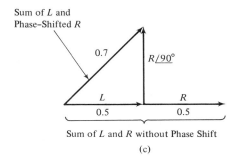

(c)

Figure 3-19. Use of 90° phase shift techniques in ensuring monophonic compatibility. (a) All-pass phase shift networks (ψ) differing by 90°. (b) Phase shift of networks with respect to frequency. The response of one network leads the other over a broad range, indicated by crosshatched area. (c) The sum of the non–phase-shifted signals is *unity* (.5 + .5), while the sum of the 90°-phase-shifted pair is 0.7, 3 dB lower in level.

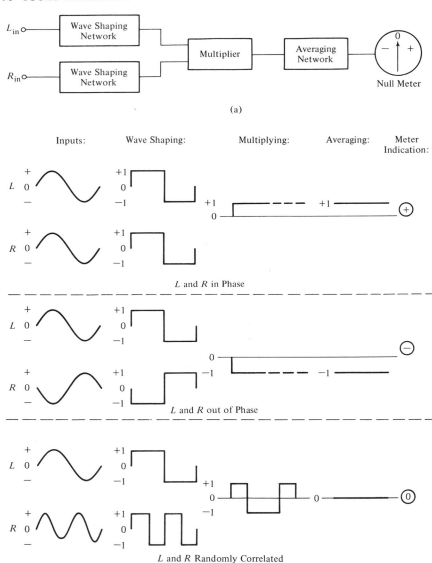

Figure 3-20. Details of the stereo correlation meter. (a) Schematic diagram of correlation meter. (b) Action of correlation meter for three signal conditions: in-phase, out-of-phase, and uncorrelated. The function of the wave-shaping network is to yield a value of +1 for any positive signal and −1 for a negative signal. The two signals are then multiplied and expressed as ±1 or zero. The averaging network filters out the rapid variations in the instantaneous product and yields a smoothed signal for actuating the meter. When in-phase signals predominate, the averaged output is *positive*; when out-of-phase signals predominate, the averaged output is *negative*. When the two signals are randomly correlated (neither in- nor out-of-phase components prominent), the averaged output is *zero*.

TECHNIQUES FOR PSEUDO-STEREO

Pseudo-stereo is the processing of monophonic program for presentation over two loudspeakers in a way that approximates, to a greater or lesser degree, some of the musical values which are implicit in stereo recordings. Normally, the goal of pseudo-stereo is to achieve a feeling of spaciousness in the processed sound, and there are a number of techniques which accomplish this rather well.

Although some of the image-broadening techniques discussed earlier may be used, the practice of pseudo-stereo usually favors approaches which are fairly unsubtle and which impress the listener directly upon first hearing as having some of the attributes of real stereo. We must, of course, realize that it is no more possible to re-create a real stereo sound field from a monophonic source than it is to add color, through video signal processing, to a black and white television signal.

Lauridsen's Method

The Lauridsen method of pseudo-stereo uses two loudspeakers oriented as shown in Figure 3-21. The rear loudspeaker, operating in an unbaffled condition, produces a figure-eight response, positive to the right and negative to the left. The signal feeding this loudspeaker is delayed some 50–100 msec, and this process creates a series of reinforcements and cancellations on each side of the array which are complementary: the reinforcements of one correspond to the cancellations of the other. The listener must be located precisely on the plane of symmetry for proper effect, and in that position he will sense a quite pronounced distribution of apparent sound sources across an arc in front of him. The width of the arc may be controlled by altering the level between the two loudspeakers; increasing the level of the closer loudspeaker narrows the arc, while lowering it widens the arc.

Variations on Lauridsen's Method

The arrangement of loudspeakers shown in Figure 3-22 can produce a reasonable simulation of Lauridsen pseudo-stereo without the need for electrical time delay. If the distance between the listener and the center loudspeaker is at least 10 feet less than his distance to the side speakers, then a time delay of $10/1130 = 8.8$ msec will be introduced into the system. This corresponds to complementary sets of reinforcements and cancellations spaced at a frequency $f = 113$ Hz, sufficiently close to give a good pseudo-stereo spread. An attenuator is provided to adjust the level of the center loudspeaker and thus the width of the pseudo-stereo effect. The left ear hears the summation of the left and center loudspeakers while the right ear hears the difference of those same signals. The effect works best in relatively absorptive acoustical surroundings.

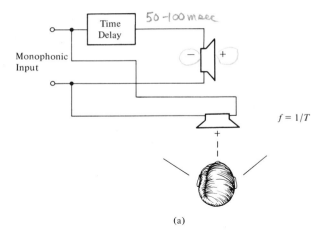

(a)

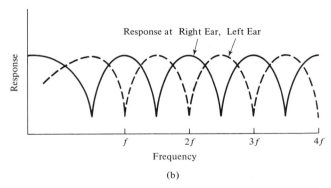

(b)

Figure 3-21. Lauridsen pseudo-stereo method. (a) Loudspeaker arrangement. (b) Sound pressures at the left and right ears.

The embodiment shown in Figure 3-23 is a practical one from the commercial point of view. It is analogous to the method shown in Figure 3-22, except that a space relationship is not used to introduce delay into the system. The important attribute of this arrangement is that the listener does not have to locate himself on the plane of symmetry. He is free to move about the listening room and appreciate the pseudo-stereo effect over a wide area.

There is another fortunate aspect—excellent monophonic compatibility is guaranteed. The criticism most often leveled at pseudo-stereo is that the original monophonic program, which is often of archival or historical nature, is somehow degraded or compromised in the effort to produce a stereo spread of sound.

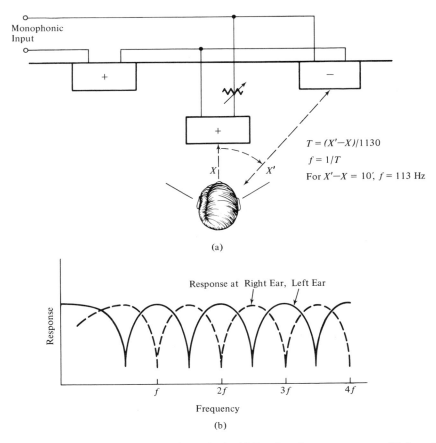

$$T = (X'-X)/1130$$
$$f = 1/T$$
For $X'-X = 10'$, $f = 113$ Hz

(a)

Response at Right Ear, Left Ear

f $2f$ $3f$ $4f$

Frequency

(b)

Figure 3-22. Variation on Lauridsen's method. (a) Loudspeaker arrangement. (b) Sound pressures at the left and right ears.

The purist, of course, wants nothing to do with pseudo-stereo processing, and he is probably justly irate when it is poorly done. The monophonic compatibility of the Lauridsen method is apparent from an examination of Figure 3-24. The original monophonic input to the system is recovered in the exact form upon simple addition of the two pseudo-stereo channels, and that should easily satisfy the purist.

The circuit arrangement for obtaining alternate reinforcements and cancellations by combining a direct and a delayed signal is called a *comb filter* because

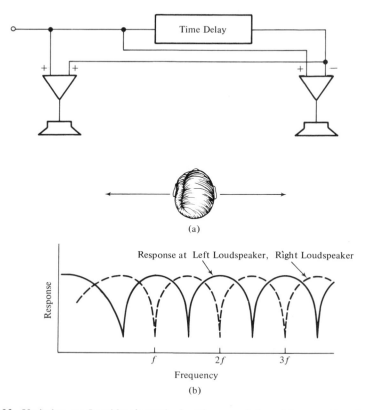

(a)

(b)

Figure 3-23. Variation on Lauridsen's method. The use of time delay provides alternate reinforcements and cancellations electrically at each loudspeaker, thus broadening the listening area.

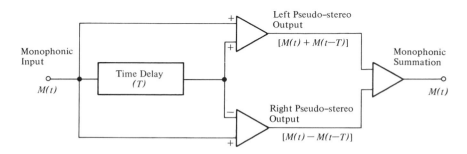

Figure 3-24. Monophonic compatibility of Lauridsen's pseudo-stereo. The monophonic summation is identical with the system input.

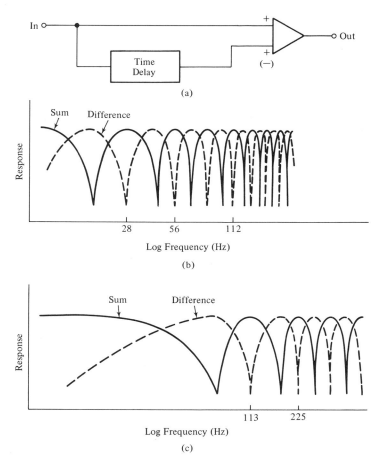

Figure 3-25. Principle of the comb filter. (a) Basic circuit. (b) Reinforcement and cancellation patterns shown on a log frequency axis for a time delay of 40 msec (reinforcements and cancellations at multiples of 28 Hz). (c) Reinforcement and cancellation patterns for a time delay of 10 msec (reinforcements and cancellations at multiples of 113 Hz). Characteristic cancellation and reinforcement frequencies are given by: $f_n = n/T$, where T is the delay time and $n = 1, 2, 3, 4, \ldots$.

of the comblike shape of its response (see Figure 3-25). Its basic characteristics are:

1. Alternate reinforcements and cancellations occur at equal frequency increments; each higher octave will contain *twice* as many reinforcements and cancellations as the preceding octave.

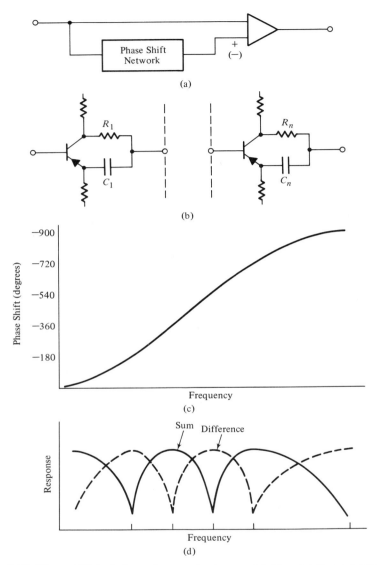

Figure 3-26. Phase shift techniques for pseudo-stereo. (a) The circuit arrangement resembles the comb filter except that an all-pass phase shift network is employed instead of time delay. (b) One section of an all-pass network. Usually a number of these sections are connected in series, providing a phase shift with respect to frequency, on the order of, say, $1000°$ as shown at (c). (d) Combining the phase-shifted signal with the nonshifted one results in cancellations at $(180° + n360°)$ and reinforcements at $(360° + n360°)$, where $n = 1, 2, 3, 4, \ldots$.

2. The pattern of reinforcements and cancellations can be made to *reverse* simply by changing the sign of the delayed component as it is combined with undelayed component.

3. The distance in frequency between successive reinforcements and cancellations is inversely proportional to the delay time. For longer delays, the reinforcements and cancellations are at closer frequency intervals than for shorter delays.

Reinforcement and Cancellation due to Wide-Band Phase Shifts

Comb filters are expensive because of the requirement for time-delay devices. For many applications, a less dense array of reinforcements and cancellations will suffice, and these can be accomplished by using an all-pass phase shift network in place of a time-delay function, as shown in Figure 3-26. Note that on a per-octave basis the density of reinforcements and cancellations is constant.

A commercial embodiment of this approach was introduced by Orban (9) and provides for adjustments in the RC phase-shift networks so that the reinforcement and cancellation frequencies can be selected for optimum effect. Two outputs (both sum and difference) are provided so that a pseudo-stereo effect is produced.

LISTENING ROOM AND LOUDSPEAKER CONSIDERATIONS

The most important requirement for proper stereo playback is the production of clear, unambiguous phantom images, and this requirement demands that several rules be followed:

1. The loudspeakers must be identical. The use of different loudspeaker types will easily produce a spacious sound, and one that is pleasant to listen to, but phantom images will tend to wander, or at best to be blurred.

2. The loudspeakers should be located symmetrically within the listening room so that the effects of acoustical treatment in the room will be the same for both loudspeakers.

3. The nominal subtended angle between the listener and the loudspeakers should be in the 60° to 90° range. There is a good bit of room here for personal preference, however.

4. The loudspeaker's directional characteristics should be utilized in such a way to make the usable listening area as large as necessary.

In Figure 3-27,a, loudspeakers having fairly directional characteristics are shown facing forward. The listening area is restricted; if an observer moves to the right, he finds himself not only closer to the right loudspeaker but also closer

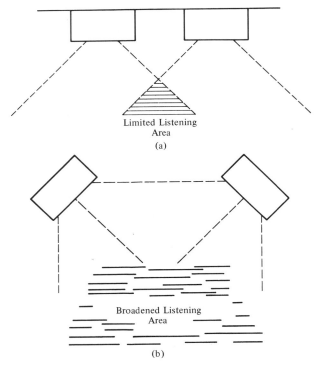

Figure 3-27. Usable stereo listening area as a function of loudspeaker orientation. (a) When directional loudspeakers are aimed forward, the area of overlap is relatively small. (b) When their patterns cross, the usable area is considerably enlarged.

to its major axis. Both of these conditions will cause phantom images to move markedly to the right. A better arrangement is shown at Figure 3-27,b. Here, the major axes of the loudspeakers are pointed toward the center of the listening area, and side-to-side movements of the listener produce minimal displacement of phantom images.

An interesting loudspeaker arrangement proposed by Bauer (1) extends the usable stereo listening area considerably. Unbaffled loudspeakers are used because they exhibit approximate figure-eight response patterns. At Figure 3-28,a, we observe what happens to phantom images for off-axis positions with forward-facing loudspeakers. With the figure-eight loudspeakers the image shift is much less pronounced. As a listener moves to the right, he approaches the null angle of the right loudspeaker while moving even more toward the major axis of the left loudspeaker. These amplitude relations tend to cancel the change in delay times, and center phantom images remain relatively stable. The effect can be

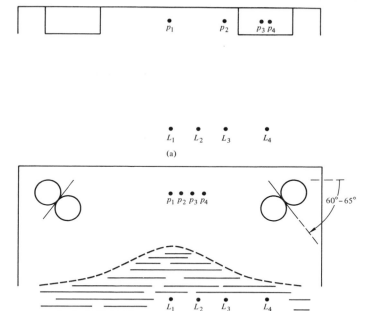

Figure 3-28. Movement of center phantom images as a function of listener location. (a) For forward-facing directional loudspeakers, listener positions $L_{1..4}$ will result in phantom images $P_{1..4}$. (b) When figure-eight loudspeakers are located as shown, phantom images remain relatively stable with respect to listener location because of the offset of arrival time differences by amplitude differences.

extended down to about 250 Hz.   Below that point, standard baffling of low frequency loudspeakers is necessary in order to provide adequate power handling capability for normal listening.

While recording control rooms are usually carefully designed to provide precise acoustical characteristics across the audio frequency spectrum, average listening rooms, even the better ones, are likely to be fairly spotty in their acoustical performance. The problem most often encountered is that of insufficient low-frequency absorption. Consider an average room in a solidly built structure. The floor may be wood or tile over concrete, and the walls and ceiling constructed of plaster on lath. This room, devoid of all furnishings, is non-absorptive over most of the audio spectrum. With the addition of carpet and draperies, the room will be deadened acoustically at middle and high frequencies, but the effect at low frequencies will be minimal. As a result, the response of even the best loudspeakers will show significant peaks and dips in the frequency region below about 150–200 Hertz. If an attempt is made to correct by electrical equalization the response for a given listening position, then it will soon be discovered that, perhaps two or three feet away, the correction may be all wrong. It is the very nature of low-frequency standing waves in an undamped room to vary considerably over short distances in the frequency region below about 150 Hertz.

Structures making ample use of wood and wallboard as internal finishing materials will typically yield smooth low-frequency response because of the high low-frequency absorption, and as a consequence stereophonic performance will be better. There is often a problem in these structures; however, the absorbed sound has to go somewhere, most often into the next room, where it may not be appreciated. Where multiple listening facilities are to be included in the same structure, special measures must be taken to provide good isolation as well as sufficient sound absorption. In a later section we shall examine some of the recommended construction techniques for these purposes.

STEREOPHONIC OSCILLOSCOPE PATTERNS

Instantaneous visual monitoring of a stereo program has always interested the engineer. While the correlation meter discussed earlier provides a time-averaged view of only the compatibility aspect of a stereo program, oscilloscope viewing provides an instantaneous picture of signal relationships.

An oscilloscope is a test instrument which provides viewing of two inputs simultaneously by means of *lateral* and *vertical* deflection of an electron beam aimed at a phosphorescent surface. Normally, the oscilloscope is used to observe wave forms, and in this mode the wave form to be viewed is introduced into the vertical input while a linear sweep signal, synchronized to the period of the wave form, is introduced into the horizontal input.

For stereo signal viewing, the sweep signal is disabled, and the stereo signals are connected directly to the vertical and horizontal inputs. The patterns which are observed are known as *Lissajous* figures. A variety of inputs is shown in Figure 3-29. At (a) the left channel only is shown connected to the vertical input; at (b) the right-channel only is connected to the horizontal input. At (c) equal in-phase signals are fed to both inputs, and at (d) equal out-of-phase inputs are shown. At (e) equal inputs with a 90° phase shift between them are applied to the two inputs. The pattern shown at (f) is typical of normal stereo program with little common information between the channels; the pattern appears to be contained roughly within a circular envelope. The pattern at (g) is for a stereo program containing strong in-phase, or center phantom, information. The pattern shown at (h) is for a stereo program containing common out-of-phase information.

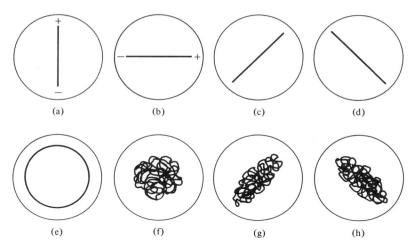

Figure 3-29. Stereophonic oscilloscope patterns. (a) Left only. (b) Right only. (c) Left and right in-phase. (d) Left and right out-of-phase. (e) Left and right at phase angle of 90°. (f) Stereo program. (g) Stereo program with significant in-phase components. (h) Stereo program with significant out-of-phase components.

BIBLIOGRAPHY

1. B. B. Bauer, "Broadening the Area of Stereophonic Perception," *J. Audio Eng. Soc.*, vol. 8, p. 91 (1960).
2. B. B. Bauer and G. W. Sioles, "Stereophonic Patterns," *J. Audio Eng. Soc.*, vol. 8, p. 126 (1960).
3. A. D. Blumlein, "British Patent Specification 394, 325 (Directional Effect in Sound Systems)," *J. Audio Eng. Soc.*, vol. 6, p. 91 (1958).
4. G. Bore and S. F. Temmer, " 'M-S' Stereophony and Compatibility," *Audio* (April 1958).
5. H. A. M. Clark, G. F. Dutton, and P. B. Vanderlyn, "The 'Stereosonic' Recording and Reproducing System," *J. Audio Eng. Soc.*, vol. 6, pp. 102–113 (April 1958).
6. J. M. Eargle, "Stereo/Mono Disc Compatibility: A Survey of the Problems," *J. Audio Eng. Soc.*, vol. 17, p. 276 (1969).
7. F. K. Harvey and M. R. Schroder, "Subjective Evaluation of Factors Affecting Two-Channel Stereophony," *J. Audio Eng. Soc.*, vol. 9, p. 19 (1961).
8. J. Mosely, "Eliminating the Stereo Seat," *J. Audio Eng. Soc.*, vol. 8, p. 46 (1960).
9. R. Orban, "A Rational Technique for Synthesizing Pseudo-Stereo From Monophonic Sources," *J. Audio Eng. Soc.*, vol. 18, p. 157 (1970).
10. M. R. Schroeder, "An Artificial Stereo Effect Obtained from a Single Audio Signal," *J. Audio Eng. Soc.*, vol. 6, p. 74 (1958).

4

Quadraphonic Sound

INTRODUCTION

For most of its history, sound recording has been a monophonic medium. Only in recent years have multichannel playback formats been introduced to the consumer marketplace, stereo in the 1950s and *quadraphonic*, or four-channel, sound in the late 1960s. The first quadraphonic releases were in the reel-to-reel tape format. They were followed by tape cartridge and, in the early seventies, quadraphonic disc formats.

There are several esthetic goals of quadraphonic reproduction ("quad," as it is generally called). Just as stereo provided a better illusion of concert hall ambience, and hence more realistic sound reproduction than could be obtained with monophonic sound, quad promises to extend the illusion even further. If stereo may be said to provide a window looking into the concert hall or onto the stage, quad attempts to recreate the original environment in the listener's living room. Just how well quad does this is a matter of considerable discussion. Where the music is clearly of an antiphonal nature with primary sources of sound located fore and aft, then there is no question of the greater illusion of accuracy which quad can provide. But if the primary sound is confined to the stage, as it is in the bulk of the symphonic repertory, then the rear channels of the quad array are relegated the role of merely providing a sound field consisting of reflections and reverberation. In order to be realistic, the back channels must be operated at a fairly low level, and their effect is apt to be a subtle one, so subtle in many cases that the cost vs. effectiveness may be seriously questioned.

However, going beyond the role of expanded realism, quad can become a vital tool in the creation of new sounds. Just as stereo techniques helped shape the pop-rock music of the sixties, quad techniques are becoming an important element in today's music making, especially as it involves electronic techniques. Much to the consternation of purists, even the hallowed ground of the concert hall is being reshaped by new quad techniques. The "direct-ambient" approach mentioned earlier is giving way, at least for the larger concerted works of the nineteenth and twentieth centuries, to a recording approach which places primary sound sources in back as well as in front of the listener.

As a consumer medium, quadraphonic sound has had more difficulty establishing itself than stereo did 15 years ago. Part of this problem has to do with physical requirements of locating four loudspeakers as well as the added expense of quad. Also, there are a number of esthetic questions which have not been answered to the satisfaction of the general record-producing community. In this chapter we shall attempt to answer some of these questions and point to future directions for growth of the medium. We shall discuss 4-2-4 stereo matrix approaches to quadraphonic sound in this chapter, but the discrete quadraphonic disc, because of its technological requirements, will be discussed in the chapter on disc recording.

Loudspeaker Arrangements for Quad

The generally preferred location of loudspeakers for quad is shown in Figure 4-1,a. The left-front and right-front loudspeakers (L_F, R_F) are located with respect to

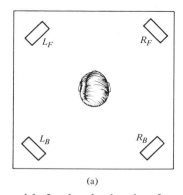
(a)

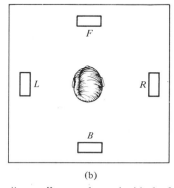
(b)

Figure 4-1. Loudspeaker locations for quad. In the "square" array shown in (a) the front pair of loudspeakers provides stereo performance as well. The "diamond" array shown in (b) can provide excellent quad performance for program material specially recorded for it. However, the array is incompatible with normal stereo performance.

the listeners as they might normally be for stereo listening, while the left-back and right-back loudspeakers (L_B, R_B) are located symmetrically behind the listener. With the "square" arrangement of Figure 4-1,a, there exist accurate phantom images in the front quadrant along with weaker and more ambiguous images in the other three quadrants. In the early days of quad, there was some experimenting with the loudspeaker arrangement shown in Figure 4-1,b. This "diamond" pattern was abandoned mainly because it did not provide compatibility with normal stereo listening and because it required the listener to perceive phantom images over a 180° frontal arc formed by three of the loudspeakers. Under this condition, frontal phantom images were precise but tended to move from side to side as the listener executed small side-to-side head movements.

Phantom Images in Quad

One of the goals of quad is to create the illusion of sound arriving from any direction in the horizontal, or azimuthal, plane of the listener, and there are a number of difficulties in doing this. Consider first an azimuthal array of eight loudspeakers symmetrically located around a listener, as shown in Figure 4-2,a; the location of real images (those existing at a loudspeaker) and phantom images (those existing between loudspeakers) will be about equally accurate and precise. Moving onto the six-loudspeaker array of Figure 4-2,b, all images intended for the frontal sextants (sixths of a circle) will be precise, while those intended for the rear sextants will be somewhat less so. In the quad arrangement of Figure 4-2,c images panned at any of the four loudspeakers will be precisely located. Phantom images in the front quadrant will be quite accurate, while those intended

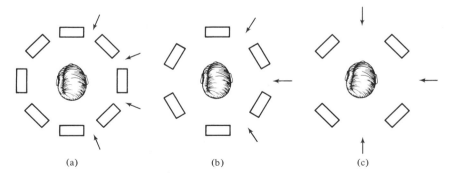

(a) (b) (c)

Figure 4-2. Phantom images in multi-loudspeaker arrays. (a) An eight-channel array produces accurate phantom images (indicated by arrows) as well as accurate real images (those existing at individual loudspeakers). (b) Phantom images in the front sextants are quite precise, while those in the side and rear sextants may be less so. (c) Phantom images in the front quadrant are precise. Those in the back quadrant are less so, and the side quadrant images are very unstable.

for the rear quadrant will be less so. In particular, a signal panned to center-back may appear somewhat overhead. In general, left-right integrity will be maintained in the back quadrant, but there will be fore-aft ambiguity.

Phantom images intended for the side quadrants are practically nonexistent. For example, as a signal is panned from L_F to L_B, the listener will hear the sound remaining at L_F until, all at once, it seems to jump back to L_B. When the signal is fed equally to L_F and L_B, the image remains clearly at L_F—unless the listener turns to face due left, at which point he will perceive a clear phantom image in that direction.

One may seriously raise the question of whether quad works at all, given the vagaries of its phantom images. Regarding overall azimuthal integrity, the question is well taken. Regarding the integrity of the four real images, there is little question that quad works, save for some reservations about the esthetics of assigning primary musical information to the rear of the listener. Regarding the presentation of direct-ambient musical relationships, again there is no question that quad works. The effect is subtle but is not primarily dependent upon phantom images in rear or side quadrants.

The Quadraphonic ("Joy Stick") Panpot

Quad panpots are the primary signal processing device for assigning directions to the elements of a quad program. Electrically, quad panpots are made up of *three* normal stereo panpots; one of these steers the signal into a "north-south" direction, and the remaining two steer these signals "east-west." Rotary controls can be used for this, but by far the most convenient form is the so-called joy stick embodiment of Figure 4-3,a; the direction of the control in space corresponds to the direction of signal assignment. The mathematics of the joy stick is based on the same principles of the stereo panpot; the acoustical output is constant and independent of the direction assignment.

Space and Time Incoherence

Students of psychoacoustics have long noticed that the interference or annoyance level of noise is greater if it appears to come from a direction *different* from that of desired signal. Specifically, for a primary sound source located in front of the listener, the annoyance value of any additional signal incoherent with it is least when it originates from the same direction as the primary sound and greatest when it is perceived by the listener as coming from the sides. The phenomenon was studied by Damaske (5), and his test results are shown in Figure 4-4.

We can all relate to Damaske's observations. At a concert, for example, minor noises, such as the rustling of programs, coughing, and so forth, originating be-

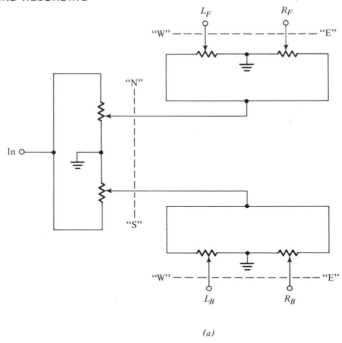

(a)

Figure 4-3. Details of a quad ("joy stick") panpot. A typical schematic diagram is shown in (a); a photo of API Model 480 is shown in (b). (*Courtesy of Automated Processes*)

hind or to the sides of a listener are more annoying to him than the same sounds would be if they originated to the front of him.

Madsen (13) observed that if a stereophonic program were processed as shown in Figure 4-5, a listener would localize primary information toward the front through the precedence, or Haas, effect, while reverberation coming from the sides would be enhanced through the Damaske effect. The effect of a delay in stereo information approaching the listener from the sides is to render its reverberant content sufficiently incoherent with that perceived from the front loudspeakers. It creates the illusion that the side information is quite different from the front information in terms of direct-to-reverberant relationships.

Tetraphonic Sound

The observations we have just made were part of a recording method introduced by Cunningham in the mid-sixties. He developed an approach to quad recording, called "tetraphonic sound," which used flanking loudspeakers slightly forward

(b)

Figure 4-3. (*Continued*)

of the lateral plane of the listener (4). His system was not so much a *direct-ambient* one, but rather was based on the notion that filling in an array of early reflections in the frontal 180° arc was in many ways more important than trying to create a continuum of azimuthal phantom image points around the listener.

Figure 4-6,a shows a typical tetraphonic recording arrangement, with the side microphones located to pick up early reflections along with direct sound delayed by no more than 30–35 msec. Figure 4-6,b shows a typical playback arrangement. The total angle subtended at the listener should be in the 120°–150° range. It is interesting to observe that many listeners who do not care for the square speaker arrangement of Figure 4-1 will find that of Figure 4-6,b perfectly satisfactory, even when the program may have been manipulated with

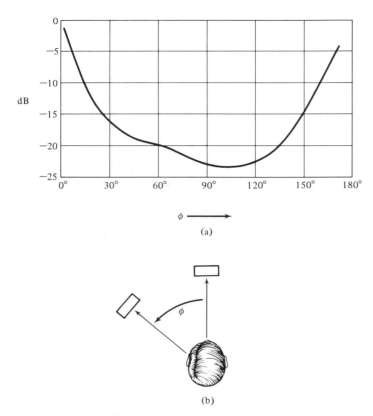

Figure 4-4. The Damaske effect. (a) the graph shows the relative annoyance level for an interfering sound source located at some angle ϕ away from a source located in front of the listener [shown in (b)]. For example, an annoyance source located at an angle between 90° and 120° from the front of the observer will be about 20–25 dB *more annoying* to the observer than it would be if it were located in front of the listener. That is, its level would have to be *lowered* 20–25 dB to have the same annoyance level as if the source were located straight ahead.

quad panpots for "around the room" effects. There is no denying the relative ease with which a tetraphonic loudspeaker array can accommodate itself to most living room environments.

Direct-Ambient Synthesis Techniques

The foregoing discussions have pointed to the feasibility of "processing" normal stereo information in such a way that a very realistic direct-ambient quad pre-

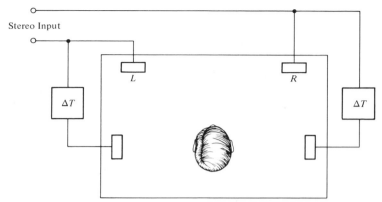

Figure 4-5. Madsen's process for recovering ambience information in normal stereo program. The delay range, ΔT, is normally no greater than about 12 msec. Listeners will localize direct sound at the front loudspeakers by the precedence effect. Reverberation, because of its random nature, will be heard principally from the side loudspeakers.

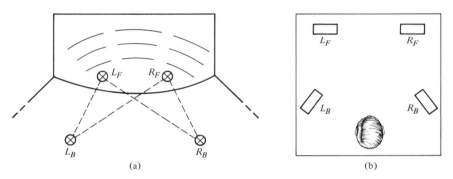

Figure 4-6. Cunningham's *tetraphonic* recording method is shown in (a). Rear microphones are carefully placed so that their distances from the front microphones do not exceed a time delay of about 25–30 msec. (b) The delayed sound and early reflections picked up by the back microphones are reproduced at the sides of the listener in playback.

sentation can be made. The author's studies (8) have shown that a combination of time delay and high-quality artificial reverberation can be used to produce a pair of ambient channels which may be barely distinguishable from the output of a pair of microphones located in an environment like the one being simulated. The basic technique is shown in Figure 4-7.

The relationships between delays, reverberation, and timbre are determined in the following ways:

1. The delay ΔT_1 establishes the distance between the front pair of micro-phones and the rear pair. If a small-scale chamber music recording is being processed, then the range for ΔT_1 may be no more than 20–30 msec; for a large symphonic recording, delays up to 45–50 msec would not be un-common. It is the purpose of ΔT_1 to establish a feeling of room size, and this it does by simulating the first early reflection from the side walls of a concert hall. The volume level of ΔT_1 should be established as about equal to the level which would be perceived in an environment with the absorp-tion characteristics of the one being simulated.

2. The adjustment of reverberation time (T_R) should be based upon the model room being simulated. It must be in keeping with the dimension established by ΔT_1 and, of course, the amount of reverberation already present in the stereo recording being processed.

3. The onset of reverberation is delayed further by ΔT_2, and the normal range for this would be 35–70 msec, depending upon the size of the room being simulated. The delay ΔT_2 establishes the normal delay between early re-flections and the onset of the dense reflections which are characteristic of reverberation. Also ΔT_2 plays a very important role in masking the charac-

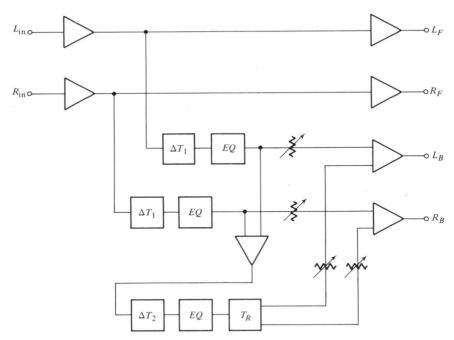

Figure 4-7. Signal flow diagram for a method of processing stereo program to simulate a quadraphonic recording of the *direct-ambient* type.

ter of the reverberation device. As we shall discuss in the chapter on signal processing, commonly available reverberation devices fall short of the characteristics of large recording environments; their defects are far less obvious when they are preceded by a direct signal component.

4. Finally, equalizers must be used to adjust the timbre of ΔT_1, ΔT_2, and T_R to match their frequency spectra to that of the model environment. The setting of relative levels of the three processed signal components is largely a matter of taste, but it must always be within the range established by the characteristics of the model environment.

Quad Microphones

As an extension of the M-S techniques of stereo, quad microphones have been designed (11), and their greatest utility has been found in the recording of environmental effects, such as sounds out-of-doors. These recordings lend themselves best to the square loudspeaker arrangement of Figure 4-1. A typical design for a quad microphone is shown in Figure 4-8. Three elements are used to produce four directional patterns spread 90° apart.

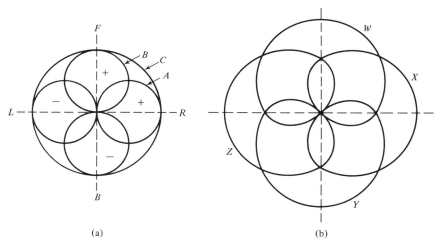

(a)   (b)

Figure 4-8. Details of a quadraphonic microphone. A typical quad microphone consists of *three* elements, two figure-eight microphones, and one omnidirectional. The three outputs can be combined to produce *four* outputs corresponding to four caridoid microphones oriented 90° apart. The outputs A, B, and C in Figure 4-8,a combine as follows to yield the patterns shown in Figure 4-8,b:

$$W = C + B$$
$$X = C + A$$
$$Y = C - B$$
$$Z = C - A$$

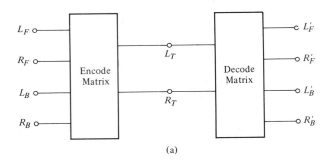

(a)

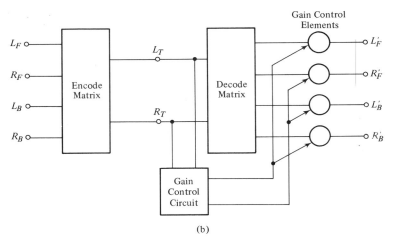

(b)

Figure 4-9. Details of the basic Scheiber 4-2-4 matrix. The four input signals are mixed into *two* transmission channels, L_T and R_T, as follows:

$$L_T = .924\, L_F + .924\, L_B + .383\, R_F - .383\, R_B$$

$$R_T = .924\, R_F + .924\, R_B + .383\, L_F - .383\, L_B$$

In the decoding matrix the signals are sorted out as follows:

$$L'_F = .924\, L_T + .383\, R_T = L_F + .707\, L_B + .707\, R_F$$

$$R'_F = .383\, L_T + .924\, R_T = R_F + .707\, L_F + .707\, R_B$$

$$L'_B = .924\, L_T - .383\, R_T = L_B + .707\, L_F - .707\, R_B$$

$$R'_B = -.383\, L_T + .924\, R_T = R_B + .707\, R_F - .707\, L_B$$

The gain control circuitry shown in (b) detects when dominant signals exist at a given output and attenuates the leakage signals at adjacent loudspeakers. For example, if L'_F is sensed as dominant, then the gain if L'_B and R'_F would be reduced in order to keep crosstalk at a low level.

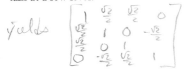

MATRIX QUAD SYSTEMS

4-2-4 Matrices

Strictly speaking, 4-2-4 matrix systems are *two-channel* systems. The notation "4-2-4" means that *four* input channels are matrixed, or mixed, into *two* transmission channels, and later "de-mixed" into *four* outputs. It is surprising how well this can be done under certain recording and playback circumstances, but in general the loss of channel separation which is incurred in the process relegates these systems to the role of simple stereo enhancement. As we discuss them in detail, we shall see how the separation characteristics can be somewhat improved through the use of program-directed gain control techniques.

Scheiber Matrix

The basic Scheiber matrix introduced in 1969 is shown in Figure 4-9,a. Here, four inputs, L_F, R_F, L_B, and R_B, are mixed into *two* transmission channels, L_T and R_T, and subsequently sorted out to yield primary information at its proper locations. In each case, the adjacent channels exist as cross-talk at a level 3 dB below the desired signal. Where one signal at a time exists, the "enhancement scheme" of Figure 4-9,b can be effective; it reduces the level of the loudspeakers adjacent to a dominant loudspeaker and gives a sense of greater separation. Since the gain-riding action is a continuous one, solely dependent upon program content, it generally produces an effect of greater separation, temporarily at least, at each loudspeaker.

Sansui "QS" Matrix

The QS matrix was introduced shortly after the Scheiber matrix and has essentially the same encoding and decoding coefficients. It corrects for the out-of-phase condition between rear channels by introducing 90° phase shifts in both encoding and decoding, thus ensuring that adjacent channel phase relationships are never more than 90°. The result is a far more natural sound than the Scheiber matrix. It is shown in Figure 4-10. Like the Scheiber matrix, the QS matrix exhibits cross-talk into adjacent loudspeakers down 3 dB.

The CBS "SQ" Matrix

The SQ matrix is significantly different from the two previously discussed in that its basic cross-talk characteristics are not to adjacent loudspeakers. Rather, left and right separation is maintained in both the front and back pairs, while the cross-talk from either front loudspeaker is into *both* back loudspeakers and from

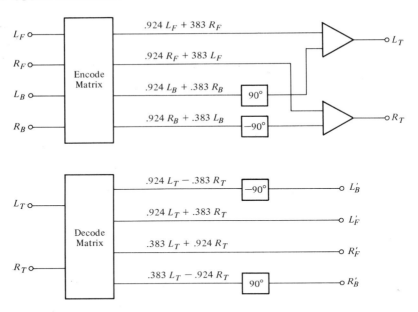

Figure 4-10. Details of the QS matrix. The coefficients are the same as in the Scheiber matrix, but out-of-phase conditions between the recovered back channels are avoided through the use of ±90° networks in both encoding and decoding.

either back loudspeaker into *both* front loudspeakers. The SQ matrix is shown in Figure 4-11,a, and the cross-talk characteristics are shown in Figure 4-11,b.

Both the QS and SQ 4-2-4 matrices are available with program-directed gain control which alters either levels or playback matrix coefficients in a manner which heightens the system separation to a greater or lesser degree. In the gain-control arrangements the trade-off is inevitable; there is a tendency for the gain manipulations to result in a "pumping" effect as signals are shifted in level.

Phantom Images in 4-2-4 Matrix Systems

Generally, because of inherently less separation, phantom images in 4-2-4 systems are even more ambiguous than in four-channel systems. Considering only phantom images intended for the front-center location, Figure 4-12,a shows the signal levels existing in a four-channel configuration. At Figure 4-12,b we see that the front-center phantom position for the SQ matrix results in *all four* loudspeakers at the same level. Localization is very imprecise unless enhanced by gain-control circuitry. At Figure 4-12,c we show the signal levels for a front-center image in the QS matrix. Here, the weight of front signals relative to the back helps to maintain the phantom image where it is desired.

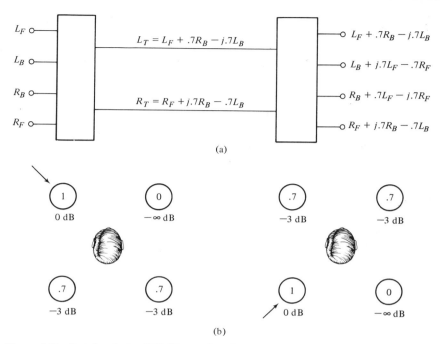

Figure 4-11. Details of the CBS SQ matrix. Basic matrix coefficients are shown in (a). The letter j ahead of a term indicates that term has been shifted 90°. The cross-talk characteristics of the SQ matrix are shown in (b). A signal intended for either of the front loudspeakers is also present in both back speakers 3 dB down in level. The same relations hold for back-intended signals cross-talking into the front loudspeakers.

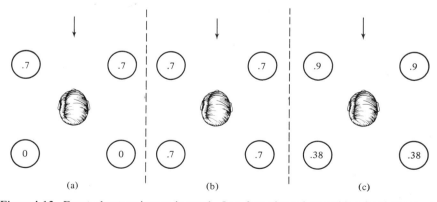

Figure 4-12. Front phantom images in quad. In a four channel array (a), a front phantom signal will result in the two front channels at a level of –3 dB (or a signal level of .7 relative to unity). In the case of the SQ matrix, (b), a front phantom signal will energize all four loudspeakers at –3 dB. In the case of the QS matrix, (c), a front phantom signal results in some leakage into the back loudspeakers, but the signal is predominately in the front pair.

Stereophonic and Monophonic Compatibility of 4-2-4 Matrices

Generally, the amplitude and phase relationships between the inputs to the SQ and QS matrices result in quite satisfactory stereo presentation. Stereo locations for the four primary inputs and front-center position are shown in Figure 4-13.

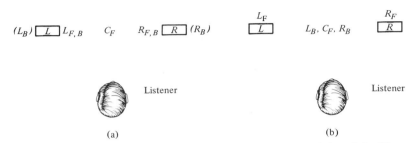

(a)   (b)

Figure 4-13. Stereo compatibility of matrix systems. The characteristics of the QS matrix are shown in (a). Under most listening conditions, both L_F and L_B signals will appear slightly panned in from the left loudspeaker. The same thing holds for the R_F and R_B signals. If the listener is precisely located on the center plane, he may localize the back signals *outside* the loudspeaker array. Characteristics of the SQ matrix are shown in (b). The L_F and R_F signals appear, respectively, at the left and right loudspeakers, while both back signals appear at the center. With both QS and SQ matrices, a signal intended for front-center (C_F) appears in the center of the stereo array.

Note that in the case of the QS matrix the L_B and R_B inputs may, under precise listening conditions, result in those signals being perceived outside the loudspeaker array. As we discussed in the chapter on psychoacoustics, this effect tends not to be a stable one.

When summed for monophonic performance the SQ matrix presents its four primary inputs at the same level; this in fact was one of the design goals of that system. On the other hand the QS matrix suffers a loss of 7.6 dB of its L_B and R_B inputs relative to L_F and R_F. The loss is, of course, inherent in the phase relationships which define the matrix.

The reader who wishes to analyze matrices in greater detail is referred to Scheiber's spherical representation of 4-2-4 matrix systems (16).

Phasor Representation of 4-2-4 Matrices

So far, we have represented various 4-2-4 matrices mathematically, listing the terms present in their transmission equations. A clearer picture results from a phasor representation of the four inputs to the encoding matrix and how the inputs determine the modulation of the two transmission channels. The representations are quite similar to the Lissajous figures shown in the chapter on stereophonic sound. The phasor representations for several matrices are shown in Figure 4-14.

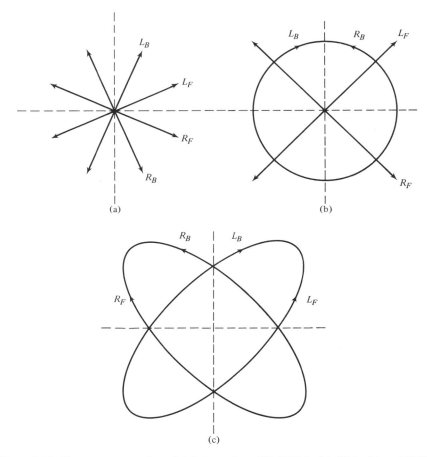

Figure 4-14. Phasor representation of 4-2-4 matrices: QS (RM) in (a); SQ in (b); and BMX in (c).

Figure 4-14,a shows the phasor representation for the four inputs to the QS matrix. As regards the four main inputs, the representation is the same as for the *Regular Matrix* (RM) standard adopted in Japan, a form to which the QS matrix best fits. Figure 4-14,b shows the phasor representation of the SQ matrix; note that the rear channels are identified by circular motion, indicating the 90° phase relationship between channels. As viewed along the groove direction of travel, the circular motions outline spiral, or helical, motions. At Figure 4-14,c, four inputs for the Cooper-Shiga BMX matrix are shown. The elliptical motions are characteristic of both amplitude and phase relationship between L_T and R_T in defining the matrix.

It is worth noting that some 4-2-4 matrix playback networks have found some favor in the playback of normal nonencoded stereo discs. Many listeners find the increased spread of sound sources musically satisfying, especially if the rear loudspeakers are played at a somewhat lower level. In general, direct signal components in a stereo program tend to be in phase between the channels, and as such will be emphasized in the front loudspeakers in both the QS and SQ matrices. Reverberation components tend to be randomly disposed in their phase relationships and accordingly may be more prominent in rear speakers. It must be emphasized that this kind of "enhancement" of stereo program is no substitute for a quadraphonic recording.

Higher Order Matrix Systems

We have examined in detail the characteristics of 4-2-4 matrix systems and seen that a degree of cross-talk is inherent in these systems. What about a 4-3-4 matrix? Four signals can be encoded into three channels and recovered with far better separation than is characteristic of 4-2-4 systems. In the following example, A, B, C, and D represent the four inputs to the input, or encoding, matrix, and X, Y, and Z represent the transmission channels. Encoding:

$$X = \tfrac{2}{3}(A + B)$$

$$Y = \tfrac{2}{3}(C + D)$$

$$Z = \tfrac{1}{3}(A - B + C - D)$$

Decoding, we recover A, B, C, and D as prime signals along with whatever cross-talk terms there may be. These combined recovered signals are indicated by A', B', C', and D':

$$A' = X + Z = A + \tfrac{1}{3}(B + C - D)$$

$$B' = X - Z = B + \tfrac{1}{3}(A - C + D)$$

$$C' = Y + Z = C + \tfrac{1}{3}(D + A - B)$$

$$D' = Y - Z = D + \tfrac{1}{3}(C - A + B)$$

The recovered signals in this 4-3-4 array exist along with the remaining terms as cross-talk at one-third the level (down 9.6 dB), as shown in Figure 4-15.

Generalization of Matrix Systems

Cooper and Shiga have generalized the theory of matrix systems as regards azimuthal presentation. It is based on the notion of *azimuthal harmonics*. The more harmonics (or channels) are present, the more accurately directional in-

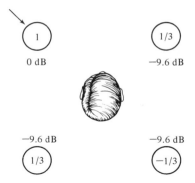

Figure 4-15. Characteristics of a 4-3-4 matrix. If a signal is intended for one loudspeaker, then cross-talk terms will exist at the other three loudspeakers down 9.6 dB. The significance of the minus sign at the *opposite* loudspeaker indicates that the cross-talk term is out of phase at that loudspeaker.

formation can be presented. The Cooper-Shiga theory takes into account any number of inputs, transmission channels, and outputs, and makes use of amplitude as well as phase angle relationships between the transmission channels. Their work is well represented in the literature (3).

As an example of their approach, we present a typical resolution of a signal in a 6-4-6 array (six signals encoded into four channels and then resolved back into six loudspeaker inputs). This is shown in Figure 4-16.

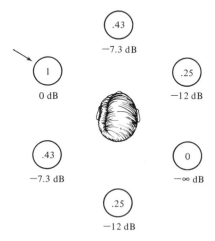

Figure 4-16. Cross-talk characteristics of a Cooper-Shiga 6-4-6 matrix. There are two cross-talk terms down 7.3 dB and two terms down 12 dB. There is no cross-talk into the opposite loudspeaker.

Systems with Height

Under the term *periphonic*, Gerzon (10) discusses multichannel systems which convey height as well as azimuthal information surrounding the listener. As an example of how this can be applied to a four-channel transmission system with six loudspeakers, we present the following 6-4-6 matrix. Four loudspeakers would be located in the horizontal plane of the listener; an additional speaker would be located *above* him and another one *below* him (for the present, we will not worry about the practicality of the arrangement). The input signals are A, B, C, D, E, and F, and the transmission channels are W, X, Y, and Z. The encoding equations are:

$$W = \tfrac{2}{3} (A - B)$$
$$X = \tfrac{2}{3} (C - D)$$
$$Y = \tfrac{2}{3} (E - F)$$
$$Z = \tfrac{1}{3} (A + B + C + D + E + F)$$

The recovered signals are then given by:

$$A' = Z + W = A + \tfrac{1}{3} (C + D + E + F - B)$$
$$B' = Z - W = B + \tfrac{1}{3} (C + D + E + F - A)$$
$$C' = Z + X = C + \tfrac{1}{3} (A + B + E + F - D)$$
$$D' = Z - X = D + \tfrac{1}{3} (A + B + E + F - C)$$
$$E' = Z + Y = E + \tfrac{1}{3} (A + B + C + D - F)$$
$$F' = Z - Y = F + \tfrac{1}{3} (A + B + C + D - E)$$

All inputs are recovered at full level, and in each output the remaining signals appear also at one-third amplitude (9.6 dB down).

A Steerable Microphone Array

In Figure 4-17 we illustrate a "steerable" four-channel microphone array, an arrangement of three figure-eight microphones and one omnidirectional microphone whose outputs can be combined in a number of ways to produce the directional characteristics of a cardioid microphone pointing in any direction in space. It is a three-dimensional extension of the steerable array which was described in the chapter on stereophonic sound.

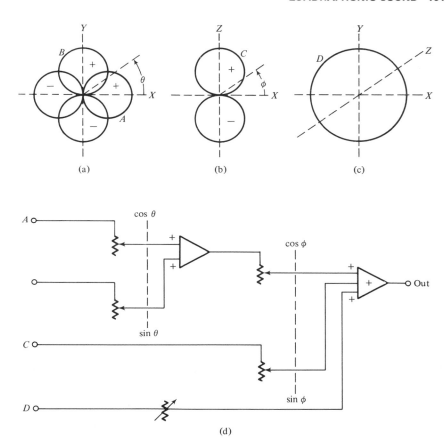

Figure 4-17. A steerable four-channel microphone array. A view of the horizontal X-Y plane is shown in (a). Angle θ is measured in that plane, and outputs A and B are combined through sine and cosine potentiometers to give a single figure-eight output oriented at any angle θ in that plane. The resulting figure-eight pattern is then combined with the figure-eight output C, which lies along the vertical, or Z-axis [shown in (b)], and a new figure-eight pattern is produced which is oriented at a vertical angle ϕ as well as a horizontal angle θ. The steerable figure-eight pattern is finally combined with the omnidirectional output D [shown in (c)] and cardioid response can thus be obtained in any direction. The significance of this quad microphone array is that the outputs, A through D, can be recorded and then later played back with resolution in any desired direction (d). The array is the basis of a system of periphonic sound reproduction suggested by Gerzon in which signals are resolved in directions parallel to the faces of a regular tetrahedron and reproduced over loudspeakers similarly placed.

CHOWNING'S METHOD OF SIMULATING MOVING SOUND SOURCES IN QUAD

Chowning has described a method of processing monophonic information for presentation over a square quad loudspeaker array so that the illusion of motion is realistically produced (2). The following parameters determine the illusion:

1. Amplitude relationships between the four synthesized channels. (This is the role played by the "joy stick" quad panpot.)
2. The simulation of *Doppler shift* proportional to the velocity of the simulated source toward or away from the listener. (Doppler shift is the *change* in frequency of a sound source as it moves with respect to the listener. For example, a fire siren rises in pitch as it moves toward the observer and falls in pitch as it moves away.)
3. *Reverberant* energy broken into two components, *global* and *local*. Global reverberation reaches the listener from all four loudspeakers equally when the simulated sound source is fairly close. Global reverberation is proportional to $(1/r)$ $(1/\sqrt{r}\,)$, where r is the simulated distance. When the source moves away from the listener, local reverberation signals follow it and are simulated to come from the same direction. Local reverberation is proportional to $(1 - 1/r)$ $(1/\sqrt{r}\,)$ and provides cues for directionality even when the simulated source is at considerable distances from the listener. Distance cues are the result of the direct-to-total-reverberant ratios established.

Most demonstrations of the Chowning synthesis scheme have been by way of rather elaborate computer processing of monophonic signals. Direct manipulation of the parameters of the Chowning scheme (so-called real-time processing) is especially difficult because of the requirements of simulated Doppler shift. There is no way that Doppler shift can be simulated on a real-time basis except in very small amounts.

Those readers whose interests include the broad field of electronic music should study Chowning's work in detail.

STABLIZING PHANTOM IMAGES IN QUADRAPHONIC ARRAYS

A continuing problem with wide acceptance of quadraphony has been the instability of phantom images in side and rear quadrants when the loudspeakers are located in a square with the listener in the middle. A number of studies have been undertaken which show that proper side image localization cannot result from standard panning to those positions via a quadraphonic panpot, but only through the construction of phasors at the listener's ears corresponding to sound sources located at those positions. Many of these studies have grown out of

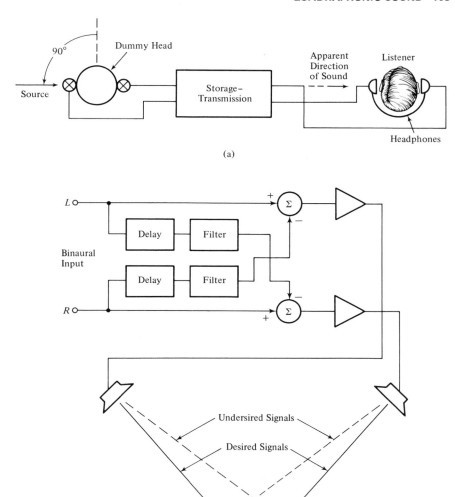

Figure 4-18. Binaural-to-stereo transformation. A binaural recording system is shown in (a). It gives accurate localization of sound sources at right angles to the listener's forward direction. In (b) the binaural signals are processed by providing both time delay and equalization simulating the acoustic path around the listener's head. These signals are then added out-of-phase so that the desired cancellation of unwanted signals will take place at each ear.

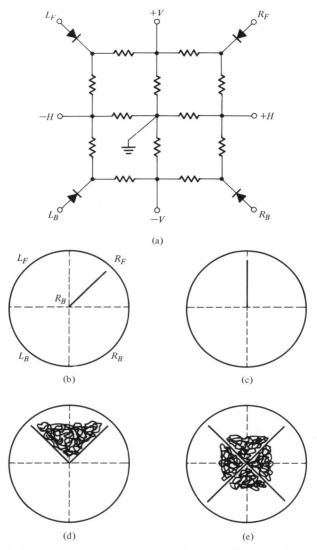

Figure 4-19. Method of visual quad monitoring using an oscilloscope. The resistor-diode network is shown in (a). The four inputs, L_F, R_F, L_B, and R_B, are applied to the indicated terminals and to the common ground point. The oscilloscope outputs of the network must be applied to the indicated horizontal and vertical inputs of a *balanced* oscilloscope. The pattern shown in (b) is for a single input applied at the R_F terminals of the network; the pattern shown in (c) is for a signal panned to center-front, feeding L_F and R_F equally with in-phase program. The direction of the oscilloscope display, as it points from the center, will correspond in direction to the individual panned signals. The pattern shown in (d) is for stereo program applied to the L_F and R_F inputs, while the pattern shown in (e) represents quad information applied to the four inputs.

binaural recording methods and subsequent transformation of binaural signals into suitable stereophonic signals by the application of inverse crossfeed terms from one stereo channel to the other. It is interesting to note that accurate side image localization can be produced from a single frontal pair of loud-speakers. The basic principle is shown in Figure 4-18. For a source located at right angles to the listener's forward direction, measurement can be made by way of a dummy head to determine frequency and phase relationships at the two ears. If these signals are recorded and then played back with headphones, the listener unmistakably hears the sound emanating at the desired right-angle direction, as is shown in (a). These two signals can then be processed as shown in (b) for reproduction over loudspeakers, with each loudspeaker's signal containing additional terms designed to cancel the unwanted signals at each ear. The technique requires a fairly rigid listener-loudspeaker relationship if the effect is to be accurate and unambiguous. These studies have yet to be applied to quadraphony in its general practice, but they hold the promise of more accurate side image localization along with an enlarging of the acceptable listening area.

It is of course possible to construct panpots which work on this principle and which would provide better azimuthal localization than current devices.

VISUAL METERING SYSTEMS FOR QUAD

A unique method for visually metering quad signals has been proposed by Patten (14). His technique uses a resistor-diode network which accepts the four quad inputs and has outputs to the X-Y plates of an oscilloscope. The approach, or variations of it, have found favor with high-fidelity manufacturers wishing to provide analytical aids for the sophisticated audiophile. The unique characteristic of the network is that it provides a vector representation of individual signals in the direction those signals are assigned. For example, a signal panned to one of the four corners will appear as a line from center to that corner; a signal panned between an adjacent pair of corners will point in the direction the phantom image is intended.

The resistor-diode network is shown in Figure 4-19,a, and typical patterns are shown in Figure 4-19,b through 4-19,f.

Along more conventional lines the Victor Company of Japan has developed a display system in which signal levels at the four corners are represented as quadrants of a circle, expanding or contracting in radius according to signal level. For professional use, this metering arrangement is calibrated in dB and can be used to determine absolute signal levels. A variety of memory functions are included along with a choice of peak or standard VU level indication. The device is shown in Figure 4-20.

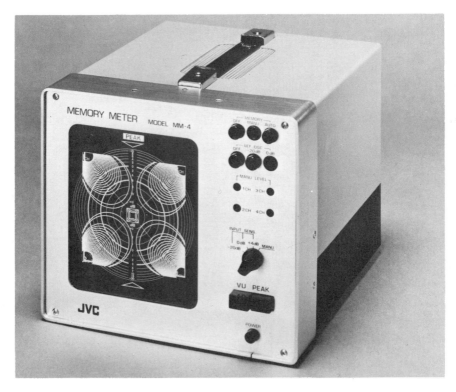

Figure 4-20. Photograph of the MM-4 visual quad metering system manufactured by the Victor Company of Japan. (*Courtesy Victor Company of Japan*)

BIBLIOGRAPHY

1. B. B. Bauer, D. W. Gravereaux, and A. J. Gust, "A Compatible Stereo-Quadraphonic (SQ) Record System," *J. Audio Eng. Soc.*, vol. 19, pp. 638–646 (September 1971).

2. J. Chowning, "The Simulation of Moving Sound Sources," *J. Audio Eng. Soc.*, vol. 19, pp. 2–6 (January 1971).

3. D. Cooper and T. Shiga, "Discrete-Matrix Multichannel Stereo," *J. Audio Eng. Soc.*, vol. 20, pp. 346–360 (June 1972).

4. J. Cunningham, "Tetraphonic Sound," *db Magazine*, pp. 21–23 (December 1969).

5. P. Damaske, "Subjective Investigation of Sound Fields," *Acustica* 19, no. 4, 199 (1967/1968).

6. P. Damaske and V. Mellert, "A Method for the True Reproduction of All Directional Information by Two-Channel Stereophony," *Acustica* 22, no. 3, 153 (1969/1970).

7. J. Eargle, "Stereo/Mono Disc Compatibility; a Survey of the Problems," *J. Audio Eng. Soc.*, vol. 17, p. 276 (1969).

8. J. M. Eargle, "On the Processing of Two- and Three-Channel Program Material for Four-Channel Playback," *J. Audio Eng. Soc.*, vol. 10, pp. 262–266 (April 1971).

9. J. M. Eargle, "Multichannel Stereo Matrix Systems: An Overview," *J. Audio Eng. Soc.*, vol. 19, pp. 552–559 (July/August 1971).
10. M. Gerzon, "Periphony: With-Height Sound Reproduction," *J. Audio Eng. Soc.*, vol. 21, pp. 2–10 (January/February 1973).
11. C. Huston, "A Quadraphonic Microphone Development," *Recording Engineer/Producer*, pp. 23–24 (September 1970).
12. R. Itoh and S. Takahashi, "The Sansui QS Four-Channel System and a Newly Developed Technique to Improve Its Separation Characteristics" (presented at the Audio Engineering Society Convention, Los Angeles, May 1972).
13. E. Madsen, "Extraction of Ambience Information from Ordinary Recordings," *J. Audio Eng. Soc.*, vol. 18, p. 490 (1970).
14. D. Patten, "A Quadraphonic Oscilloscope Display Technique," *J. Audio Eng. Soc.*, vol. vol. 20, pp. 483–489 (July/August 1972).
15. P. Scheiber, "Suggested Performance Requirements for Compatible Four-Channel Recordings" (presented at 40th Audio Engineering Society Convention, April 1971).
16. P. Scheiber, "Analyzing Phase-Amplitude Matrices," *J. Audio Eng. Soc.*, vol. 19, pp. 835–839 (November 1971).

5

Microphones

A microphone is a *transducer*, a device which converts energy from one form to another, namely, acoustical to electrical. Other transducers used in recording are loudspeakers (electrical to acoustical), disc cutting heads (electrical to mechanical), and phonograph playback cartridges (mechanical to electrical).

CARBON

The use of microphones began with the advent of the telephone in the last quarter of the nineteenth century. The requirements were merely those of speech intelligibility, and the *carbon* microphone developed early in that art is still used today. The carbon microphone acts as a variable resistance. Particles of carbon are alternately compressed and relaxed by the diaphragm under the influence of sound pressure (Figure 5-1), and the resulting alteration of resistance gives rise to a signal current proportional to the change in resistance. Carbon microphones are noisy, have limited dynamic range, and produce high levels of distortion, but none of these defects is really serious in its application to telephony.

CAP
(CONDENSER)

The demands of broadcasting in the early years of this century called for higher quality levels; music and speech entertainment demanded more accurate translation of sound pressures into electrical signals and better microphones were needed. The *capacitor* or "condenser" microphone was developed, and the principle of magnetic induction was applied to

108

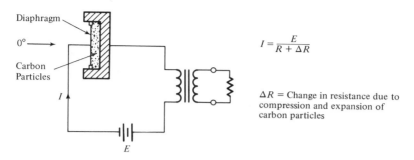

$$I = \frac{E}{R + \Delta R}$$

ΔR = Change in resistance due to compression and expansion of carbon particles

Figure 5.1. Schematic of a carbon microphone.

moving coil and ribbon devices. Their refinement over the last seventy years has formed the basis of the present-day microphone art.

Another principle has been used in microphone design: *piezo-electricity* (from the Greek *piezo*, meaning pressure) (see Figure 5-2). Certain crystalline sub- *CRYSTAL* stances, when flexed or compressed, develop a voltage difference between opposite surfaces. Coupled to a diaphragm they can function as microphones. They have been used mainly for paging and various hand-held applications. The fidelity of these is poor, and they have never been used for serious recording. Certain *ceramic* materials also exhibit piezo-electricity; the field of *sonar* makes use of ceramic elements in the construction of *hydrophones*, underwater acoustical transducers.

It is surprising that the microphone did not become a part of recording until about fifty years after its introduction. The art of sound recording developed as a purely *acousto-mechanical* process from the last years of the nineteenth century until the introduction by Western Electric of electrical recording in the mid-twenties. Up to this time the performance characteristics of the acoustical medium had been at least the equal of the corresponding electrical art as applied to radio and telephony.

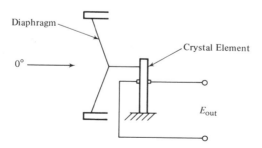

Figure 5-2. Schematic of a crystal microphone.

Radio broadcasting developed around the various moving coil and ribbon devices, and those microphone types were the mainstay of recording in the United States through the mid-forties. The most significant engineering of microphones during the thirties was accomplished by RCA and Western Electric, essentially for their broadcast and motion picture interests. Development of capacitor types was more or less restricted to calibration and measurement applications.

Capacitor microphones thrived in Europe during the thirties, and after the war they made a significant impact on American recording practice. The introduction of tape recording and the long-playing record in the latter forties pointed up the frequency response limitations of the magnetic microphones which had been designed in the thirties, and capacitor devices, with their extended high-frequency response, were quick to fill the need. The fifties and sixties saw the introduction of numerous excellent magnetic devices with extended response, and today's recording practice draws heavily from both magnetic and capacitor microphone types. In the last ten years microphones have become both better and cheaper; increased demand for all types has resulted in improved mass production techniques and the development of better materials.

ANALYSIS OF MAGNETIC MICROPHONES

The principle of *magnetic induction* shown in Figure 5-3 has formed the basis for a number of microphone types. When a conductor moves in a magnetic field in such a way that it crosses the field, a voltage will be developed across the conductor. The equation which governs this principle is:

$$E \text{ (voltage)} = Blv$$

where B is the flux density of the magnetic field, l the length of the conductor in the field, and v the velocity of the conductor as it moves across the field.

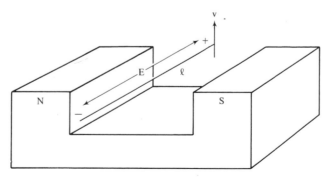

Figure 5-3. Magnetic induction. A wire of length l moving across a magnetic field of flux density B at a velocity v, produces a voltage in the wire proportional to Blv.

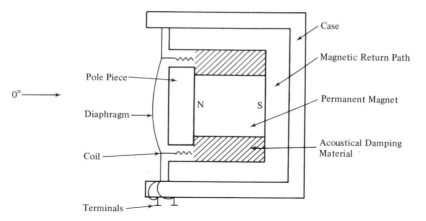

Figure 5-4. Diagram of a dynamic microphone.

For high voltage output, the flux density and the length of the conductor should be as great as possible consistent with the requirements of low mass of the moving system.

The simplest magnetic device is the *moving coil* microphone, often called a *dynamic* microphone. A typical form of this is shown in Figure 5-4. A small coil, usually no wider than half to three-quarters of an inch, is attached to a very thin diaphragm and placed in a narrow magnetic gap. Sound pressure causes a to-and-fro motion of the diaphragm, and the motion of the coil in the magnetic gap produces an output voltage proportional to the velocity of the diaphragm. The simple device we have described is essentially omnidirectional. At low frequencies there is sufficient diffraction of sound around the microphone so that diaphragm motion is insensitive to the direction of the sound. At high frequencies, and correspondingly shorter wavelengths, the microphone becomes acoustically larger and shows a preference for sound arriving perpendicular to the diaphragm. Thus, the smaller we make the microphone, the higher in frequency its behavior remains omidirectional. Dynamic microphones of early design were fairly large, perhaps $1-1\frac{1}{2}$ inches in diameter, because of inefficient permanent magnet structures. As a result, large voice coil-diaphragm structures restricted the high-frequency response. Today's dynamic microphones are far smaller and more sensitive, with excellent response up to the 15–20 kHz region.

Another very important type of magnetic device, the *ribbon microphone*, is unique in that it yields a "figure-eight" response pattern. A corrugated ribbon is suspended between two magnetic pole pieces and behaves as a single-turn coil in a magnetic gap. Sound arriving at 0° and 180° incidence will produce maximum motion of the ribbon and thus maximum electrical output. Sound arriving at angles of 90° and 270° will result in equal pressures on both sides, and there will be no resultant motion of the diaphragm.

Details of the ribbon microphone and its directional characteristics are shown in Figure 5-5. (The figure-eight pattern, also known as a *cosine* pattern, is evi-

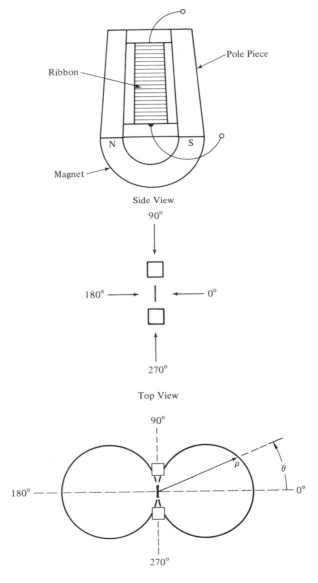

Figure 5-5. Diagram and directional characteristics of a ribbon microphone.

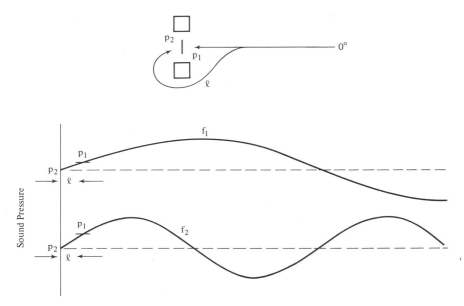

Figure 5-6. Operation of a ribbon microphone. For sound arriving at zero-degree incidence there is a path length, l, between the two sides of the diaphragm. At some frequency, f_1, there is a pressure difference, or gradient, equal to $p_1 - p_2$ acting on the ribbon. At f_2 (twice f_1) the $p_1 - p_2$ gradient is about 6 db greater. The ribbon is *mass controlled* because of its subsonic resonance, and the net output is a flat electrical signal with respect to frequency, as shown in Figure 5-7.

dent and is mathematically expressed as $\rho = \cos \theta$, in polar coordinates.) The ribbon microphone is also referred to as a *pressure gradient* microphone in that the force acting on the diaphragm is proportional to the difference between the pressures on both sides of the diaphragm. This relationship is shown in Figure 5-6. In addition to the designation "pressure gradient," the ribbon microphone is often referred to as a *velocity* microphone, its output being dependent on the air particle velocity at the ribbon. Figure 5-7 illustrates the force acting on a ribbon microphone to produce flat output with respect to frequency.

Ribbon microphones designed in the thirties exhibited significant response out to the 10–12-kHz region, but later designs have extended the useful range out to the 15–20-kHz region. Because of the general need for separation in multitrack recording, there is relatively little demand for ribbon devices today. There is, however no question of their usefulness in certain types of classical recording in rooms with sympathetic acoustics.

The earliest *directional* microphones were built around the characteristics of the omnidirectional and figure-eight devices. The basic directional pattern is the

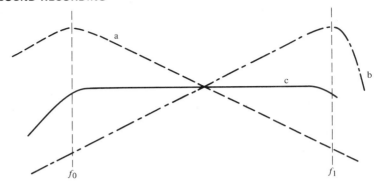

Figure 5-7. Forces acting on a ribbon microphone producing flat output with respect to frequency. Curve *a* is the velocity of the ribbon exposed to a constant pressure gradient. The term f_0 is the subsonic resonant frequency of the ribbon and defines the lower useful frequency limit of the device; it diminishes 6 dB/octave with rising frequency. Curve *b* is the pressure gradient acting on the ribbon; it rises 6 dB/octave, leveling off and finally reaching a null point where the wavelength for f_1 is equal to *l*. The net output is shown at Curve *c*.

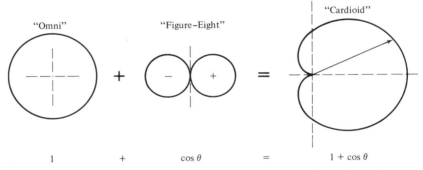

Figure 5-8. Derivation of the cardioid pattern. At zero-degree incidence, the cosine pattern and omni pattern are in phase and add to give a value of *two*. At 90° the cosine pattern is zero, and the output of *unity* is due only to the omni pattern. Going from 90° through 180° to 270°, the output of the cosine pattern is negative (since the diaphragm is driven from the back side), and it is in opposition to the omnidirectional pattern. At 180°, it is equal to, but out-of-phase with, the omni pattern, and total cancellation occurs.

cardioid (heart-shaped) curve shown in Figure 5-8. It is the sum of the response of an omni element and a figure-eight element.

By varying the amount of omnidirectional and cosine components, we can create a variety of response patterns, as shown in Figure 5-9. This is the principal on which many microphones with selectable response patterns are based.

It is possible to arrive at various directional patterns using a single ribbon or dynamic element by providing complex acoustical paths to the diaphragm or ribbon. Effectively, the vibrating element functions both as an omnidirectional and a figure-eight device at the same time. Varying the amounts of both actions produces the family of response curves shown in Figure 5-9. Figure 5-10 shows how the acoustical paths can be modified around a single ribbon to arrive at a cardioid pattern.

Such techniques can be elaborated upon for even greater directionality. Line, or so-called shot-gun, microphones employ a long slotted tubular structure in front of the diaphragm. Sounds arriving in line with the tube reach the diaphragm relatively unattenuated, while those arriving at other angles reach the

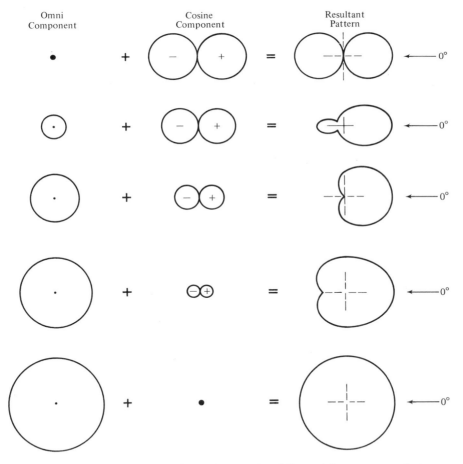

Figure 5-9. Various combinations of omnidirectional and figure-eight patterns producing a variety of polar patterns.

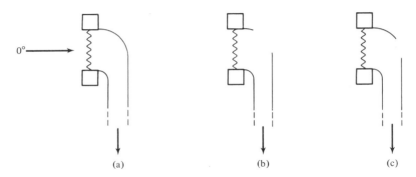

0°⟶

(a)   (b)   (c)

Arrow indicates path to acoustical damping

Figure 5-10. Modifications around a single ribbon to produce a cardioid pattern. In (a) the back of the ribbon is sealed with an acoustically inert tube; the ribbon thus behaves like a simple dynamic element. In (b) the opening in the tube is large enough that the ribbon behaves as a pressure gradient device with its characteristic figure-eight pattern. With an opening of intermediate size, as shown in (c), both actions are combined with a resultant cardioid response.

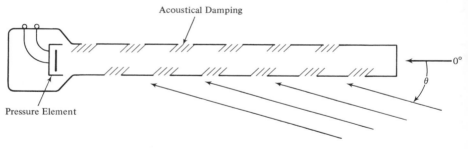

Acoustical Damping

Pressure Element

θ ⟵ 0°

(a) Principle of the Line Microphone

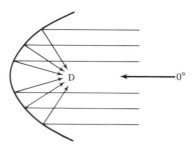

D ⟵ 0°

(b) Principal of the Parabolic Reflector

Figure 5-11. Diagram of a line microphone (a) and a parabolic reflector (b).

diaphragm through a multiplicity of paths, with resultant interference and cancellation of sound pressure. Parabolic reflectors, which focus on-axis sound on a microphone, are also used for highly directional pickup in long-throw, out-of-doors situations. These devices, along with line microphones, are quite effective at shorter wavelengths, but at low frequencies they tend to lose their directivity. They are shown in Figure 5-11.

ANALYSIS OF CAPACITOR MICROPHONES

Capacitor microphones are mechanically the simplest types used in recording; their only moving part is an extremely light diaphragm, which acts as one electrode of a *capacitor*. A capacitor is an electrical component consisting of two electrodes, separated by a very small distance, capable of storing an electrical charge according to the equation $Q = CE$. Moving the electrodes (see Figure 5-12) alters the capacitance and voltage according to the following equation:

$$\Delta C = \frac{Q}{\Delta E}$$

For small changes in C (indicated by ΔC), there is a voltage change (ΔE) which is *inversely proportional* to the capacitance change.

In the capacitor microphone shown in Figure 5-13, the back plate acts as one electrode of the capacitor, and the diaphragm acts as the other. The charge is maintained through an electrical biasing network. The diaphragm is made of a

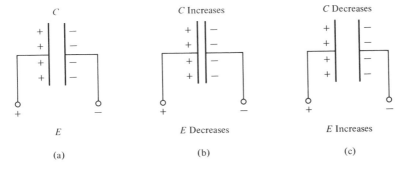

Figure 5-12. Relations between capacitance and voltage in a variable capacitor with fixed charge. The term Q is the charge in coulombs, C is the capacitance in farads, and E is the applied voltage. The closer the electrodes are spaced, the higher the capacitance. In (a), a a capacitor has been charged by a voltage E. If the charge remains constant and the electrodes are moved closer together, the voltage between the electrodes will *decrease*, as shown in (b). If the electrodes are moved farther apart, the voltage *increases*, as shown in (c).

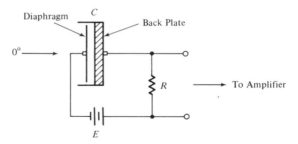

Figure 5-13. Basic principle of the capacitor microphone.

thin piece of plastic, usually Mylar, metallized so that it becomes a conductor. As sound pressure causes the diaphragm to move to and fro, there is a very slight change in capacitance, and a minute signal voltage is developed. The resistor R is usually quite large in order to ensure that the charge on the electrodes of the capacitor does not change as the diaphragm moves in and out. The signal voltage is always amplified and converted to a low impedance level as near the capacitance element as possible in order to minimize signal losses.

DIRECTIONAL CAPACITOR MICROPHONES

Various directional patterns for capacitor microphones can be produced by applying techniques similar to those used with magnetic devices. In order to explain this in the clearest way, a set of *analogies* between mechanical and electrical systems will be developed as shown in Table 5-1.

Table 5-1. Analogous Electrical and Mechanical Quantities

Electrical	Mechanical (Impedance Analogy)
Voltage (E)	Force (F)
Current (I)	Velocity (V)
Resistance (R)	Damping (dash pot) (D)
Capacitance (C)	Compliance (C)
Inductance (L)	Mass (M)

Figure 5-14, shows a simple electrical circuit and its equivalent, or analogous, mechanical circuit. Figure 5-14,d shows a weight suspended on a spring; when a force is applied to the mass, it will oscillate up and down at a frequency given by:

$$f_0 = \frac{1}{2\pi} \sqrt{\frac{1}{MC}}$$

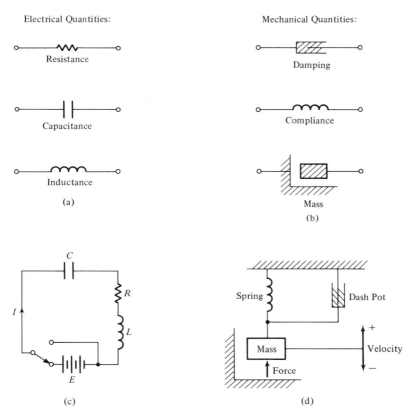

Figure 5-14. Electrical elements, L, C, and R (a) and a resonant circuit composed of them (c). Mechanical elements M, C, and D (b), and a resonant circuit composed of them (d). The combinations of L, C, and R determine the *impedance* of electrical circuit, the ratio of applied voltage to current flow. In a like manner, the analogous mechanical quantities provide mechanical impedance, the ratio of applied force to velocity. Both circuits are examples of *resonance*.

where M is the mass of the weight and C the compliance of the spring. For the electrical circuit of Figure 5-14,c, if voltage is applied to the circuit, it will oscillate at a frequency given by:

$$f_0 = \frac{1}{2\pi} \sqrt{\frac{1}{LC}},$$

where L is the inductance (in henrys) and C the capacitance (in farads). These two circuits, electrical and mechanical, are called analogs because equations of the same form determine their behavior. Typical resonance curves for both mechanical and electrical circuits are shown in Figure 5-15.

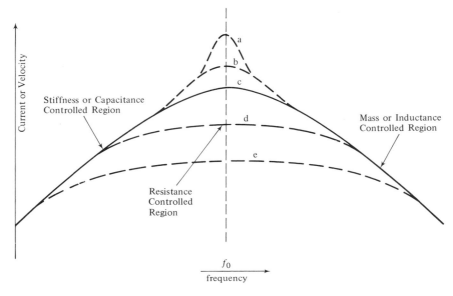

Figure 5-15. Family of resonance curves for the circuits of Figure 5-14 showing the effect of going from low resistance or damping (a) to high resistance or damping (e). Where there is little resistance or damping in the circuit, the oscillation increases rapidly in the region of resonance. When there is considerable resistance or damping in the circuit, the response flattens out in the region of resonance, and the response is said to be *resistance controlled* in that region. Above that region the response falls off 6 dB per octave and is said to be mass or inductance controlled. Below the resistance controlled region the response falls off 6 dB per octave and is said to be stiffness or capacitance controlled.

In combining the elements of omidirectional and figure-eight response in a capacitor microphone, the compound structure shown in Figure 5-16 is used.

For omnidirectional response the electrodes are connected as shown in Figure 5-17; for figure-eight response the connection shown in Figure 5-18 is used. In comparing Figures 5-17 and 5-18, observe that the difference between omnidirectional and figure-eight response is simply the polarity of one of the batteries shown in the schematic drawings. The circuit can be conveniently rearranged as shown in Figure 5-19 to provide for both types of actions.

The principle of the compound capacitor microphone discussed here was developed by Braunmühl and Weber. As with magnetic devices, specific directional patterns can be arrived at by providing a number of acoustical paths to a single capacitive element. The control of acoustical impedances allows the single element to respond both as an omnidirectional and as a figure-eight device, yielding a cardioid pattern. This approach has been favored in new capacitor designs because it allows a smaller overall structure and provides the convenience

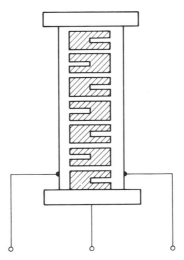

Figure 5-16. Basic structure of the Braunmühl-Weber dual capacitor structure. Important features: (1) there are two diaphragms, one on each side of the back plate; (2) there are perforations in the back plate which connect both cavities; and (3) there are holes on both sides of the back plate which provide damping for the diaphragms.

of a device whose axis of major sensitivity is in line with the microphone structure rather than perpendicular to it.

THE ELECTRET MICROPHONE

In recent years the *electret* capacitor microphone has become popular. An electret is a material which exhibits a permanent electrical charge and is the electrical analog of a magnet. Certain materials, most notably fluorocarbons, develop a permanent charge if subjected to heat under the influence of a high polarizing voltage. They can be used as elements of a capacitor microphone, and because of their permanent polarization they do not require a polarizing power supply. Electret microphones are inexpensive and exhibit excellent frequency response and noise characteristics. Details of the electret design are shown in Figure 5-20.

RANDOM ENERGY EFFICIENCY OF MICROPHONES

The *random energy efficiency* (REE) of a microphone is a measure of its sensitivity to random, or reverberant, energy relative to its on-axis sensitivity. For an omnidirectional microphone this value is unity, since the device is equally sensitive in all directions. A cardioid microphone is one-third as sensitive, and

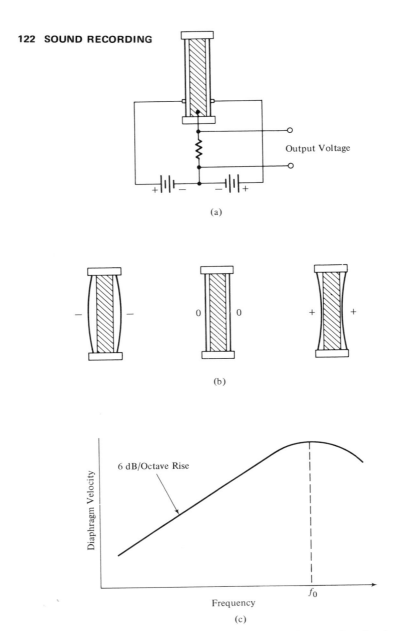

Figure 5-17. Connection of the dual capacitor element for omnidirectional response (a). The microphone is sensitive only to pressure conditions which are the *same* at both diaphragms, shown in (b). The diaphragms are operating in the stiffness controlled portion of their resonance curve, and this ensures that, when placed in a sound field of *constant pressure,* the diaphragm motion will exhibit the *constant displacement* necessary for flat output with respect to frequency. The stiffness controlled region, shown in (c), defines the useful frequency range of the microphone, and it extends upward to the resonant frequency, which is well beyond the range of hearing.

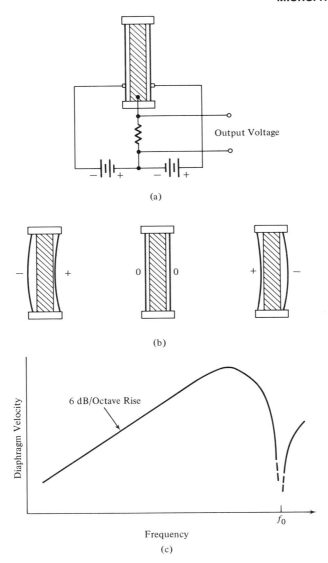

(a)

(b)

(c)

Fig. 5-18. Connection of the dual capacitor element for figure-eight response (a). The microphone responds only to the pressure conditions shown in (b) and behaves like two ribbons moving in parallel. Because of the damping provided by the perforations in the back plate, the diaphragm motion is resistance controlled. However, because of the difference in path length around the microphone the sound pressure difference at the two diaphragms rises 6 dB per octave with frequency as shown in (c). This results in a constant displacement of the microphone with respect to frequency and thus a constant output up to the frequency region where the wavelength approaches the path length difference between diaphragms (f_0) for a zero-degree incident signal. Again, this region is usually well above the range of hearing.

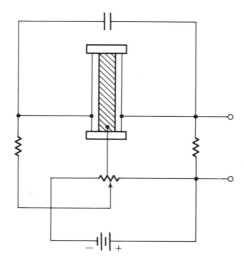

Figure 5-19. Connection of the dual capacitor element for variable polar patterns. By adjusting the wiper on the center-tapped potentiometer, we can vary the response from omnidirectional (wiper at full right position), through cardioid (wiper at center-tap), to figure-eight (wiper at full left position), providing the array of polar patterns shown in Figure 5-19 and all positions in between. Note that when the potentiometer wiper is at center tap, only the right diaphragm is electrically effective. The left diaphragm, however, is effective acoustically by ensuring the proper stiffness control to the omnidirectional aspect of the microphone.

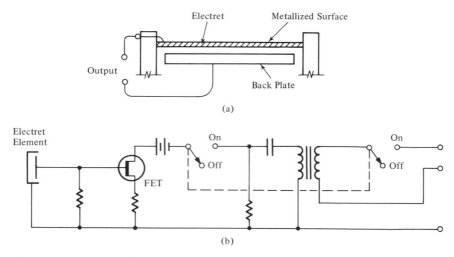

Figure 5-20. Structure of the electret microphone (a) and a typical electrical circuit associated with it employing a field-effect transistor (FET) at (b). The electret material is metallized on one side to form an electrode, and the resulting diaphragm and back plate combination behaves like a capacitor in series with a DC voltage source.

its random or reverberant response will be 4.8 dB down relative to its on-axis sensitivity. A *hyper-cardioid* microphone minimizes the random energy efficiency, while a *super-cardioid* microphone has the greatest ratio of total front pickup (±90°) to reverberant pickup. The cardioid family is shown in Figure 5-21, along with useful data concerning each type.

It is possible to construct microphones which exhibit even lower random energy efficiency, as in the case of line microphones and parabolic reflectors. Such devices, at least over portions of their operating frequency range, can easily exhibit random energy efficiency of 0.15 to 0.2, corresponding to 6-8 dB rejection of reverberant energy relative to on-axis response. Normally, it should not be necessary to use such devices in recording inasmuch as performer and

CHARACTERISTIC	OMNIDIRECTIONAL	BIDIRECTIONAL	CARDIOID	HYPERCARDIOID	SUPER-CARDIOID
POLAR RESPONSE PATTERN	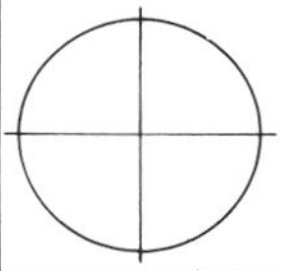	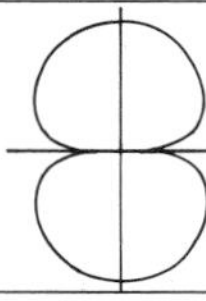	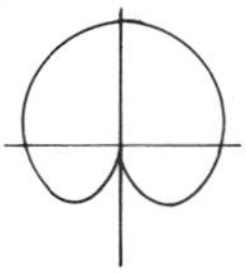	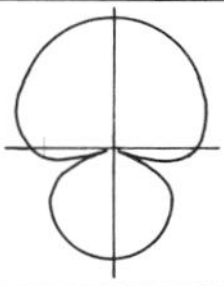	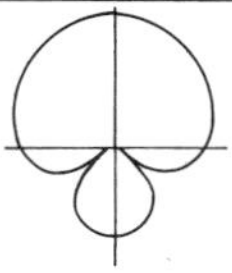
POLAR EQUATION F (θ) $\propto$	1	COS θ	1/2(1+COS θ)	1/4(1+3COS θ)	.37+.63 COS θ
PICKUP ARC 3 dB DOWN (θ3)	360°	90°	131°	105°	115°
PICKUP ARC 6 dB DOWN (θ6)	360°	120°	180°	141°	156°
RELATIVE OUTPUT AT 90° (dB)	0	$-\infty$	-6	-12	-8.6
RELATIVE OUTPUT AT 180° (dB)	0	0	$-\infty$	-6	-11.7
ANGLE AT WHICH OUTPUT =0 (θ₀)	—	90°	180°	110°	126°
RANDOM ENERGY EFFICIENCY (RE)	1 0dB	.333 −4.8 dB	.333 −4.8 dB	.250 ① −6.0dB	.268 ② −5.7 dB
DISTANCE FACTOR (DSF)	1	1.7	1.7	2	1.9

① MINIMUM RANDOM ENERGY EFFICIENCY FOR A FIRST ORDER CARDIOID
② MAXIMUM FRONT TO TOTAL RANDOM ENERGY EFFICIENCY FOR A FIRST ORDER CARDIOID

Figure 5-21. Data on the family of first-order cardiod patterns. Polar equations are given along with the pickup angle between the 3 dB and 6dB down points. Relative outputs at 90° and 180° are given along with the angular value for which the output is zero. (Courtesy Shure Bros.)

microphone placement are usually under the control of the engineer. But certain broadcast applications, pick up out-of-doors or in a large room, for example, will require their use.

The random energy efficiency of a microphone is related to the directivity factor (Q) of a loudspeaker. The value Q is a measure of a loudspeaker's penetration, or "throw," into the reverberant field, while the random energy efficiency of a microphone is a measure of its ability to "reject" the energy of the reverberant field. The two quantities are *reciprocals*. If a given loudspeaker exhibits a cardioid pattern, its Q is 3; a microphone with a cardioid pattern has a random energy efficiency of $\frac{1}{3}$. Or, expressed as equations: $Q = 1/REE$ and $REE = 1/Q$, for the same pattern.

MICROPHONE REFERENCE AND IMPEDANCE LEVELS

Microphone sensitivity ratings state either the microphone's output power into a specified load or the open-circuit voltage developed when the microphone is placed in a known sound field. A sound pressure of 10 dynes/cm² is standard for most measurements today and is equivalent to 94 dB-SPL. The output voltage may be stated either in terms of its actual value or in dB relative to a reference voltage. The term dBV is sometimes used to express voltage levels relative to one volt: Value in dBV = 20 log V_0. (One volt is 0 dBV; 0.1 volt is −20 dBV; 0.01 volt is −40 dB, and so forth.) Figure 5-22 shows the open-circuit measurement method schematically.

When output power is used for expressing microphone sensitivity, it is usually stated in dBm. DBm refers to power levels above or below *one milliwatt* (one-thousandth of a watt) and is expressed as: Value in dBm = 10 log (Power level in watts/0.001 watt). For example, assume that a given dynamic microphone is

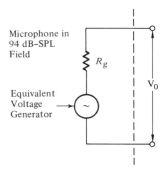

Figure 5-22. Equivalent circuit for a microphone in a sound field looking into an open circuit. Because there is no current flow there is no voltage drop across the generator impedance R_g.

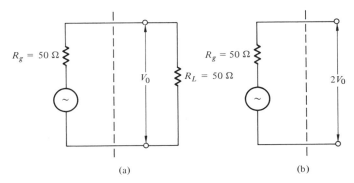

(a)   (b)

Figure 5-23. Illustration of the doubling of output voltage between a loaded microphone (a) and an unloaded microphone (b). In (a), the microphone is viewed as a signal voltage generator in series with a source resistance of 50 ohms loaded externally with another 50-ohm resistance. Computing the voltage across the load:

$$\text{Power } (P) = -53 \text{ dBm} = .001 \text{ antilog}_{10} \, (-53/10) \text{ watts}$$
$$= 5 \times 10^{-8} \text{ watts}$$
$$\text{Voltage } (V_0) = \sqrt{PR_L} = 5 \times 10^{-4} \text{ volts}$$

Operating this microphone into an open circuit, rather than a matching impedance, the voltage would *double*. When $R_L = R_g$ the voltage drop across R_L is the same as that across R_g, and *sum* of the two voltages is equal to the generator voltage. In (b), R_L has been removed, and there is no current flow or power transfer; in this case the full generator voltage appears unattenuated at the output terminals.

rated as follows:

Impedance: 50 ohms
Sensitivity: −53 dBm *re* 10 dynes/cm²

This implies that the microphone can deliver a power level into a load of 50 ohms of −53 dBm and is shown schematically in Figure 5-23.

In the early days of recording and broadcasting, it was customary to operate microphones into matching loads to maintain maximum power transfer from the microphone and proper signal-to-noise ratios. In most of today's applications, microphones are operated essentially into an open circuit. A microphone rated at say, 50 or 200 ohms would operate into an input impedance of perhaps 3,000 or 4,000 ohms, and this would hardly alter the microphone's output voltage.

The situation is quite different with capacitor microphones because their "rated impedance" is not the same as their generator impedance. Because of the internal amplifier, the effective generator impedance, R_g, of the microphone is reduced to a low value, and its rated impedance is instead the load value for which the rated power in dBm is calculated. As an example, assume that a capacitor microphone is specified:

> Impedance: 200 ohms
> Sensitivity: -36 dBm *re* 10 dynes/cm^2

This means that when the microphone is placed in the 10 dynes/cm^2 sound field it will develop an open circuit voltage which, if applied to a 200-ohm load, would produce a power level of -36 dBm:

$$\text{Power } (P) = -36 \text{ dBm} = .25 \times 10^{-6} \text{ watt}$$

$$\text{Voltage } (E) = \sqrt{PR_L} = \sqrt{.25 \times 10^{-6} \times 200}$$

$$= 7 \times 10^{-3} \text{ volt}$$

Loaded or unloaded, the microphone would effectively produce this output voltage since there would be an insignificant voltage drop across the generator impedance when it was loaded.

It is rarely necessary for the recording engineer to calculate microphone output voltages; his main concern is the relative differences between microphones, and this he can appreciate merely by looking at manufacturer's data. Most professional microphones are rated as we have discussed here, so comparisons are easy to make.

As general information the engineer should know that typical outputs of dynamic devices in a 10 dyne/cm^2 field are about 50–55 dBm, while the outputs of most current capacitor microphones, because of internal amplification, are typically around 35–45 dBm. As a result, the engineer should be aware of the possibility of overloading certain input transformers or preamplifiers in mixers which were designed in an earlier day. Additional padding or attenuation of level may be necessary between microphone output and mixer input if capacitor microphones are to be used for picking up loud rock performances at short distances. Usually the operating instructions which come with capacitor microphones explain how this can be done.

Some capacitor microphones have output transformers which can be connected for either 50-ohm or 200-ohm operation. In either case, the dBm rating for a given sound field will be the same, but the engineer should be aware that there is a 6-dB difference in open-circuit output voltage between the two positions. Normally, the 200-ohm connection should be used because of its higher voltage output, as shown in Figure 5-24.

Other matters of operational concern with microphones are: polarity (phasing), grounding practice, remote powering of capacitor microphones (provision of power for polarization and amplification via shield and signal paths between microphone and mixer), and effect of excessive cable length. Because of the

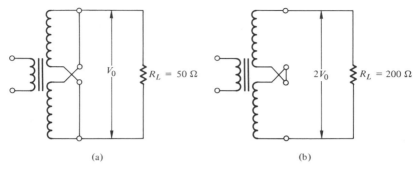

(a)   (b)

Figure 5-24. Illustration of transformer strapping for 50 ohms (a) and 200 ohms (b). In either case the power is the same:

$$\text{Power} = E^2/R = V_0^2/50 = (2V_0)^2/200$$

wide variety of these situations, the engineer is referred to the operating instructions for the various microphone types that he will use.

MICROPHONE APPLICATIONS

The selection and placement of microphones is usually one of the first decisions made by a recording engineer working in a given environment. Recording engineers often rely too heavily on certain microphone models, even at times favoring specific units because of subtle differences between them. A good engineer should be able to use whatever microphone resources are at hand, and there are certain fundamentals of microphone usage which must be learned early. After these are mastered, he is then in a position to discover the subtleties for himself and make good use of them.

Microphones tend to be very personal instruments; many performers are known to travel on tour with their own microphones which they insist be used for all their performances. Usually there is some characteristic of the microphone which complements the singer's voice, but very often the microphone functions as a good luck charm as well. The situation is much the same with many recording engineers.

In this section a number of microphone applications will be analyzed, and recommendations for good practice will be made. The topics to be discussed are:

1. Proximity Effects
2. Cancellation due to multiple acoustical paths
3. Cancellation due to multiple microphones
4. Choosing appropriate directional characteristics
5. Recording at large distances

Proximity Effects

All microphones exhibit a rise in bass response when used close to a sound source, but the phenomenon, known as the *proximity effect*, is most pronounced with ribbon microphones (or capacitor microphones operating in their pressure gradient mode). A typical rise in bass response because of the proximity effect is shown in Figure 5-25. The reason for the increase is rather complicated mathematically, but it is essentially due to the fact that both the microphone and source are within each other's near fields. The effect is used to advantage by

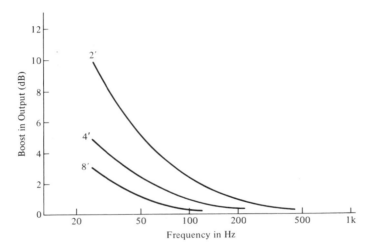

Figure 5-25. Illustration of proximity effect as a function of distance and frequency for a ribbon microphone.

vocalists, who often appreciate the full low end it may add to their voices. Since many vocalists have a tendency to move in close to a microphone when singing softly and to back away when singing loudly, the engineer must expect the low frequency content to vary accordingly. The best way to avoid this is to stabilize the microphone-to-vocalist distance.

Bass drums and string basses often yield "bigger than life" sounds because of the proximity effect. In the case of the bass drum, subsonic frequencies, which are rarely audible at any normal listening distance, can be quite pronounced through very close microphone placement and can cause trouble later on in the recording process. Unless the control room monitor speakers have extended low-frequency response, these frequencies may go totally unnoticed during the recording process, only to resurface later and cause phonograph tracking problems.

Close microphone placement is often necessary for good separation, but the engineer should always be aware that with such placement, even small movements of the sound source may cause significant variations in level at the microphone because of inverse-square fall-off.

There is another problem to be avoided at all costs, low-frequency blasts of wind against the microphone case because of sudden movements of performers or instruments, or in the case of vocalists, a breath blast into a microphone (the sounds "b" and "p" are the worst offenders here). Many microphones have accessory windscreens which effectively minimize these effects.

As a further measure against excessive low-frequency response, some microphones are provided with a switch, often with two or three positions, which provides a gentle roll-off of low frequencies. The slope is usually 6 dB per octave, and the range where it becomes effective is most often 100–250 Hz. Many microphones with two-position switches bear the legends "voice" and "music." The "voice" position inserts the roll-off, while the "music" position maintains flat response.

Cancellations Due to Nearby Reflecting Surfaces

If a listener is standing close to a large reflecting surface, he is usually unaware of reflections from that surface. As we saw in Chapter 2, his capability of binaural hearing allows him to distinguish the arrival angle of direct sound and focus his attention on it. Sounds arriving later are minimized by the precedence effect. But if the listener closes one ear he will hear some rather strange things; reverberant sound becomes more obtrusive and interferes with direct sound perception; he can no longer isolate sounds according to their directions of arrival. In a sense, a microphone behaves like a one-eared listener, and Figure 5-26 illustrates the problem.

The remedy will vary with the application, but in the case of pick up of sound on stage it is always best to locate the microphone *on the floor*. Figure 5-27 shows the effects of moving the microphone closer to the floor; note that $D - R$ becomes progressively smaller and the interferences become farther apart. Finally, when the microphone is on the floor, $D - R$ is equal to zero, and there is no interference.

A number of companies manufacture special floor mounts, the simplest being a flexible polyurethane foam holder which will accommodate a number of microphone sizes.

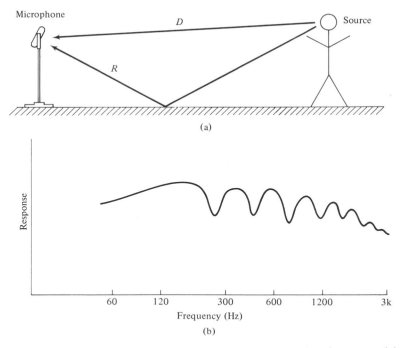

(a)

(b)

Figure 5-26. Illustration of reinforcement and cancellation at a microphone caused by a path-length difference between direct and reflected sound. (a) Sound from the talker arrives at the microphone by way of a direct path (D) and a reflected path (R). Assume that the difference in path length, $D - R$, is equal to three feet. Then the sounds arriving at the microphone will reinforce at the frequency where $\lambda = D - R$ and c is the speed of sound in air:

$$f = \frac{c}{\lambda} = \frac{c}{D - R} = \frac{1130}{3} = 377 \text{ Hz}$$

At multiples of this frequency ($2f$, $3f$, $4f$, and so forth), reinforcement will also take place. At frequencies halfway between ($1/2f$, $3/2f$, $5/2f$, and so forth), sound will arrive at the microphone from the direct and reflected waves out of phase, and some degree of cancellation will take place, as is shown in (b).

Cancellation in Combining Two or More Microphones

Another cancellation problem is shown in Figure 5-28. For certain kinds of stereophonic pickup, microphones may be spaced apart as shown, and certain performers will be located approximately equidistant from the microphones. In stereophonic playback there will be no cancellation problem, but when the two stereophonic channels are combined to produce a monophonic signal, there may be significant wavelength-dependent cancellation because of differences in the

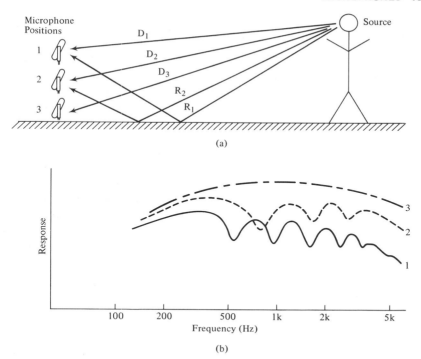

(a)

(b)

Figure 5-27. Illustration of the effect of microphone height above a floor on the reinforcement-cancellation pattern.

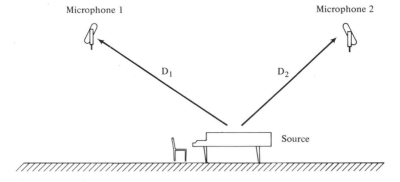

Figure 5-28. Illustration of different path lengths between a sound source and a pair of microphones. When the microphones are combined for monophonic reproduction, reinforcement takes place at the frequency (and its multiples) whose wavelength is equal to $D_1 - D_2$. Partial cancellation will take place at points between those frequencies.

path length, $D_1 - D_2$. A simple analysis will show that the case is analogous to the one discussed in the previous example.

The effect is most likely to occur when a solo instrument, perhaps a piano, is being recorded in stereo. The best "cure" for the problem is simply to be aware that it exists. The engineer should monitor the monophonic summation of the two channels and not be satisfied with his final microphone placement until both stereophonic and monophonic requirements can be satisfied. If this solution is not feasible, the engineer can always add a third microphone, panned to the center of the stereophonic array. This arrangement will produce a phantom image in the stereophonic array which adds in the monophonic mode without cancellation and which tends to predominate in that mode.

The monophonic summation problem can also be alleviated by using closely spaced microphones. The coincident microphone techniques discussed in the chapter on stereophonic sound effectively eliminate the problem because these techniques produce no wavelength-dependent cancellation when their outputs are combined.

Taking Advantage of the Directional Characteristics of Microphones

The first thing an engineer learns about a cardioid microphone is that it does not cancel sound arriving at an angle of 180°. The cardioid realization is only approximate, and it always varies with frequency. Even if the response were an ideal cardioid, total rejection would take place only at one precise angle and only for a source of sound located some distance away in a free field. For typical cardioid microphones, the effective 180° response may be anywhere between 15 and 30 dB down. It is usually most effective in the frequency range from 100 Hz to 3–5 kHz, with less rejection below and above those frequencies.

It is more important for the engineer to think of a cardioid microphone's behavior in a diffuse, or reverberant field. The cardioid microphone has a random energy efficiency of $\frac{1}{3}$; it picks up $\frac{1}{3}$ as much diffuse or reverberant energy as an omnidirectional microphone if both are set for the same on-axis sensitivity (the equivalent in dB is -4.8). If the problem is insufficient separation between adjacent performers, the engineer should not look for a microphone which would provide the desired separation; his only recourse is to place the microphones *closer* to their respective instruments or move the performers *farther* apart.

If a single microphone is to be used to pick up two instruments preserving the natural balance between them, a figure-eight pattern may be useful. In this case the microphone would be located between the performers oriented so that the performers were at 0° and 180°. Since the random energy efficiency of a figure-eight device is $\frac{1}{3}$, this arrangement would pick up 4.8 dB less reverberant energy than an omnidirectional microphone.

When recording in reverberant locations, the main problems facing the engineer are those of providing a proper musical balance between direct and reverberant sound and maintaining proper balance between the components of the performing ensemble. To a degree these aims are in conflict; the requirements of ensemble and balance demand that microphones be located far enough away from the performers so that their musical balances are maintained, and this demand may require the microphones to be located well in the reverberant field. The super-cardioid and hypercardioid patterns discussed earlier may be effectively used in these circumstances.

In summary, the recording engineer must learn to think of specific microphone polar patterns in terms of the effective on-axis-to-reverberant response ratio. Separation *per se* is usually a more important goal in the recording of pop-rock program material in relatively dead studios and is easy to come by through the use of close microphone placement, adequate spacing of performers, and the use of acoustical "traps" in the studio.

Recording at Large Distances

On occasion the recording engineer is forced to make recordings at distances up to 40 or 50 feet from the source. For example, it is not unusual to find pipe organs arrayed on both sides of a church or auditorium. In an effort to preserve natural perspectives the engineer may prefer to locate a stereo pair of microphones not more than 10 or 15 feet apart, and he may find his microphones at distances up to 40 or 50 feet away from the sound sources. Cardioid patterns would be preferable, and the engineer should provide extra microphone equalization as well. He may need upwards of a 5 to 8 dB boost at 10 kHz in order to preserve natural spectral balances because of losses of high frequencies by air absorption. Figure 5-29 shows losses that are due to inverse square law and air absorption at distances of 4, 13, 40, and 130 feet from a sound source. If equalization is added later in the recording process, high-frequency noise will probably intrude. It is best, therefore, to boost high frequencies as needed in the microphone inputs at the time of recording.

Another effect is also obvious when recording at distances of more than, say, 15 to 20 feet; the microphone is operating in a diffuse, or reverberant, field, and the engineer must consider the difference in the microphone's response when it is used close to a source (its direct or free field response), and away from a source (its diffuse field response). Figure 5-30 shows the fall-off of diffuse response typical for many microphones; differences of 10 dB at 10 kHz are not

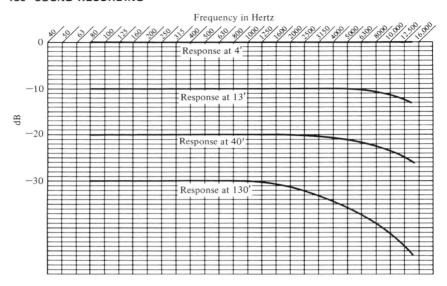

Figure 5-29. Losses due both to inverse square fall-off and atmospheric attenuation at high frequencies at distances of 4', 13', 40', and 130'. (At 20% Rel. Humidity and 20°C.)

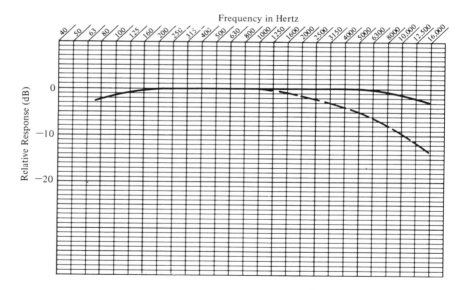

Figure 5-30. The difference between the direct, or free field, response of an omnidirectional microphone (solid line) and its diffuse field response (dotted line).

uncommon, and the signal must be boosted by this amount as well if proper spectral balances are to be maintained.

Thus, taking into account losses that are due to air absorption and diffuse field microphone response, the engineer must be prepared to compensate high frequencies by as much as 10–15 dB in the 8–15 kHz region.

BIBLIOGRAPHY

1. F. Bauch, "New High-Grade Condenser Microphones," *J. Audio Eng. Soc.*, vol. 1, no. 3 (1953).
2. L. Beranek, *Acoustics* (McGraw-Hill, New York 1954).
3. L. Burroughs, *Microphones: Design and Application* (Sagamore Publishing, Plainview, New York, 1974).
4. J. M. Eargle, "How Capacitor Mics Produce Cardioid Patterns," *db Magazine* (April 1971).
5. M. Thorne, "Studio Microphone Technique," *Studio Sound*, vol. 15, no. 7 (1973).
6. H. Tremaine, *Audio Cyclopedia* (Howard W. Sams, Indianapolis, 1969).

6

Monitor Loudspeakers and the Monitoring Environment

INTRODUCTION

To a large extent today's monitor loudspeakers are an outgrowth of the cinema tradition which began in the late twenties. The requirements of the early theater sound systems were efficiency, controlled directivity, and reliability. Power was at a premium in the early days; few amplifiers were greater than 10 watts, so high efficiency was essential in attaining realistic sound pressure levels. Controlled directivity, aiming the sound at the audience area, also helped in conserving power. High reliability was essential inasmuch as equipment down-time could be expensive as well as embarrassing.

It was natural that the early broadcast and recording industries inherit scaled-down versions of the larger theater systems, because of similar requirements. In the last ten to fifteen years, as recorded music has changed so significantly, more demanding requirements have been placed on monitor loudspeakers. The bandwidth has been extended at low frequencies; good response is required down to the 35-Hz region. Music has become louder as a result of the use of many amplified instruments; thus due attention must be paid to system linearity and power handling throughout the frequency spectrum. There is a growing concern for spatial and time-domain relationships between system components as the quest for greater accuracy continues; these were matters scarcely thought of in earlier days. Because of the ready availability of large amounts of high-quality amplifier power, the demands of system efficiency have been relaxed somewhat in the quest for greater bandwidth. More attention is being paid to the design of dividing networks, tailoring them specifically for the transducers at hand. A growing concern for the way loud-speakers interact with the environment has led to proper concern for monitor system installation and integration into control rooms and for how monitors may be electrically equalized so that the response in one location will not be too different from that in another.

BASIC MONITOR SYSTEM ELEMENTS

Almost exclusively, monitors make use of horn-loaded mid-range (MF) and high-frequency (HF) sections, whether they are two-, three-, or four-way systems. Low-frequency (LF) requirements (or low- and mid-low-frequency requirements in four-way systems) are met with moving coil loudspeakers mounted in either sealed or vented enclosures. There has been some limited use of quasi-horn-loading for LF elements, but the excessive space requirements for doing this properly have made the approach an unpopular one.

Horn loading is a method of coupling a fairly small vibrating diaphragm area to a large radiating area in a way that maximizes the system's efficiency as well as directivity. (Recall the effect of a megaphone and its projection of the voice by transforming the small area of the speaker's mouth to the much larger mouth of the megaphone.) A typical HF horn driver, designed for use from 500 Hz upwards, is shown in Figure 6-1. The design concept dates back to the early thirties, when Western Electric commanded a large segment of the motion picture sound business. In its original form, the diaphragm was four inches in diameter, and subsequent models were three and 1.75 inches in diameter. In the United States, so-called Western Electric–type high-frequency drivers are currently manufactured by Altec, James B. Lansing, Electro-Voice, and Gauss, as well as a number of smaller companies. The most significant aspect of the phasing plug is the close spacing of its annular slits, which ensures the best compromise between good high-frequency response and high power-handling capability.

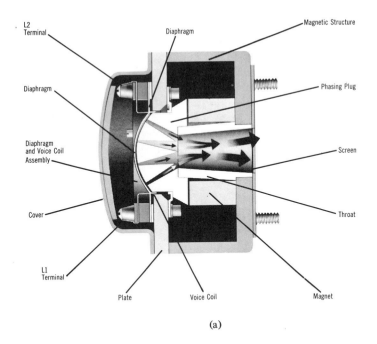

L2 Terminal

Diaphragm

Magnetic Structure

Diaphragm

Phasing Plug

Diaphragm and Voice Coil Assembly

Screen

Cover

Throat

L1 Terminal

Plate

Voice Coil

Magnet

(a)

(b)

POWER REQUIREMENTS

Until recent years, the rule in monitor design seems to have been "one monitor channel—one amplifier." Today, the trend is toward biamplification, or even triamplification, in an effort to prevent intermodulation distortion at high levels. As an example of how effective the approach may be, Figure 6-2 shows how two 100-watt amplifiers may be as effective *under certain program conditions* as a single 400-watt amplifier.

Output power capability of an amplifier depends upon the voltage swing available at its output. If a signal has a high crest factor then the average power output capability will be limited proportionally. Biamplification effectively lowers the crest factors of LF and HF signal components relative to the *sum* of the two, and both HF and LF amplifiers are able to operate at relatively higher average power levels.

In general, the benefits of biamplification will extend to triamplification if the overall statistical power requirements of all three system elements are about the same. As a rule, however, there is little advantage in going beyond biamplification in powering monitor systems.

Absolute power requirements will depend upon a number of considerations; namely, room size and absorption characteristics, desired listening level, and loudspeaker sensitivity. We shall discuss these factors in considerable detail in the following sections.

ANALYSIS AND SPECIFICATION OF COMPONENTS

If the recording engineer is to gain a thorough understanding of monitor systems, he must know the limits of the various HF and LF components used in their design. He must understand how such components are specified for given applications. Tables 6-1 and 6-2 show the important specifications for a number of HF and LF devices and horn-driver combinations which have been used in designing monitor systems. Note the similarity between components in terms of sensitivity, frequency response, and power handling. This similarity is largely the result of common engineering points of view, and even common engineering traditions among the manufacturers.

Frequency Range

These figures represent the useful limits of frequency response of the devices, allowing for response being no more than 3 dB down. The extent of useful LF

Figure 6-1. Details of the "Western Electric" high-frequency driver. A cut-away drawing is shown in (a); the diaphragm assembly is located at the rear of the driver. Details of the phasing plug and diaphragm assembly are shown in (b). [Both (a) and (b) *courtesy Altec Corp.*]

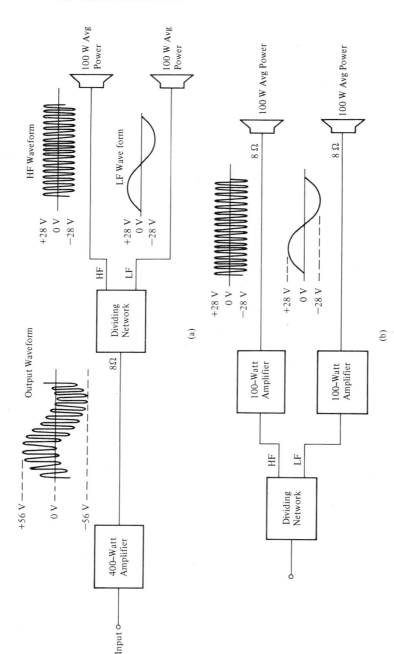

Figure 6-2. Advantages of biamplification. In (a) a 400-watt amplifier is fed a signal composed of equal amounts of low-frequency and high-frequency components. The 400-watt amplifier can produce a ±56 volt RMS signal before clipping. A sine wave output of ±56 volts RMS across an 8-ohm load produces 400 watts ($W = E^2/R = (56)^2/8 = 400$). However, when separate high and low frequencies are combined, the total power available will be less because of the increased crest factor (or peak-to-RMS ratio) of the waveform. The amplifier still maintains its ±56-volt output capability, and at the output of the dividing network this is the equivalent of *two* signals, HF and LF, of ±28-volts RMS amplitude. Since ±28-volts RMS across 8 ohms is 100 watts ($W = E^2/R = (28)^2/8 = 100$), the total output power available under this signal condition is 100 watts each for the HF and LF loudspeakers, a total of 200 watts. With biamplification, shown in (b), the input signal is split into HF and LF bands *before* amplification, and each amplifier is able to deliver its full output.

Table 6-1. High-Frequency Components Used in Monitor System Design

Manufacturer, Model Number, Description	Frequency Range	Sensitivity Power Rating	Impedance	Horizontal Coverage				Vertical Coverage			
				1 kHz	2 kHz	4 kHz	8 kHz	1 kHz	2 kHz	4 kHz	8 kHz
JBL, 2420/2391, Driver/horn	800–15,000 Hz	106 dB-SPL 30 watts	16 ohms	130°	120°	110°	80°	45°	40°	35°	30°
JBL, 2440/2391, Driver/horn	800–9,000 Hz	106 dB-SPL 60 watts	16 ohms	130°	120°	110°	80°	45°	40°	35°	30°
JBL, 2405, HF Transducer	7 kHz–20 kHz	103 dB-SPL 20 watts	16 ohms	7 kHz 120°	10 kHz 100°	14 kHz 90°	20 kHz 65°	7 kHz 60°	10 kHz 45°	14 kHz 35°	20 kHz 30°
Altec, 802/811, Driver/horn	800–15,000 Hz	104 dB-SPL 30 watts	8 ohms	1 kHz 60°	2 kHz 80°	4 kHz 85°	8 kHz 80°	1 kHz 220°	2 kHz 80°	4 kHz 55°	8 kHz 55°
Altec, 802/511, Driver/horn	500–15,000 Hz	104 dB-SPL 10 watts	8 ohms	100°	85°	85°	75°	120°	70°	45°	40°
Altec, 288/511, Driver/horn	500–14,000 Hz	107 dB-SPL 40 watts	8 ohms	100°	85°	85°	75°	120°	70°	45°	40°
Altec, 802/32A, Driver/horn	1 K–15 kHz	104 dB-SPL 30 watts	8 ohms	125°	90°	85°	90°	125°	135°	85°	55°
EV SM-120 Driver/horn	500–5,000 Hz	105 dB-SPL 30 watts	8 ohms	115°	125°	120°	120°	180°	62°	55°	38°
EV ST-350A HF Transducer	3,500–18,000 Hz	100 dB-SPL 10 watts	8 ohms	3 kHz 115°	7 kHz 125°	10 kHz 125°	14 kHz 115°	3 kHz 120°	7 kHz 100°	10 kHz 60°	14 kHz 55°

Table 6-2. Low-Frequency Components Used in Monitor System Design

Manufacturer, Model Number, Description	Frequency Range	Sensitivity	Impedance	Power Rating	Resonant Frequency
Altec, 411, 15″ Long Throw	20–1000 Hz	92 dB-SPL	8 ohms	100 watts	20 Hz
Altec, 515, 15″ Vented-type	20–1000 Hz	98 dB-SPL	16 ohms	75 watts	25 Hz
JBL, 2215, 15″ Long Throw	20–1000 Hz	91 dB-SPL	16 ohms	150 watts	20 Hz
JBL, 2205, 15″ Vented-type	30–2000 Hz	94 dB-SPL	8/16/32 ohms	180 watts	25 Hz
EV Sentry-III 15″ Vented type	30–1000 Hz	97 dB-SPL	8 ohms	50 watts	25 Hz

response will depend upon room size, location, and conditions of loudspeaker baffling.

Sensitivity

Sensitivity ratings in these tables are based upon one watt of pink noise, band-limited to the normal frequency range of the unit, measured at (or referred to) a distance of four feet using the flat ("C") scale of a Sound Level Meter. Some manufacturers use a rating method suggested by the Electronic Industries Association (EIA) which specifies one milliwatt of power input measured at 30 feet. Since the desired input signal for the EIA test method is a "warble tone" instead of pink noise, a conversion from EIA sensitivity to 1-watt-at-4-feet may not be exact. Generally, we can convert EIA ratings to 1-watt-at-4-feet simply by adding 47 dB to the EIA rating, and the error should be no more than ±1.5 dB. Published LF sensitivity ratings are made with the unit mounted in a sealed or vented enclosure of some volume specified by the manufacturer, while sensitivity ratings for horn/driver combinations are normally made in an unbaffled condition.

Impedance

Ideally, the nominal impedance of a unit is the *lowest* value in ohms that it will present to an amplifier over its operating frequency range. Many so-called

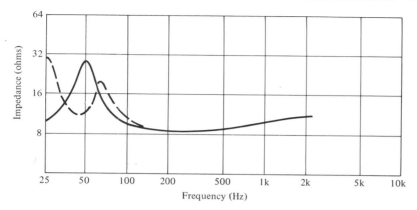

Figure 6-3. Variation in impedance of an LF loudspeaker. The impedance of an LF loud-speaker mounted in a sealed enclosure is shown by the solid curve. It exhibits one resonant peak, and impedance is at a maximum at the frequency of resonance. The nominal imped-ance is 8 ohms. The dotted curve shows the characteristic twin resonance peaks of a loud-speaker mounted in a vented enclosure.

8-ohm loudspeakers may present impedances as low as 5 or 6 ohms over some part of their frequency range, and there is a possible danger of improper ampli-fier performance if it is overdriven at those frequencies. With the better crop of today's amplifiers, this is not likely to be a problem, and the maximum power which can be delivered to the unit may simply be said to be that value rated by the amplifier manufacturer for that impedance level.

The impedance of a loudspeaker varies with frequency and is a function of the electrical, mechanical, and acoustical parameters of the device. Figure 6-3 shows the impedance characteristic of an LF loudspeaker for both sealed and vented mounting.

Power Handling Capability

There is considerable disagreement among manufacturers in the U.S. concerning loudspeaker power ratings. A given HF driver may be able to sustain a sine wave input of 20 watts, while it may only sustain a pink noise input of, say, 10 watts. The average heating value of the 10-watt input would, of course, be 3 dB less than the 20-watt input, but the natures of the signals are entirely different. The peak-to-RMS ratio (crest factor) for the sine wave input is only 3 dB, while the crest factor for the pink noise signal may be as high as 10 dB. Thus the peak power input to the driver with a 20-watt sine wave will be 40 watts, while the peak power input with the noise signal will, on a statistical basis, be 100 watts. Since HF driver failure is normally due to mechanical fatigue of the diaphragm material, it is easy to see how a rating based upon a noise signal may be significantly lower than one based upon a sine wave input at some frequency within the operating bandwidth.

An LF unit may be safely rated at, say, 100 watts for signals within its normal operating frequency range; yet a 30-watt signal at a frequency of 10 or 15 Hz may damage it because of excessive cone motion at those frequencies.

The usable bandwidth of a device has a great deal to do with its rated power-handling capability. Since displacement of loudspeaker diaphragms is inversely proportional to frequency, the higher the LF cutoff can be maintained, the higher its power handling can be. For example, HF drivers rated at 15 watts over the 500 Hz to 10 kHz bandwidth may easily be rated at 40 watts over a 1 kHz to 10 kHz bandwidth.

Other methods of power rating consider both HF and LF elements as a system. A 20-watt HF driver may be incorporated into a "150-watt" system; because of the substantial attenuation in series with the HF unit in order to have it match the sensitivity of the LF unit, the actual power reaching the HF unit may be no more than 8–10 watts. In any event, it may be assumed that one could safely use a 150-watt amplifier with the system—provided that the operating bandwidth is not exceeded. In terms of system performance, ratings should be based upon a noise spectrum which is shaped the same as the most demanding program spectrum likely to be encountered. For monitoring pop-rock program we must assume a reasonably flat spectrum from 50 Hz to 10 kHz.

Thus, the published power ratings of similar items by different manufacturers can vary significantly depending upon the test conditions specified by the manufacturer. Although information concerning these conditions is not usually provided as catalog data, most manufacturers are willing to give this information to qualified engineers and consultants on a need-to-know basis. Generally, components used in monitor systems are conservatively rated by their manufacturers, and as we shall see, they are rarely specified for operation at or even near their power-handling limits.

Coverage Angles

Effective coverage angles given in Table 6-1 are the included angles at which the response of the HF units is 6 dB down relative to maximum on-axis response. For example, if the effective horizontal coverage angle of a device is $80°$, then the response would be down 6 dB at $\pm 40°$ off axis in a horizontal direction.

Dividing Networks

For systems powered with a single amplifier a dividing network is used to split the spectrum into two or more bands as required for the various transducers. In earlier days, dividing networks were designed for ideal resistive loads which

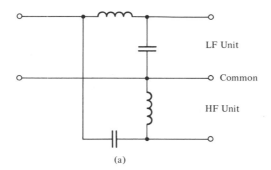

(a)

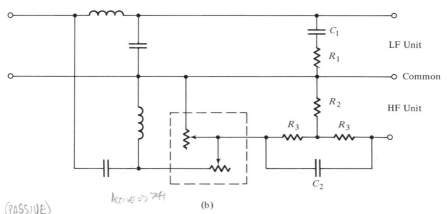

(PASSIVE)   Active => 741   (b)

Figure 6-4. Two-way dividing networks. Older network design, as shown in (a), provided only for simple high-pass and low-pass action with slopes of 12 dB/octave. A network typical of newer designs is shown in (b) and contains a number of circuit elements for smoothing the impedance curve as well as shaping the acoustical response. R_1 and C_1 are tailored to the LF unit and help maintain a smooth impedance curve. R_2, R_3, and C_2 comprise an HF shelving-type boost for maintaining flat HF output. The HF attenuator (enclosed in dotted lines) provides for proper HF-LF balance in a variety of acoustical environments.

did not vary with frequency. Typical of this design practice is the circuit shown in Figure 6-4,a. As we have seen, loudspeakers are not ideal loads, and newer dividing network designs are based upon due attention to impedance control and response tailoring as well as frequency division. Figure 6-4,b shows a typical design of the newer type.

SPECIFICATION OF A MONITOR SYSTEM

From the information presented in Tables 6-1 and 6-2, let us select LF and HF components suitable for a two-way stereo monitor system satisfying the following specifications: (1) levels of 105 dB-SPL are required at a distance of 8–10 feet from the loudspeaker pair in an acoustically inert control room; (2) in developing these levels, the system must operate with at least 6 dB "headroom" below the power limits of the HF and LF components as well as the amplifiers specified; (3) system frequency response limits are to be 40 Hz to 15 kHz.

Normally, the power handling of a monitor system is limited by the LF component, so let us begin with the LF requirements. The Altec model 411-8A unit, mounted in a sealed enclosure, has a 4-foot-1-watt sensitivity of 92 dB-SPL. The unit is rated at 100 watts; allowing for 6 dB headroom we would expect to operate the LF unit at an average power level of 25 watts (6 dB down from 100 watts). At 4 feet, with 25 watts input, the 411-8A will produce 106 dB-SPL. At a distance of 8 feet the level will be about 6 dB *lower*, or 100 dB, because of inverse square law fall-off, and this value represents the maximum average output, consistent with a 6-dB headroom factor, which we can expect from a single LF element. The meaning of headroom is, of course, that the loudspeaker can produce peaks of 106 dB-SPL (but no more than that) to satisfy peak program demands.

We now consider the effects of adding the system elements together acousti-

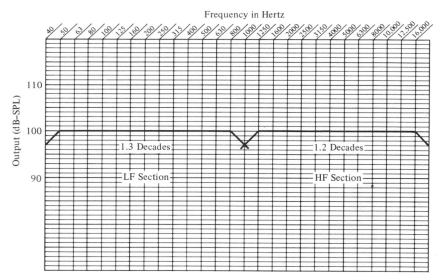

Figure 6-5. Acoustical summing of HF and LF outputs. The LF system produces a level of 100 dB-SPL at 8′ with an input of 25 watts, and the HF section produces the same level at 8′ with 1.5 watts input. Since the bandwidths of both LF and HF systems are effectively the same, we can expect their acoustical summation to be 3 dB greater than either one alone, a level of 103 dB-SPL. In addition, there are two systems in operation, a stereo pair, and there will be an effective doubling of acoustical power to 106 dB-SPL. A decade is a 10-to-1 range of frequencies and is equal to $3\frac{1}{3}$ octaves.

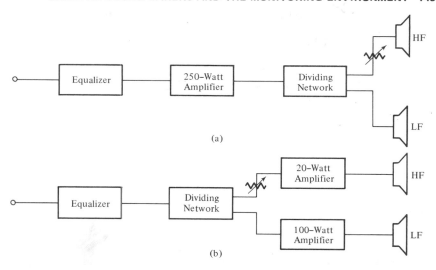

Figure 6.6. Implementation of the monitor design. A single wide-band amplifier is shown in (a), while biamplification is shown in (b). The wide-band power handling capability of the 250-watt amplifier is roughly equal to the 100-watt and 20-watt pair since the crest factor requirements in biamplification are reduced.

cally. If we divide the LF and HF elements at 1 kHz, then the acoustical burden will be shared equally between the two elements, assuming equal acoustical spectral requirements across the entire 40 Hz to 15 kHz range, as shown in Figure 6-5. Choosing either the 811/802 or the 32A/802 HF combination, we observe a 4-foot-1-watt sensitivity of 104 dB-SPL. At 8 feet, only 1.5 watts would be required for a level of 100 dB-SPL. With both HF and LF units contributing equally to the acoustical output, the resultant level would be 103 dB-SPL; and with both stereo channels operating, the level would be 106 dB-SPL, thus satisfying the specification. Block diagrams of the system, realized both in biamplified and standard configurations, are shown in Figure 6-6. Note the respective power requirements for the two realizations for equivalent performance. A similar analysis can be made using the equivalent JBL components, the HF 2420/2391 combination and the LF 2215. Since the sensitivity and power ratings are, item for item, within 2 dB of each other, the two analyses are almost identical. Similarly, a three-way analysis may be made with the EV components.

The biamplified realization shown in Figure 6-6,b calls for a dividing network ahead of the two power amplifiers. These networks are most often of an active configuration and are known as electronic dividing networks; however, passive forms may be used as well. Normally, these devices are of simple high-pass, band-pass, or low-pass form with slopes of 12 dB/octave and contain no response

basic RC has 6 dB/octave.

tailoring for given systems. Accordingly, a system which is biamplified may sound quite different in its unbiamplified state, and prospective users of biamplification should consult the loudspeaker manufacturer for recommendations before proceeding.

INCREASING THE ACOUSTICAL OUTPUT

We can increase the power-handling capability of the system just described by using multiple LF units. If 2 LF units are placed close together, we will observe a 3-dB increase in output because of the doubling of power-handling capability. But there will also be an added benefit because of *mutual coupling* between the units, the tendency they will exhibit to behave as a single larger unit. The effect of mutual coupling may be as much as 2 dB at low frequencies.

Another effect will be noticed when two LF units are placed side by side, a narrowing of the polar radiation pattern in the plane of the two units. Figure 6-7,a shows the polar behavior of both single and double 15″ LF units. Figure

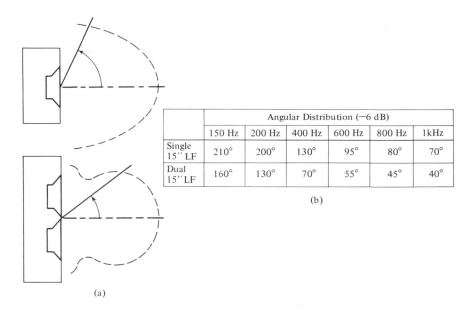

	Angular Distribution (−6 dB)					
	150 Hz	200 Hz	400 Hz	600 Hz	800 Hz	1kHz
Single 15″ LF	210°	200°	130°	95°	80°	70°
Dual 15″ LF	160°	130°	70°	55°	45°	40°

(b)

(a)

Figure 6-7. Narrowing of polar response of LF units used in combination (a). When LF units are paired for greater LF output, the polar response is narrowed *in the plane of the two LF units*. The polar response in the plane perpendicular to the pair will be about the same as for a single unit. The chart in (b) shows the narrowing of polar response (the angular spread between the 6-dB-down points) for single and double 15″ LF units (data courtesy Altec Corporation).

6-7,b shows the angular distribution for both cases from 150 Hz to 1 kHz. Where two LF units are to be used, they should ideally be placed one above the other. In this configuration the narrowing of the polar radiation angle is in the vertical plane, and the horizontal angle will be about as wide as for a single LF unit. The narrowing in the vertical plane will not be noticed as such but will be appreciated as an *increase* in output because of the increase in directivity factor.

All things considered, there may be an effective increase in power output capability of 6 dB because of mutual coupling and increase of directivity factor. Since the power input to the pair of LF units is only a 3-dB increase relative to a single one, this represents a net increase in sensitivity of 3 dB.

When LF units are used in pairs in control room monitor systems, vertical space requirements almost always require that the LF units be mounted horizontally rather than vertically. In order that the reduction of horizontal coverage angle not interfere with proper listening, it is important that the baffle be angled in toward the primary listening area and that the LF crossover frequency be kept as low as possible.

Vented enclosures can also result in a significant increase of LF capability by providing extra acoustical loading of the LF unit. The recommendation of the manufacturer should be carefully followed since many LF units, especially of the "long-throw" low-resonance type are unsuited for vented enclosure. The

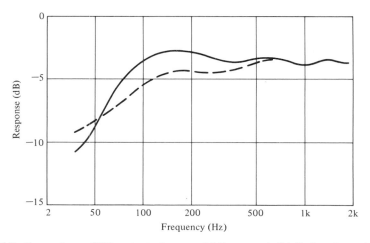

Figure 6-8. Comparison of LF output of a vented LF system (solid line) and a sealed system (dashed line). Where the parameters of the LF unit and enclosure volume allow, venting may result in a substantial increase in LF output capability over a sealed system. The price paid for this increase may be a reduction in output capability at extremely low frequencies. Manufacturer's specifications should be carefully studied; many LF units of the so-called long-throw, or high-excursion, type are engineered for use in sealed enclosures.

degree of increase in LF output will depend on a number of parameters including: LF unit free-air resonance, enclosure volume, and the exact nature of the venting. Figure 6-8 illustrates the difference in LF output typical of a 15″ LF unit operating in both sealed and vented modes. Note that there is a price paid for the overall increase in output, and that is a more rapid fall-off of extreme LF response below 50 Hz.

CURRENT DESIGN PRACTICE

Our previous discussion of the characteristics of LF and HF elements used in monitor system design should not tempt the neophyte into designing his own systems. The calculations we gave are only the basic ones; much attention must be paid as well to the spatial relationships between components and, more important, the response of dividing networks. The significant monitor system designs used today have been put in final form only after long and detailed listening tests and evaluations by recording engineers and producers.

Wherever possible, existing designs should be specified and carefully integrated into the listening environment. Flush mounting is desired since it eliminates cavity resonances around and behind the enclosures. The practice of hanging enclosures from the ceiling or tilting them out from the wall is frowned upon because it gives rise to many undesirable peaks and dips in response at mid-low and low frequencies.

In Figures 6-9, 6-10, and 6-11 we show details of minotor systems manufactured by Altec, Electro-Voice (EV), and James B. Lansing (JBL). Component locations are apparent from the photographs and fore-aft relationship from the side-view cut-away drawings. In general, the choice of whether a system should be two-, three-, or four-way is largely a reflection of the manufacturer's philosophy. There are certain inevitable trade-offs in making the choice. For example, a four-way system will likely exhibit uniform dispersion throughout the frequency range because the elements would be assigned only that part of the frequency spectrum over which they exhibit wide dispersion. All components, LF or HF, tend to narrow their coverage angles as they are operated toward the upper end of their pass band, and the assignment of the spectrum to a number of elements is one way to get around the problem. However, the more bands the

Figure 6-9. Views of the Altec Model 9846-8A 2-way monitor system. A side-view cutaway drawing is shown in (a), and a photograph of the front with grille removed is shown in (b). The system crosses over at 500 Hz. In the biamplified version (9846-B), the crossover can be set to either 500 Hz or 800 Hz, depending upon system application. The 9846-8A has a sensitivity of 93 dB-SPL (4′-1-watt); the HF components are the 511/802 combination, and the LF loudspeaker is the 411. (*Courtesy Altec Corporation*)

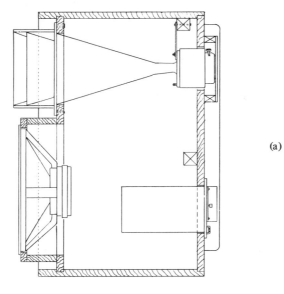

(a)

(b)

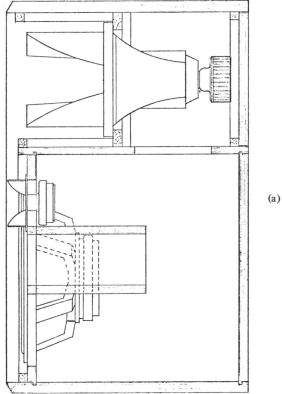

(a)

Figure 6-10. Views of the Electro-Voice Sentry III 3-way monitor system. A side-view cutaway drawing is shown in (a), and a drawing of the front with grille removed is shown in (b). Crossover frequencies are 600 Hz and 3500 Hz. Provision is made for biamplification, which includes an adjustment in venting the enclosure to optimize LF performance if a specified external LF boost is used. Sensitivity of the Sentry III is 95 dB-SPL (4'-1-watt) in the non-biamplified mode. The acoustical components in the Sentry III are those Electro-Voice items listed in Tables 6-1 and 6-2. (*Courtesy Electro-Voice Inc.*)

spectrum is divided into, the more likely will be interferences between elements in the region of the crossover frequencies. Manufacturers are generally very careful to choose crossover frequencies as well as spatial relationships between components which minimize these problems. Crossover frequencies in the 1K to 5 kHz region are generally avoided, since interferences between components in that range tend to be more noticeable than interferences in the 500 Hz to 1 kHz or 5 to 8 kHz range.

Two-way systems minimize the problems described above by having only one crossover frequency, usually in the 500 to 1 kHz region. Most HF horn-driver

(b)

Figure 6-10. (*Continued*)

combinations designed to handle the range from 500 or 800 Hz to 15 kHz generally tend to narrow their coverage angles at high frequencies, perhaps to 75° to 80° in the 10-kHz region; a notable exception is the Altec 32A horn, a Western Electric design which maintains a 90° horizontal radiation angle beyond 15 kHz.

EQUALIZATION OF MONITOR SYSTEMS

The prime purpose of monitor system equalization is to provide a degree of consistency between monitoring environments so that musical balances made in one location will not be too unlike those made in another. In general, only those systems which are adequately powered, and can handle that power, will benefit from equalization. Attempts to correct for gross system deficiences or for significant variations in acoustical absorption are likely to be disastrous.

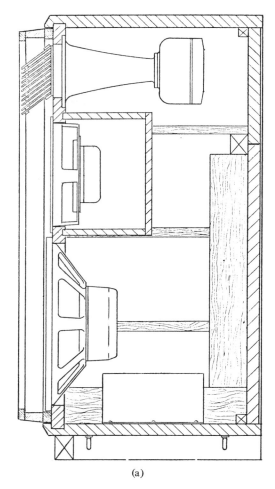

(a)

Figure 6-11. Views of the JBL Model 4341 4-way monitor system. A side-view cutaway drawing is shown in (a), and a drawing of the front with grille removed is shown in (b). Crossover frequencies are 300 Hz, 1250 Hz, and 9500 Hz. Sensitivity of the 4341 system is 91 dB-SPL (4'-1-watt). The Model 4341 can be biamplified, crossing over at 300 Hz, with provision for special external equalization for proper LF transition. The LF and MF components are specially made for the system; HF components are the 2420/2391 combination and 2405 unit. The 2405 can be located either to the right or left of the 2420/2391 combination in order to maintain symmetry. (*Courtesy James B. Lansing Sound Inc.*)

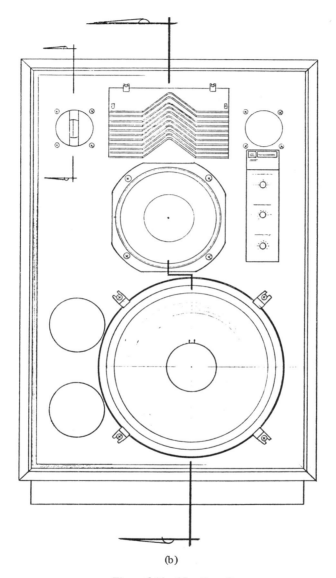

(b)

Figure 6-11. (*Continued*)

Equalization may correct *broad* variations in response caused by deviations from ideal room absorption characteristics, but standing wave phenomena in the room will not be altered. Variations in response between positions in the room will be the same after equalization as before. Similarly, broad variations in loudspeaker response can be corrected consistent with power handling capability and power availability.

It is wise to remember that the least equalization is usually the best. Equalization will not make a mediocre system good; it *may* make a good system exceptional.

Equalizer Characteristics

The equalizers which have usually been chosen for monitor system equalization are of the *band rejection* type centered on preferred ISO third-octave frequencies. In addition, *broad band* equalizers may be used to attenuate or boost large portions of the spectrum, and sharp LF cutoff filters should be used to prevent subsonic overloading of amplifiers and loudspeakers. The equalizers are of the *minimum phase* type; they introduce the minimum amount of phase shift possible for the amplitude correction they produce. Equalizer sections are connected in series, and their interaction can produce a smooth curve with a total phase shift rarely exceeding ± 90 degrees. The basic passive form of an adjustable "bridged-T" notch filter is shown in Figure 6-12,a. Tandem, or series, connection of the filter elements is shown in Figure 6-12,b. Note that when the filter is adjusted for minimum action there is direct feed-through, and the device is effectively out of the circuit. The same holds for the active configuration shown at Figure 6-12,c.

It is possible to produce a desired amplitude response by using an assemblage of *parallel-band-pass* devices as shown in Figure 6-12,d instead of the *series-band-rejection* arrangement of Figure 6-12,b. While the parallel arrangement may be very useful in certain instrumentation applications, such as the shaping of noise spectra, it should *never* be used in monitor equalization because of its time-delay characteristics. It is not a minimum phase device, and the time delays in its filter section may audibly affect transient signals in the program.

Phase and amplitude responses for various filter settings are shown in Figure 6-13. Typical professional devices used in monitor equalization are the Altec Model 9014 (passive bridged-T), Altec Model 9860 (active configuration), and UREI Model 529 (active configuration).

Instrumentation

Monitor systems are normally equalized by feeding pink noise (equal energy per octave) into the monitor chain and observing the response at the prime listening

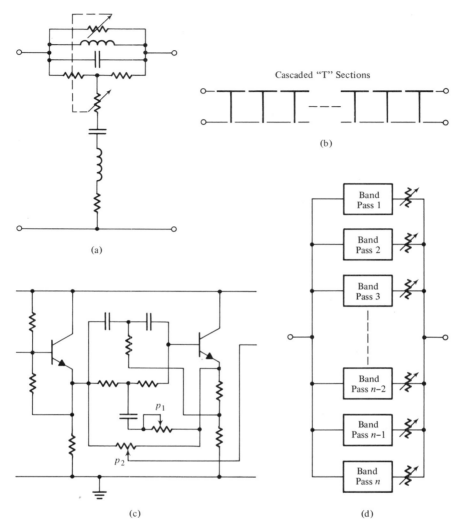

Cascaded "T" Sections

(b)

(a)

(c)

(d)

Figure 6-12. Filters used in monitor system equalization. The basic form of the "bridged-T" filter is shown in (a). In practice, these filters are spaced on $\frac{1}{3}$-octave center frequencies and connected in tandem as shown in (b). An active, or electronic, realization of the same band rejection filter action is shown in (c). In this form, potentiometer p_1 is used to adjust the maximum *depth* of the filter action, while p_2 is used in adjusting the amount of rejection required in the equalization process. When the wiper is at full left, the filter section is by-passed; when at full right, maximum action is obtained. An adjustable parallel-band-pass equalizer is shown in (d). Although useful for shaping noise spectra, it is not recommended for monitor equalization because of non-minimum phase response.

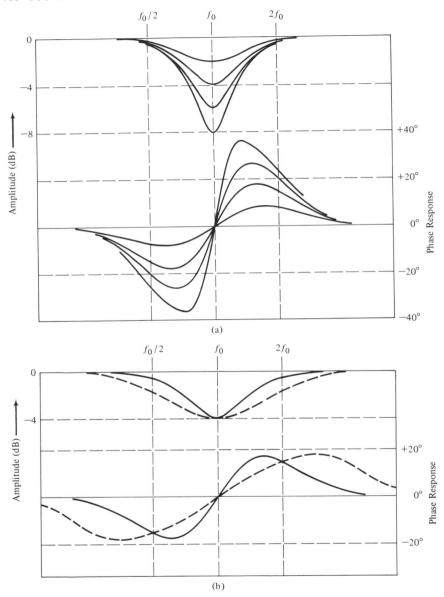

Figure 6-13. Phase and amplitude characteristics of band rejection filters used in monitor equalization. For amplitude settings up to –8 dB, phase variation is no more than ±40°. When three adjacent sections, located on $\frac{1}{3}$-octave centers, are adjusted for a total response of –4 dB [dashed curves in (b)], the effect is the same as that for a single *broader* filter. A –4 dB setting of a single filter centered at f_0 is shown (solid curves) for comparison. The ability of filter sections to combine to produce smooth amplitude and phase response is essential to their application to monitor equalization.

position via a real time spectrum analyzer (RTA). The RTA consists of a set of one-third-octave band-pass filter sections on ISO preferred frequencies whose outputs are averaged and scanned for visual presentation on a cathode ray tube. Scanning rates are usually 20 times per second, so adjustments of filter sections are seen immediately on the cathode ray tube.

Figure 6-14 shows the application of the RTA to monitor system equalization.

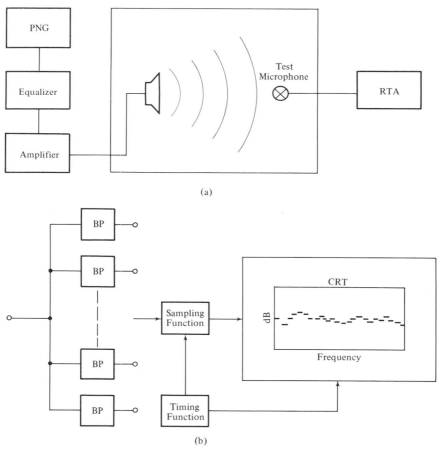

(a)

(b)

Figure 6-14. Instrumentation for equalization. In (a) a pink noise generator (PNG) is inserted ahead of the equalizer, and wide-band pink noise (equal energy per third-octave) is fed into the system. A test microphone is located at the primary listening area and its output observed on a Real Time Frequency Analyzer (RTA). Details of the RTA are shown in (b). A set of $\frac{1}{3}$-octave band-pass filters are sampled (after rectification and integration) and fed to the *vertical* input of a cathode ray tube display (CRT). A timing function controls both the sampling of the band-pass filters and the *horizontal* sweep of the CRT. The result is a continuous display of the processed band-pass filter output vs. frequency, updated as much as 20 times per second.

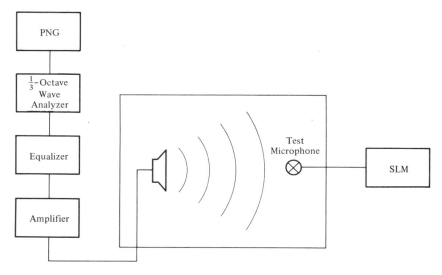

Figure 6-15. An alternate method. Individual bands of $\frac{1}{3}$-octave noise may be fed into the monitor system one at a time, observed on a Sound Level Meter and plotted on a graph. The method is equivalent to that shown in Figure 6-14 but does not permit the direct observation of the total spectrum while individual frequency bands are being adjusted.

A variation of the method consists of feeding individual third-octave pink noise signals through the monitor system and observing the acoustical output on an SLM set for a flat weighting curve. The method, shown in Figure 6-15, is equivalent to that using the RTA but is somewhat more time-consuming.

Another method, the "Sonipulse" technique, has been introduced by United Recording Industries Corporation (UREI). It replaces the pink noise signal with a rapid series of pulses, 5 per second, which are shaped through filtering to contain an array of frequencies over the audible spectrum, 5 Hz apart, with equal energy per octave. The pulsed signal permits detailed equalization of the same order as the pink noise-RTA combination.

Equalization Practice

Many things become apparent during the equalization process. The pink noise signal, with its relatively high crest factor of perhaps 10 dB, will show up amplifier limitations by clipping of the signal and the consequent "dirtiness" or "grittiness" of the amplifier's output. In some cases, fuses or circuit breakers will go, and this should be a clear warning that available monitoring "horsepower" is somewhat on the shy side. If the pink noise signal is generated at the 100–105 dB-SPL levels typical of current monitoring practice, then HF power handling limitations may become apparent as well.

The movement of the measuring microphone in and around the primary listening area will give a reasonable view of smoothness, or the lack of it, of the room's acoustical absorption characteristics. Since the primary aim of equalization is to provide a degree of consistency between monitoring environments, it is wasteful to attempt to equalize a room which has not been properly designed physically to provide smooth acoustical response over reasonably large areas. The normal location of the prime listening area toward the middle of the room, be it a remix or a control room, does not help matters; LF response is invariably lower toward the middle of a room because of the tendency for LF room modes, or preferred frequencies, to exhibit *maxima* close to the room boundaries. As a result, equalization requirements as well as loudspeaker power-handling capability will often be increased substantially below 80 Hz.

With modern instrumentation, monitor equalization has been made to look easy, deceptively so. In any event, the least equalization usually turns out to be the best, and the process should never be hurried.

We now present a number of examples of monitor-system response, both before and after equalization. Figure 6-16 shows 1/3-octave acoustical response before and after equalization along with the amplitude and phase characteristics of the equalizers.

On some occasions both room and loudspeaker seem to complement each other, and the response is fairly flat without benefit of equalization. Figure 6-17 illustrates this situation.

Figure 6-18 shows before and after acoustical response for the same monitor loudspeakers of Figures 6-16 and 6-17 in still a different environment. In this case, the loudspeakers were mounted away from the nearest wall in such a manner that interferences took place in the 630–1250 Hz part of the spectrum. The ideal solution of course would have been a combination of both equalization and physical rearrangement to minimize the acoustical problem.

The data of Figure 6-19 show the effect of equalization in a motion picture theater. Equalization is performed toward the center of the audience area, in this case about 80' from the loudspeaker, and the effects of HF absorption caused by distance, through-the-screen losses, and acoustical characteristics of the house are evident. There is no attempt to maintain flat response above 2 kHz at the measuring position in the house. The desired contour is flat out to 2 kHz and then rolls off at the rate of about 3 dB/octave.

Cinema requirements are significantly different from those of the recording studio both in frequency response and SPL demands. Note that power requirements place an extra burden at high frequencies, whereas in studio monitoring applications more power is usually required at low frequencies. The bandwidth of a typically good cinema system would be 50 Hz to 10 kHz, and maximum SPL's would normally be no more than 90 dB-SPL.

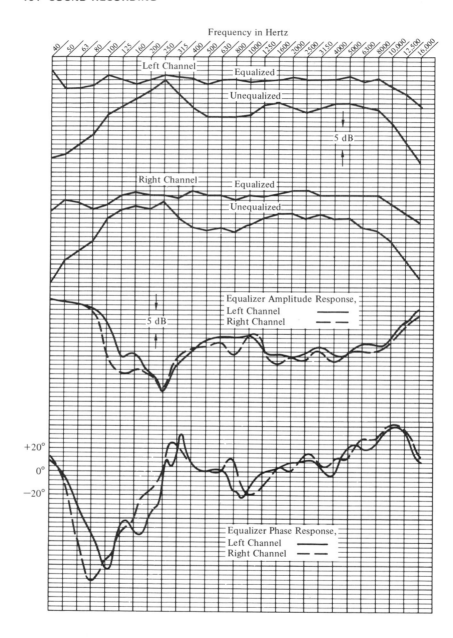

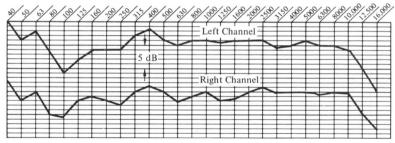

Figure 6-17. The same monitors in a second environment. Here, the loudspeakers are shown in environment which is far smoother acoustically. Measurements were made at a distance of about 12′ from the monitors, which were suspended by chains above the control room window. The ±2 dB response from 160 Hz to 10 kHz is due to the even specification and dispersion of acoustical absorption in that range. The variations below 160 Hz are due to local cancellations and reinforcements between the loudspeakers and neighboring walls. The rapid fall off above 10 kHz is due to increased acoustical absorption at high frequencies as well as slightly off-axis location of the measuring microphone.

Equalization Contours

Should HF response of monitor systems be flat or rolled off? An argument in favor of flat acoustical response is that the monitor-to-producer link in the recording chain should be just as flat and consistent as the response of amplifiers, microphones, and cutter heads. An argument in favor of rolled-off response is that most consumer record-playing equipment exhibits a greater or lesser degree of roll-off, and recordings should be balanced accordingly.

Let us assume that a record company has been producing records using monitor loudspeakers exhibiting a response contour which rolls off, say, 3 dB/octave

Figure 6-16. Typical acoustical and electrical characteristics. These curves show the acoustical and electrical responses of a pair of Altec Model 9846-B biamplified monitor systems located in a typical recording facility. Acoustical response, before and after equalization, is shown in the upper two sets of curves. Note that both left and right channels show response peaks in the 200 to 250 Hz region before equalization. This response is due to inadequate acoustical absorption in the room, and it is clearly a case where electrical equalization can make a profound difference. As stated before, the best results are obtained when acoustical absorption is evenly distributed across the spectrum, minimizing the need for this degree of equalization. The third set of curves shows the amplitude response of a set of Altec 9860 active equalizers used to flatten the response as shown in the upper two sets of curves. Note that the equalizer response (measured with a swept sine wave) covers a 20-dB range, while the corresponding acoustical response has been altered by a considerably smaller degree. The difference is due mainly to the fact that the acoustical response is measured with $\frac{1}{3}$-octave filters with a significant degree of overlap between sections and a consequent smoothing of response. The fourth set of curves shows the phase response of the equalizer; note that the response is within the fairly narrow limits of +40° to –100°.

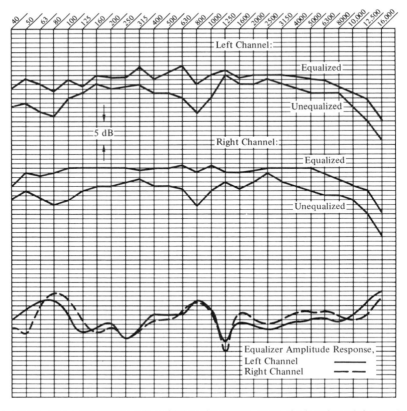

Figure 6-18. The same monitors in a third environment. Here, the location of the monitors relative to nearby surfaces caused substantial response variations in the 630–1250 Hz region, and $\frac{1}{3}$-octave equalization provided a reasonable flattening of the variations as measured at the prime listening area.

above 1 kHz. Then what the engineer hears during the final balancing and equalizing of a recording will not be too different from what an average consumer may hear. Now, let us assume that flat monitors are installed in the remix room. The engineer, relying on his previous conditioning, will attempt to alter the response to put himself back on more familiar ground; he will tend to use the program equalizers available to him to roll off the HF content of the recording *to the degree that his previous monitors were rolled off.* As a result, things will sound to him as they did before, but the recorded product his company issues may sound somewhat dull and lifeless on the average consumer set as a result of the "double roll-off."

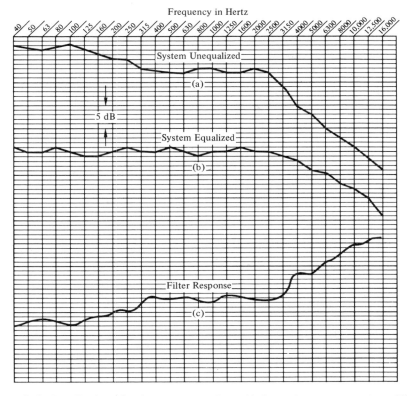

Figure 6-19. Equalization of a cinema system. Curve (a) shows the response at about 80' in a large motion picture theater of an Altec A4-X theater system. Room volume was 450,000 ft³, surface area 45,000 ft², and average reverberation time 0.4 seconds. A desired equalization contour, flat from 50 Hz to 2 kHz rolling off at the rate of 3 dB/octave above 2 kHz, is shown at (b). The electrical response of the equalizer system necessary for this response is shown at (c).

There is a gradual shift in the recording industry toward flat monitoring, and it is being met by a trend among the better high-fidelity manufacturers toward loudspeakers exhibiting flat energy output as a function of frequency.

Figure 6-20 shows typical equalization contours for a variety of systems. Figure 6-20,a shows the contour generally recommended for sound reinforcement systems measured at some position well into the listening area. Figure 6-20,b shows a curve which has been suggested as appropriate for cinema use. Curves shown in Figure 6-20,c and d have been suggested for studio monitoring. Noting the ease with which monitors may be equalized, it makes sense for the basic system to be equalized flat from 40 Hz out to 15 kHz with switchable roll-offs

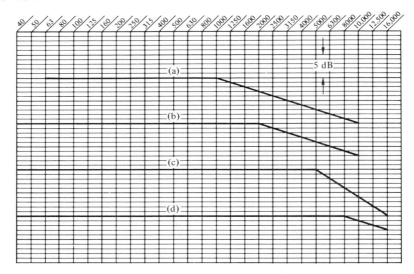

Figure 6-20. Suggested equalization contours, At (a), sound reinforcement systems; a suggested tolerance is ±2 dB, 63 Hz to 10 kHz. At (b), cinema systems; a suggested tolerance is ±1.5 dB, 40 Hz–10 kHz. Contours which have been suggested for studio monitoring are shown at (c) and (d), with a preference for the contour shown at (d). Reasonable tolerances would be ±1½ dB above, say, 200 to 250 Hz, while tolerances should be maintained +2, −4 below those frequencies. Where special attention has been paid to structural details, smoother response may be expected below 200 Hz.

to alter the contour as desired. While departures from the ideal curves of Figure 6-20 are certainly allowable, tolerances *between* stereo pairs of loudspeakers should be held to within ±½ dB on a ⅓-octave basis in the prime listening area. Where symmetry has been observed both architecturally and in the arraying of loudspeaker components, this is not difficult to achieve.

THE MONITORING ENVIRONMENT

In past years, improper attention has been paid to the monitoring environment, its acoustical properties, the integration of loudspeakers into the space, and even the superficial details of interior decor. Up until fairly recently, monitoring environments, both control rooms and remix rooms, tended to be on the small side, with numerous square corners, and with either free-standing loudspeakers or loudspeakers hanging on chains from the walls or ceiling. These conditions invite unsatisfactory performance from even excellent loudspeakers, and the trend today is toward environments which exhibit the following important characteristics: symmetry, flush mounting of loudspeakers, specification of similar absorption characteristics throughout the frequency spectrum, and attention to

Figure 6-21. Plan view (a) and side view (b) of a control room designed for quadraphonic monitoring. (*Courtesy Westlake Audio.*)

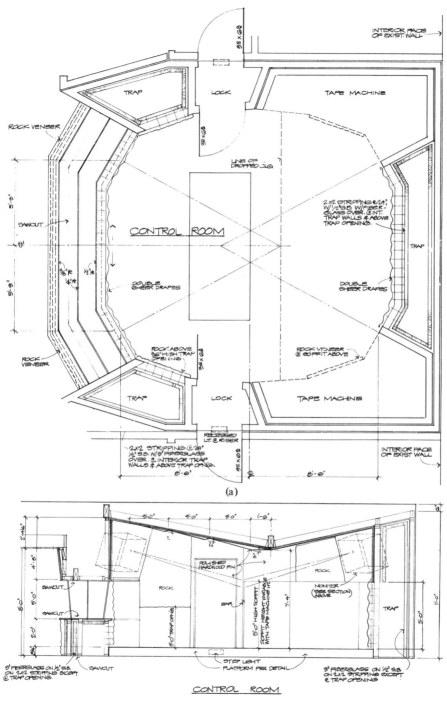

(a)

(b)

CONTROL ROOM

esthetic details. Ideally, if loudspeakers exhibiting flat acoustical energy output over their operating range were used in rooms with constant acoustical absorption over the same range, then little or no equalization would be necessary. But practical loudspeaker and room designs depart from these ideals, and there are many pitfalls for inexperienced designers. A number of acoustical consultants and contractors have specialized in these areas of design, and the neophyte is strongly advised to seek their help rather than attempt a design on his own.

Figure 6-21 is an example of quadraphonic control room design incorporating the above characteristics. The room is roughly circular in shape, and the prime listening area is toward the middle, equidistant from the four loudspeakers. The acoustical aim was to create the largest possible listening area consistent with smooth response from all loudspeakers, thus helping to stablize stereo and quad imagery.

It is important to note that the actual space occupied by the control room is much smaller than the total space into which the structure was built. This is always bound to be the case if proper attention is given to absorption of LF energy. The goal is to provide sufficient LF absorption so that response peaks and dips due to normal room modes will be minimized. The loss of LF energy is compensated for through the specification of monitoring components of high sensitivity and power-handling capability along with any required electrical equalization. Note that the monitors are flush-mounted and angled toward the listening area in both horizontal and vertical planes.

The angled ceiling puts to good acoustical use space which is ordinarily wasted. Sight lines from the listening area to the loudspeakers are preserved, and this arrangement lends an illusion of space while the enclosed overhead volume functions as a low-frequency absorber. Diffusion in the room is provided by the many angled plane surfaces as well as the varied array of finishing materials such as glass, stone, wood, and the recording equipment itself. These materials and their disposition promote a feeling of acoustical intimacy in the room through their low HF absorption coefficients, and this is an essential ingredient for extended listening ease and comfort. On the other hand, the excessive use of HF absorption would create an environment far "too dead" for extended listening.

Finally, after due attention has been given to the requirements of monitoring, the final choice of colors, lighting, and textures can be made with the eye in mind. A room can be as visually attractive as it is acoustically functional.

BIBLIOGRAPHY

1. "Symposium on Auditory Perspective," *Electrical Engineering,* pp. 9–32, 214–219 (January 1934).
2. "Acoustics Handbook," Hewlett-Packard Applications Note 100 (November 1968).
3. G. Augspurger, "The Importance of Speaker Efficiency," *Electronics World* (January 1962).

4. G. Augspurger, "Versatile Low-Level Crossover Networks," *db Magazine* (March 1975).
5. L. Beranek, *Acoustics* (McGraw-Hill, New York, 1954), pp. 313–322.
6. J. M. Eargle, "Equalizing the Monitoring Environment," *J. Audio Eng. Soc.*, vol. 21, no. 2 (1973).
7. J. Eargle and M. Engebretson, "A Survey of Recording Studio Monitoring Problems," *Recording Engineer/Producer,* vol. 4, no. 3 (1973).

7

Audio Control Systems

INTRODUCTION

Audio control systems are the means by which audio signals are routed, processed, and assigned to the desired monitor and recording output channels. In the early days of electrical recording, rarely more than one or two microphones were used, and the signal routing was to a single output channel. (The terms "line out" and "output buss" are also used and refer to the main signal outputs of the control system.) The audio control system was indeed a simple one, probably no more than an array of volume controls, or *faders*, some kind of metering, and perhaps a few switches for routing signals to different recording devices. Audio control systems used in the motion picture industry were more complex from their inception because of the necessity of recording dialogue, sound effects, and music at different times. In a sense this recording represented the beginning of multichannel recording even though the final product was a monophonic one.

As recording developed after World War II, engineers demanded greater input capability so that more microphones could be used. Along with this flexibility came the rudiments of program equalizers, limiters, compressors, and reverberation devices. The simple mixing panel was thus transformed into the familiar mixing desk or *console* configuration of today.

The three- and four-channel consoles of the early sixties provided for perhaps 20 or 24 microphone inputs. Since all inputs were mixed down to only a few output channels, the recording engineer, or "mixer" as he is usually known, had to establish most of the musical balances at the time of the original recording session. Selective use of reverberation or equalization on individual microphone inputs was possible only at the time of the recording session, and it is significant to note that in those days the engineer and producer left the session virtually with finished product in their hands. Not much remained for the final remix, or mix-down, session. The overall balance of the tracks as they were reduced to either monophonic or stereo, broad changes in equalization, and perhaps some additional dynamic range compression were usually the extent of what could be done. These operations often made the difference between a successful recording or an unsuccessful one, but the bulk of the work had previously been done in the studio.

The types of music current in the early sixties demanded no more flexibility than these simple, straightforward consoles provided. But as the pop-rock styles of the mid-sixties gained in popularity, more capability in the studio was essential. To a large extent rock music was shaped by the recording tools available, and much of the "new music" had its first existence not in live performance but over the control room monitor loudspeakers. With 8- and 16-track recording capability it became possible to store the outputs of individual microphones, putting off until a later, and less harried, remix session the critical balances of the final stereo or monophonic product.

The newer consoles provided vast flexibility in monitoring functions. Eight- and 16-channel tape recorders provided for "sel-sync"* (*selective synchronization); tracks could be added later in synchronization with the originals (a technique to be explained in the next chapter). Monitoring could be done with the benefit of equalizers, compressors, and reverberation, while the recorded tracks themselves remained uncommitted. Although some will argue with its esthetic justification, a producer working with these new tools could change his entire concept of a piece of music as he got into the many phases of its recording and enjoy the flexibility of reshaping it altogether.

The most recent developments in audio control systems include the function of storing information concerning the positions of faders, allowing a final mix-down to be made in stages while all interim fader positions are recorded. At any point in the process, a given fader position can be altered by any degree without disturbing the recorded positions of the others. The technique has added another dimension of freedom to the mix-down process. An essential element in these automated functions is a voltage-controlled amplifier (VCA), a device

*TM Ampex Corporation.

whose gain can be precisely controlled over a wide range (100 dB) by an applied DC control voltage. Depending upon how the control voltage is generated, the VCA can combine the many functions of fader, compressor, limiter, and "noise gate" in a single element. In the future it may be commonplace for consoles to control directly only DC signals, which are then used to control the audio signals at some remote point. This aspect of audio control is still in its infancy, and the shape of its ultimate impact on recording is yet to be seen.

To a large extent, the choice of whether to invest in 16- or 24-track tape recorders has become academic. Synchronizing techniques have been developed which enable tape recorders to be interlocked with each other. Thus, two 16-track machines can be combined (at the cost of one track each for synchronizing purposes) to yield 30-track recording capability.

Before we discuss typical audio control systems in detail, we must present a number of fundamental concepts: noise considerations, division of gains and losses, reference levels and metering, operational amplifiers, and symbol conventions.

Equivalent Input Noise (EIN)

Any audio control system is limited in dynamic range by noise at low levels and distortion at high levels. The noise level in a properly designed system is always established at its input. Assuming that noise due to the microphone is negligible, the microphone signal level and the noise generated in the first steps of amplification will establish the operating signal-to-noise ratio for the system. There is a limit to how low the noise floor can be made, and that is the so-called *thermal noise* level of the input device, the noise that is due to thermal agitation of its molecular structure. The thermal noise level of a resistor, expressed as a voltage, is given by the equation: $E = \sqrt{4kTR\Delta f}$, where k (Boltzmann's constant) is 1.38×10^{-23}; T is the temperature of the device measured in degrees Kelvin; Δf is the bandwidth over which the measurement is made; and R is the value of resistance. Typical values for T, R, and Δf are $T = 300°K$ ($80°F$), $R = 600$ ohms, and $\Delta f = 20$ kHz. These values yield a thermal noise level of 0.45 microvolts. Expressed in decibels relative to 0 dB = 1 milliwatt, this value is -125 dBm. (The designation dBm indicates a power level relative to 1 milliwatt.) Equivalent input noise and its measurement are shown schematically in Figure 7-1. No device operating under these conditions can exhibit a noise level lower than -125 dBm, and in practice, state-of-the-art devices do not approach this value closer than about 1 dB.

Like loudspeaker power ratings, noise specifications are not always clear. Measuring conditions may not be specified, and some manufacturers choose to use weighting curves which result in lower readings than those given by the foregoing calculations. For most preamplifiers, stated values of EIN will usually be

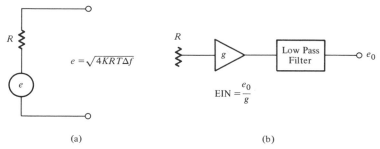

(a)   (b)

Figure 7-1. Equivalent input noise. A resistor exhibits a noise voltage at its terminals because of thermal agitation of its molecular structure. All sources of audio signals have a resistive component, and this value establishes the ground noise level behind the signal, as shown in (a). Measurement of *equivalent input noise* (EIN) for an amplifier is shown in (b). When measuring the EIN of a preamplifier, a resistor R, equal to the nominal impedance of the microphone normally used, is placed across the input. The output voltage is band-limited to the audio frequency range and is measured by a sensitive electronic volt meter. The gain of the preamplifier must be high enough so that the output voltage reading is free of any noise contributed by the meter itself.

in the -120 to -124 dBm range. In some cases, an equivalent input noise voltage will be given, usually without reference to the effective noise generator resistance, and values on the order of 0.5 microvolt are common.

Division of Gains and Losses

In general, EIN in a well-designed audio control system is negligible relative to noises accompanying the input signals themselves or the noise inherent in tape recorders. Figure 7-2 shows the input-to-output path for a typical audio control system. Note that there are sources of *gain*, indicated by *positive* decibel values, and sources of *loss*, such as equalizers, faders, and combining networks, indicated by *negative* decibel values. The input signal level is given, along with the input noise level and clipping level. They are followed throughout the system. Losses indicated by the three faders (input, submaster and master) are variable depending upon the fader position, and they would be altered during the recording process as required.

The normal program output level is +4 dBm; however, amplifiers used in console design often have maximum output capability of +24 dBm before the onset of clipping, representing a margin, or "headroom," of 20 dB. This headroom may seem quite generous, but in reality it is not. Certain transient signals, tambourines and triangles, for example, may easily exhibit peak-to-average ratios on the order of 15–18 dB, and this is precisely why the headroom is necessary— to let the complex waveform pass through the system without clipping.

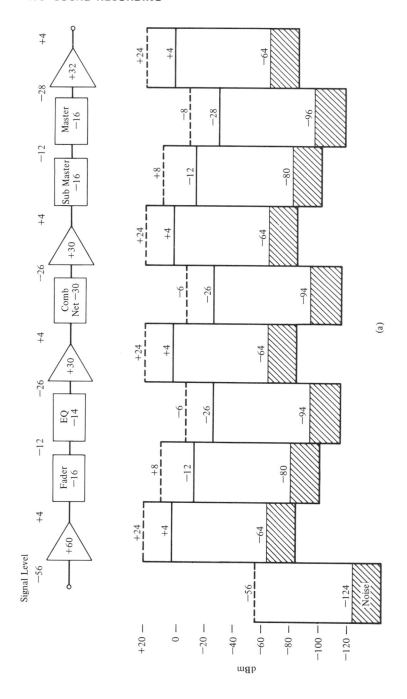

(a)

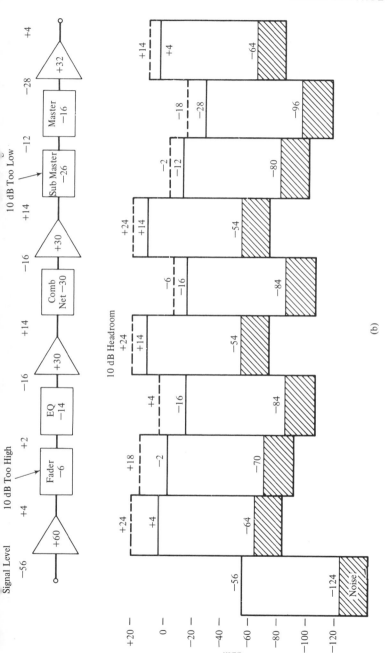

Figure 7-2. A typical input-to-output flow diagram for an audio control system. At each interface the total system dynamic range is shown graphically. The noise levels are shown by crosshatching at the bottom; nominal signal levels are shown by solid lines, while overload or clipping points are shown by dashed lines. A properly operated system is shown in (a); its 88-dB dynamic range is preserved from input to output. In (b), the same system is operated improperly. The input fader is set 10 dB too high, resulting in overload of the second amplifier with only 10 dB headroom over the nominal signal level. This 10-dB penalty is then carried through the rest of the system, and the overall dynamic range is diminished by 10 dB.

In the diagram of Figure 7-2,a, note that the output levels of all four amplifiers are +4 dBm for an input of −56 dBm with nominal settings of all faders. This means that all amplifiers will reach their output clipping level of +24 dBm at the same time, and the widest possible dynamic range is thus assured. However, if the input fader is set, say, 10 dB *higher* than nominal for a −56 dBm input, and the submaster set 10 dB *lower* than nominal in order to maintain the same system gain, then the overall dynamic range, as shown at Figure 7-2,b, will have been reduced by 10 dB. A level of +14 dBm at the output of the third amplifier corresponds to +4 dBm at the output of the fourth amplifier, and this means that +14 dBm at the system output is the maximum attainable level. At higher settings, the output amplifier is merely amplifying the distorted output of the previous amplifier. This problem is a fairly common one, especially when inexperienced mixers are working at unfamiliar consoles.

At the other extreme, signal-to-noise ratios can be degraded if signals at any point in the system are attenuated to a level corresponding to the input level. When this happens, the input noise of an amplifier later in the chain becomes as significant as that of the input amplifier. This situation is not very likely with most current console designs, but on rare occasions one does encounter a bad design, such as that shown in Figure 7-3. This design contains the same gain and loss elements shown in Figure 7-2; two elements have been transposed, and as a result the signal level is reduced to −56 dBm at the input of the second amplifier. Because of this, the EIN of the second amplifier becomes as significant as that of the first, and the overall signal-to-noise ratio is degraded by 3 dB. The situation can be much worse if the input fader is operated too low.

In addition to those sources of noise which are inherent in the control systems, there are a number of others external to the system. The most prevalent is *hum*, the induction of the 60-Hz power line frequency into microphone inputs. Its cure is proper attention to shielding of microphone cables and proper grounding practice. A more difficult problem to solve is that caused by RF (radio frequency) interference from nearby transmitters or equipment in which there are frequent discharges of fairly high voltages. Again, the problem is usually solved through proper shielding; but occasionally in dense urban areas with a high concentration of radio and TV transmitters, there is significant radiation of RF energy directly into preamplifier input stages. These are often the most elusive problems of all, entailing significant rewiring and even mechanical redesign of equipment.

Remote recording sessions are prey to all kinds of noise problems because of the rather hasty way in which they are set up. Microphone lines are often inadvertently placed next to power lines, and interference from lighting-control equipment is very common. The only cure is to take more time in set-up and to make sure that all performance conditions are considered *before* the recording takes place.

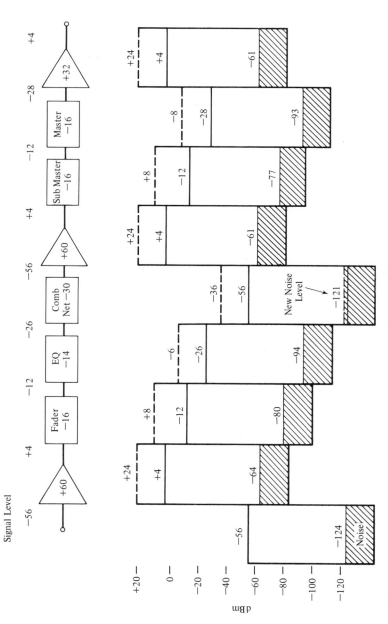

Figure 7-3. A poorly designed audio control system. The same elements of the system shown in Figure 7-2 are rearranged differently so that the signal level is excessively attenuated at the input of the second amplifier. The result is a 3-dB degradation of the noise floor of the system caused by the input noise level of the second amplifier.

We can make the following general observations concerning the division of gains and losses:

1. Mixers should familiarize themselves with nominal signal levels at all points in an audio control system and strive to maintain the standard settings of all faders on which the basic gain-loss calculations for the system were made.

2. The mixer's concern for gains and losses begins at the input to the control system. Microphones of higher than normal output level, due either to internal amplification or to their placement in high sound pressure fields, must be attenuated, or "padded," ahead of the console so that the intended levels will be presented to the input stages.

3. When a number of microphones are assigned to one output channel through a combining network, the signal level at the output of the combining network will be proportionally higher. Input faders should be lowered accordingly, so that the signal level at the output of the combining network will be near the nominal level. In this way, both signal-to-noise ratio and dynamic range can be maintained.

4. The mixer's knowledge of gains and losses must extend beyond the console itself. Feeds to tape recorders are usually directly off the main outputs, but signals to and from peripheral devices such as reverberation units can be significantly lower with respect to both level and clipping point.

Reference Levels and Metering

We have stated before that recording technology had common origins with the broadcast, motion picture, and telephone industries. Most passive components used in recording, such as faders and certain filters, are still designed around the impedance level of 600 ohms characteristic of telephone and broadcast transmission lines. Such devices present a 600-ohm load and are required to be loaded themselves by 600 ohms. The standard method of metering in a 600-ohm system is the VU (Volume Unit) meter, one of the most ubiquitous devices in the recording and broadcasting industries. In its basic form the VU meter registers *zero level* on its scale when the voltage corresponding to one milliwatt in 600 ohms is applied (0.775 volts). In its usual application in recording an attenuator is placed ahead of the meter so that its zero level reading corresponds to +4 dBm (1.23 volts).

As recording developed through the mid-sixties, the VU meter was adequate for monitoring signal levels. In the last ten years, however, engineers have become more aware of distortion as the very nature of recorded music has changed, and the VU meter has shown its inherent weakness of not responding quickly enough to certain transient program material. The ballistic characteristics of the

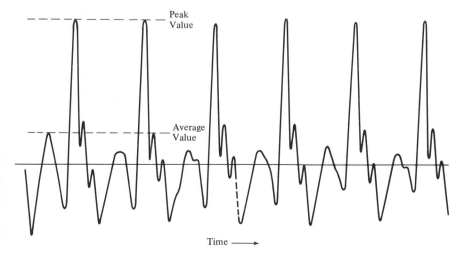

Figure 7-4. Waveform of a trumpet tone (about 400 Hz). The spread between average and peak values of the waveform is 13 dB.

device do not permit it to register transient signals accurately which are shorter than about $\frac{1}{3}$ second. In recent years there has been a growing interest in so-called *peak program indicators* because of their more accurate reading of transient program signal, but simple peak reading devices are not necessarily the answer to the problem. Figures 7-4 and 7-5 illustrate the difficulties.

The waveform illustrated in Figure 7-4 is a steady state trumpet tone, and its peak and average values are indicated. If this signal were monitored on a VU meter, the indication would be proportional to the average signal level. Actual peak levels would, of course, be some 13 dB *greater*. If the nominal level were +4 dBm, then peak levels of +17 dBm could easily result in some magnetic tape saturation, if not amplifier clipping. The situation can be far worse with transient program, as shown in Figure 7-5. Because of meter ballistics or electrical time constants, an average reading device may altogether miss a sudden transient in the program. The margin between peak and average levels can easily be in the 15-18 dB range when microphones are placed close to certain percussion instruments.

Why not then simply use peak metering for all applications? If the standard VU meter does not go far enough, then it can be said that peak metering of the sort described here goes too far. An engineer monitoring levels via peak reading devices would tend to be too cautious in setting levels; he might well end up trading noise for distortion. Actually, certain characteristics of the sluggish VU meter work to the engineer's benefit. It has long been observed that occasional

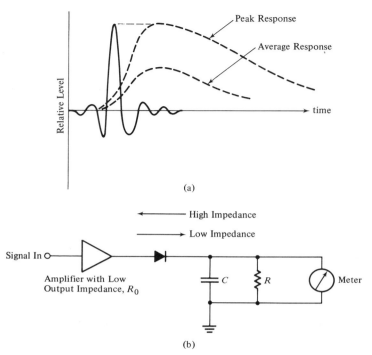

Figure 7-5. Peak indication of transient signals. A typical transient signal is shown in (a). The upper dotted line indicates the response of a true peak-reading meter, indicating the peak level at some short time later. The lower dotted line indicates the response of an average reading device. Details of a peak reading meter are shown in (b). The signal is amplified and fed through a rectifier to the RC parallel combination across the meter; since the charging time constant (R_0C) is low, the capacitor is quickly charged. The discharge time constant (RC) is longer, and the meter has time to reach the full signal value.

transients can undergo a slight degree of distortion and remain unnoticed in the process. Accordingly, the slow response of the VU meter tells the engineer that he can record at a higher level than the peak reading device would indicate.

The dynamic characteristics of a standard VU meter are such that it reaches 99% of its 0-dBm deflection in 0.3 second if a steady sine wave of 0-dBm level is applied to it. Obviously, transients of less than 0.3 second duration will result in a lesser deflection of the meter. The ballistics of a standard VU meter as well as a typical peak indicating device are shown in Figure 7-6.

What are the ideal ballistics for metering the recording process? There may be several, depending on the application. For recording individual tracks on 16- or 24-track tape, the ballistics of the VU meter are quite satisfactory. Instantaneous overloads may be tolerated because with individual tracks intermodulation

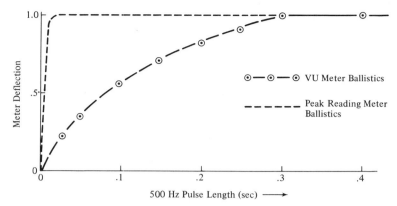

Figure 7-6. Response of meters to 500 Hz pulsed signals. Below about $\frac{1}{3}$ second the response of a standard VU meter does not indicate peak levels. By comparison, a quasi–peak reading device gives a more accurate account of shorter pulses.

distortion is all but nonexistent. For monitoring composite program channels, then some degree of peak metering is desirable because of the susceptibility of complex musical textures to intermodulation distortion.

For critical transfer processes, such as disc recording and the preparation of tape duplicating masters, peak reading devices are essential. These mediums contain significant HF pre-emphasis, and accurate monitoring of high-frequency transients is important in determining suitable transfer levels.

Another problem associated with signal level monitoring has to do with operational aspects. How can one operator adequately keep 16 or 24 meters in his direct view? Edgewise meters have been devised which result in a significantly smaller horizontal angle for the mixer to observe; even then, it is difficult for a mixer to be aware of signals which are out of control. In recent years a number of manufacturers have used TV monitors for displaying signal levels. The outputs of the several detection circuits are scanned rapidly and displayed, usually as vertical bars on a TV screen. A color mask on the screen enhances the display by showing clearly (usually the color *red*) any signal over the nominal zero reference point. These displays are quite compact, usually 12 to 15 inches wide and handling up to 20 channels. Normally, both peak and VU-type response are available.

Operational Amplifiers

Operational amplifiers (op amps) provide a convenient and extremely flexible means of signal routing and processing and are used in the design of most present-day audio control systems. The term *operational* derives from the role these devices play in performing analog mathematical operations, such as the arithmetic functions of addition, subtraction, multiplication, and division, as well as the functions of integration and differentiation in calculus.

The basic symbol of an op amp is shown in Figure 7-7,a. Ideally, it has the following characteristics: infinite gain, infinite input impedance, and zero output impedance. Actually, the gain of a typical op amp is in the range of 100 to 110 dB, its input impedance in the range of 10 megohms (10,000,000 ohms), and its output impedance on the order of a few ohms. These are "sufficiently close"

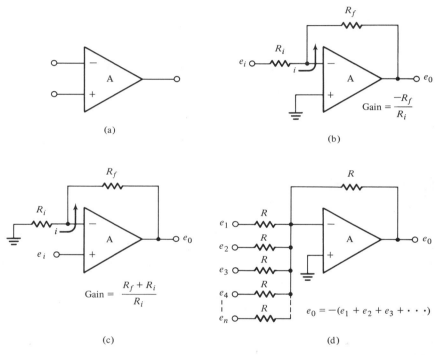

Figure 7-7. The operational amplifier. The basic symbol is shown in (a). When the op amp is used as an inverting amplifier, as shown in (b), input and feedback resistors (R_i and R_f) are connected as shown. Because of the effectively infinite input impedance, the input current i is equal through both R_i and R_f. Because the gain of the amplifier is effectively infinite, a zero voltage between the input terminals results in full output. Thus, the input voltage is zero for all output levels. Thus, $e_i = iR_i$ and $e_0 = iR_f$, and gain $= e_0/e_i = R_f/R_i$. Accordingly, the simple ratio of external passive components determines the gain of an operational amplifier. Rearranged as shown in (c), the op amp becomes a noninverting amplifier. Since the input voltage (the difference between the positive and negative terminals) is zero, $e_0 = i/(R_f + R_i)$ and $e_i = i/R_i$. The gain, $e_0/e_i = (R_f + R_i)/R_i$. In (d) the normal connection for a combining amplifier is shown. As a rule, the feedback resistor is made equal to the summing resistors to that unity gain results. Thus, any number of inputs, e_i through e_n, can be combined. In the unity gain mode, the isolation between inputs can be maintained on the order of the open-loop gain of the op amp, typically 100–110 dB.

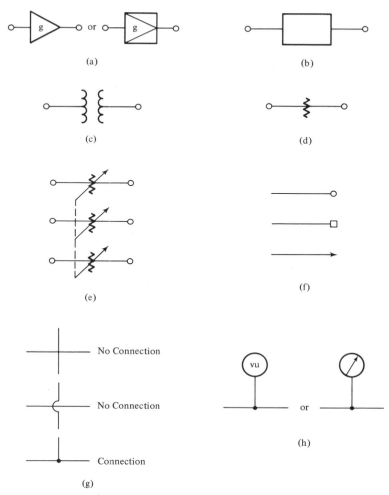

Figure 7-8. Symbol conventions. An amplifier is almost always shown as a triangle or a triangle enclosed in a square, as in (a). Its gain is usually indicated in dB by a number inside the triangle. A rectangle (b) is normally used to indicate a signal processing device, and it is always labeled as to function. If it is a passive device, its loss in dB is usually indicated internally in parentheses or in terms of respective input and output levels. A transformer is shown at (c). With no indications, the impedance ratio is assumed to be unity, and the transformer is used for purposes of DC isolation. A terminating resistor, as required by some amplifiers, is shown at (d). Ganged or grouped control functions are shown by dotted lines. In (e), three faders are grouped for ganged operation. Various symbols are used to indicate tie points, reference points, and abbreviated connections between devices. Some of these are shown in (f). Reference to further figures in this chapter will illustrate their use. (g) Wire connections in flow diagrams are always shown by a heavy dot at the point of connection; the simple crossing of lines *does not* indicate a connection; in older schematics a hoop or wicket was used to indicate no connection. A meter placed across a line is shown in (h); the indication *VU* or the arrow in a circle indicates the function.

approximations to infinity and zero to enable us to make a number of simplifying assumptions and to establish its gain in terms of the external resistances, R_i and R_f, which are used in conjunction with it. Figure 7-7,b, c, and d show typical op amp connections as inverting and noninverting amplifiers as well as a unity-gain combining amplifier. This last configuration is an extremely useful one which allows any number of inputs to be combined with virtually no interaction between them.

There are many excellent texts and handbooks on op amp applications, covering their use not only for mathematical operations but also for specific audio applications. Integrated circuitry has made possible the construction of low-cost high-quality op amps, and these have in turn contributed to the increased operational flexibility and lower cost of modern audio control systems.

Symbol Conventions

Unfortunately, there is no universal set of standards in the audio industry regarding symbol conventions used in laying out block diagrams of audio control systems. To a large extent, each manufacturer relies upon his own conventions, and an experienced audio engineer can easily make the transition from one schematic diagram to another. There are a few conventions which seem to be universally understood, and they are shown in Figure 7-8.

Ring-tip-sleeve patching conventions are universally indicated as shown in Figure 7-9.

The greatest confusion is apt to occur in symbols of combining networks or other arrays involving extensive switching. In Figure 7-10 the combining network shown in (a) in its complete form is often simplified as shown in (b) and (c). For the most part the same information is conveyed, and the latter symbols are easier to use. One bit of information which is not clear with the simplified forms is whether or not a microphone output can only be assigned to one channel at a time, or to two or more simultaneously. By comparison, the representa-

---

Figure 7-9. Patch bay conventions. Patch bays, known also as jack bays and jack fields, provide access to the inputs and outputs of most active devices in an audio control system. The patch bay provides additional flexibility for signal routing as well as the ability to "patch around" a defective component. The terminals in a patch bay are called jacks, and the schematic diagram of a jack is shown in (a). The input terminals 1 and 4 are normally connected to 2 and 3, respectively, providing signal continuity as shown in (b). When a patch cord is inserted into the jack, as shown in (c), the normally shorting contacts are lifted, and the signal is connected from terminals 1 and 4 to the tip and ring of the connecting patch cord. The arrangement shown in (d) is normally connected internally from jack 1 to jack 2. When a patch cord is inserted into either jack, the normal connections between terminals 2 and 3 of the two jacks are lifted, and the signal can be rerouted or a piece of auxiliary gear may be inserted.

Schematic

Symbol

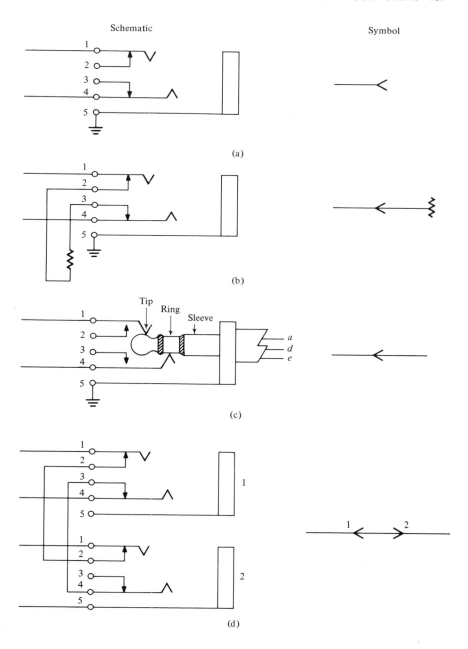

(a)

(b)

(c)

(d)

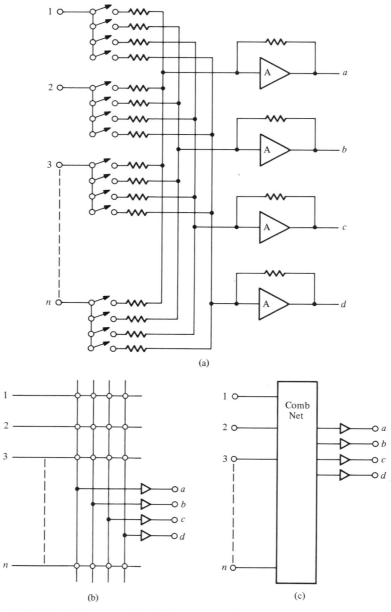

(a)

(b)

(c)

Figure 7-10. Combining networks. The representations shown in (a), (b), and (c) are equivalent.

tion in (a) explicitly indicates that each input can be assigned to all outputs simultaneously. In all forms, dotted lines are used to indicate repeated inputs for the sake of simplicity.

TYPICAL AUDIO CONTROL SYSTEMS

A 20-by-4 Console

In this section we shall examine the demands of studio recording flexibility as they have progressed from the early sixties to the mid-seventies. In the early sixties, a typical recording console had perhaps 20 inputs and 4 outputs. Four-channel recorders provided the maximum channel capability, but many recordings were made directly into the 2-track stereo format.

A typical console is shown in Figure 7-11. Such a system would most likely have been designed and fabricated by the studio personnel themselves out of individual components. Input flexibility includes adjustable pads so that microphones of varying sensitivity can be used, resulting in normalized settings of the input faders. High-level inputs are provided for feeds from tape recorders or other high-level devices. (The first seven high-level inputs would be permanently assigned to the outputs of the 4-track, 2-track, and monophonic tape recorders.) The equalizers in the inputs would normally be fairly simple, probably no more than three-knob devices providing LF boost and roll-off, MF boosting at two frequencies, and HF boost and roll-off.

Note that program assignments can be made independently of reverberation send assignments, and this capability enables a mixer to assign a primary signal to one output (channel 1, for example), while the reverberation return signal can be placed elsewhere (perhaps channel 4). This provides a degree of flexibility in establishing natural acoustical perspectives between direct sounds and reflections and reverberation generated from them. Reverberation return is normally back into the corresponding program channel just ahead of the master fader, but patching allows the reverberation return to be brought back to one of the high-level inputs for added flexibility.

It is essential to remember that when the outputs of 20 microphones were mixed down to 4 output channels, many final balances had to be made at the time of the original session itself. Typically, in the recording of a vocalist the rhythm instruments would be assigned to one channel, the remaining instruments assigned to two of the channels, while the vocalist would be assigned to the remaining channel. In the final stereo mix-down, vocalist and rhythm would be panned to the center position, while the two remaining instrumental tracks would be assigned left and right.

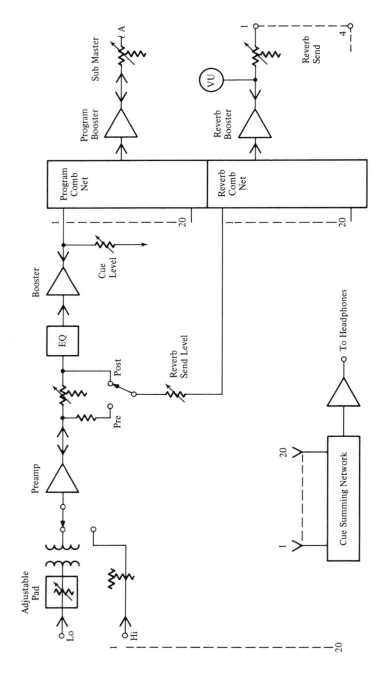

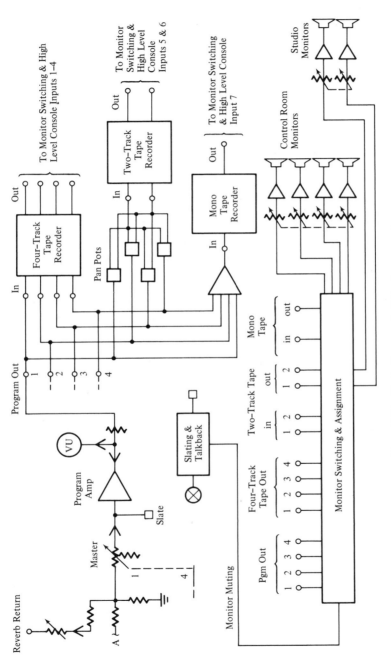

Figure 7-11. Block diagram of a 20-in-4-out console.

Let us assume that, for whatever reason, the recording producer was not satisfied with the performance of the vocalist. If the vocalist had been isolated, say, in a vocal booth, there would have been no acoustical "leakage" into other microphones. Thus, a new vocal track could be recorded, or overdubbed, at a later date. This process was accomplished by playing back the instrumental tracks using the *record* heads on the tape recorder as *playback* heads, assigning them to their respective high-level inputs in the console. Wearing headphones, the vocalist could sing in synchronism with the three instrumental tracks, while a new vocal track was recorded. This technique will be explained in detail in the following chapter.

It was essentially this requirement, and its extension to other instruments and musical resources, which led to the "multitrack explosion" of the mid-sixties. We can easily appreciate how limited these early consoles and tape recorders were in this regard.

Headphone monitoring in the studio established itself early as a means for musicians to hear each other more easily, especially in large studio setups where the players are often widely separated. Of course for a vocalist isolated in a vocal booth such monitoring is essential. The cue function shown in Figure 7-11 accomplished this; the mixer could establish auxilliary balances, entirely apart from the program balances, and these were fed to headphones worn by the musicians.

The functions of *slating* and *talk-back* enable the engineer and producer to communicate with the musicians in the studio and to indicate take numbers on the master tape. (The term "slating" derives from motion picture practice of holding a slate tablet with scene and take numbers written on it in front of the camera at the beginning of a take.) The slating and talk-back functions override the program at the inputs to the program amplifiers. The control room monitors are muted, but the studio monitors remain on so that the musicians can hear the announcements. The slating function adds a low-frequency tone (about 30 Hz) which at high rewind speeds is transposed upward in pitch so that the beginnings of recorded segments on the tape can be easily identified.

The feed to the 4-track tape recorder is directly from the four main outputs of the system. The feed to the stereo tape recorder is via panpots so that the four channels can be positioned anywhere in the stereo array, and the feed to the monophonic machine is the summation of the four outputs.

The monitoring switching provides the following modes: The outputs of the console (program out) and the 4-track tape recorder are assigned respectively to the four control room loudspeakers. These were invariably arrayed across the front of the control room. The output of the 2-track tape recorder would normally be assigned to loudspeakers 1 and 4, at the extremes of the array, while the monophonic tape recorder output would be assigned to the two center loudspeakers.

The feeds to the two studio loudspeakers would be channels 1 and 2 for the *left* loudspeaker and 3 and 4 for the *right* loudspeaker. The studio loudspeakers would be turned on only for tape playback.

A Modern 16- or 24-Track Console

The demands of rock recording as they developed in the mid-sixties called for increased track capability because of the necessity of recording different instruments at different times. The difficulty of interfacing an 8-track recorder with the console shown in Figure 7-11 is obvious, but many a recording was made that way. Sixteen-track machines required a far more complex approach to signal routing and control, and the complexity of building such consoles was beyond the capability of most studios. In the mid-sixties a number of companies were formed specializing in the building of multitrack consoles. Design philosophies centered largely around stock modular components, and this enabled consoles to be easily specified and built at reasonable cost.

A comprehensive signal flow diagram for one of the 16/24-track consoles is indeed complicated, and little purpose would be served by including one in this book. However varied the approaches of individual console builders may be, the basic requirements are much the same, and the general diagram of Figure 7-12 shows how the basic signals are routed through the system.

Input modules may provide any or all of the following functions:

 1. High-low level input switching
 2. Microphone padding
 3. Phase reversal switch
 4. Level control
 5. Reverb send level control
 6. Reverb pre-post switch
 7. Equalization
 8. Overload indicator
 9. Cue level control (one or more)
10. Preview or solo switch
11. Buss assignment (Program & Reverb)

The preview or solo function enables the mixer to audition one input simply by pressing a button on the input module which mutes the normal monitor output, overriding it with the output of the module. Program busses are not affected, so this can be done during the course of a recording without altering the

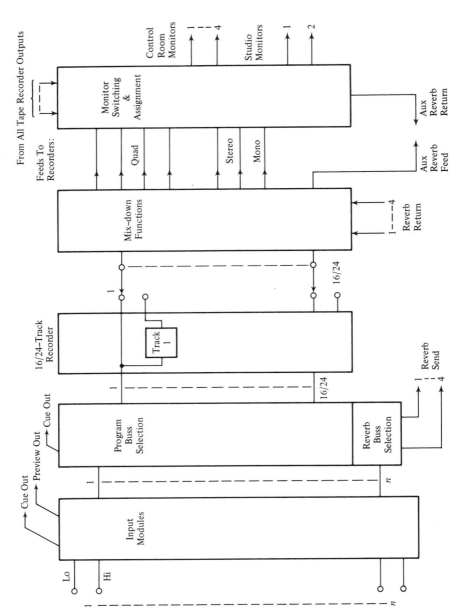

Figure 7-12. Diagram showing the major functions of a 16- or 24-track console.

inputs to the recorder. It is a diagnostic tool enabling the mixer to isolate individual pick-up problems in the studio.

Buss assignment in the newer consoles takes a number of forms. Some builders provide for only one buss assignment per input module while others allow multibussing and panning between a pair of busses.

Buss outputs are then fed directly to the multitrack recorder. Individual switching on each track facilitates the overdub function without having to route the recorder output back to the high-level inputs of the console.

The output busses and recorded tracks are then routed to the format assignment function, and monitoring during the recording process is usually done in one of the standard formats (usually stereo or monophonic). If a recording were being conceived primarily for the quad format, then monitoring would take place in that mode. The monitor switching provides for assignment of all signals to any or all of the four monitoring channels. Many consoles provide for an auxiliary reverberation feed out of the mix-down networks which is returned to the monitor switching function. This arrangement allows monitoring a signal with reverberation without having to make a commitment on the master recording.

When all components have been recorded on the multitrack master tape, the final mix-down would then proceed by routing the tracks back to the high-level inputs, thus giving the engineer and producer the benefit of all the input signal processing capability. The important difference between the 4-track system shown earlier and the multitrack approach is that the program recorded on the 4-track recorder was, for all intents and purposes, the finished product. The recorder was located at the output of the console. In the multitrack approach, the recorder is viewed as a storage medium, an interim process located midway in the console flow diagram.

AUTOMATING THE MIX-DOWN FUNCTION

General Requirements

Multi channel recording holds the promise of greater musical flexibility by allowing the producer and engineer more musical options. It is not an unmixed blessing, and many an engineer has found on occasion that there were simply too many tracks on the master tape to be handled intelligently during the mix-down process. Another problem is that of the complicated mix-down, achieved after several grueling hours, which the producer listens to a day or so later—and wishes to alter at one point. The agony of setting balances all over again is one that neither producer nor engineer wants to face, but it has been the only way to correct the problem.

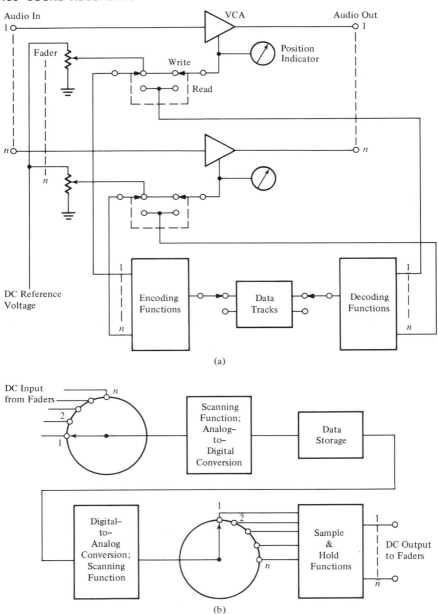

Figure 7-13. Console automation. A basic flow diagram for automatic control of levels is shown in (a). Detail of the sample-and-hold function is shown in (b).

Automated mix-down was conceived as a way of solving this problem by providing a means of *recording the physical positions of the faders* and, in a sense, letting the console do its own mix-down during the final transfer. A general plan for this is shown in Figure 7-13,a. In the *write* mode, the faders function as they normally do, and the mixer performs as usual. In this mode, data on the positions of the faders can also be stored on a data track on the multitrack master. In the *read* mode, the information on the data track is converted back into positional information for automatic operation of the faders. For updating, a fader may be taken out of the *read* mode back into the *write* mode while the new data are being recorded on another track. Thus, a correction may be made in the position of a single fader without altering any of the others. It is required, however, that there be *two* tracks available for data purposes, with the information being transferred from one to the other as data changes are made. Some means must be provided for indicating the recorded fader position so that switching from *read* to *write* mode can be accomplished without level mismatches. The basic encoding process is shown in Figure 7-13,b.

Selecting a Code

In designing an automated mix-down system, the engineer must take into account the following considerations:

1. How many tracks are to be controlled?
2. How often must these tracks be updated?
3. What degree of resolution is required?
4. Is the encoding format compatible with normal audio recorders?
5. What will be the effects of drop-outs or other mechanical problems on the repeatability of data as it is transferred from one track to another?

The first three questions determine the basic data rate of the system, while the last two determine its reliability.

The Allison Research Automated System

The Allison Research Automated System uses a scanning rate which varies according to the number of functions being sampled. The functions can be accommodated in groups of 16, so the update rate for 16 functions would be twice that of 32 functions and three times that of 48 functions. The basic "word" structure is based upon four cycles of an 8-kHz signal. The first cycle is used as a reference marker, and the next three are quantized on five levels, giving a total of $5 \times 5 \times 5 = 125$ possible states. This system is shown in Figure 7-14,a. Four full cycles at reference level serve as a marker or beginning of a frame or sequence, as shown in Figure 7-14,c, and the number of words in a frame is in multiples of 16. With a frame of 16 words, the total time required is 500 μsec for the marker and 16 × 500 μsec for the 16 words. Thus for 16 functions, the frame rate is:

$$\frac{1}{(16 + 1)(500 \ \mu sec)} = 117.6 \ \text{times per second}$$

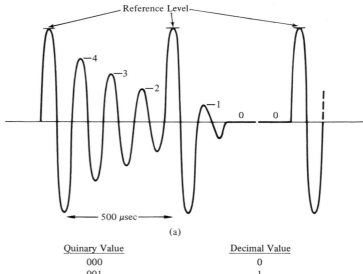

(a)

Quinary Value	Decimal Value
000	0
001	1
002	2
003	3
004	4
010	5
011	6
012	7
013	8
⋮	⋮
444	125

(b)

Figure 7-14. The Allison system. The basic quinary word structure is shown in (a). The quinary values are related to decimal values as shown in (b). A sequence or frame is initiated by four cycles of 8-kHz signal at reference level (c). Each word is initiated by one cycle at reference level. Possible errors include dropouts and the effects of overshoot in the data track, as shown in (d).

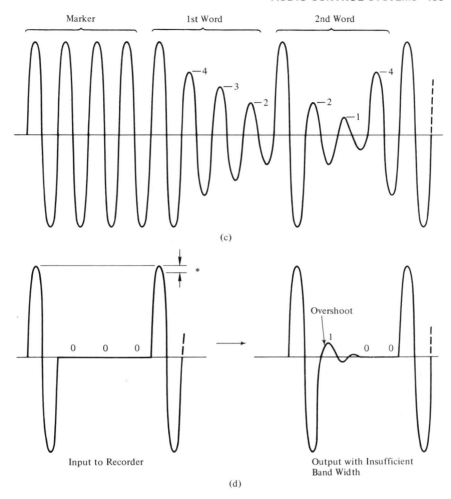

(c)

(d)

Input to Recorder

Output with Insufficient Band Width

*Note: Word is discarded if any reference level differs from previous one by 2 dB.

Figure 7-14. (*Continued*)

Most gain control requirements vary fairly slowly in practice, so it is possible to program many functions with an adequate frame rate.

Number of Functions	*Frame Rates*
16	117.6 times per second
32	60.6 "
48	40.8 "
64	30.7 "
80	24.7 "
96	20.6 "
112	17.7 "
128	15.5 "
144	13.8 "
160	12.4 "
176	11.3 "
192	10.4 "
208	9.7 "
224	8.9 "
240	8.3 "
256	7.9 "

For 256 functions the frame rate of 7.9 times per second is quite adequate for general audio purposes.

The bandwidth requirements of the Allison system are somewhat in excess of 8 kHz. The rapid indexing of signal levels can cause significant overshoot if the bandwidth is limited, and this can give rise to erroneous readings, as shown at Figure 7-14,d. The transfer characteristics of the recording channels must be optimized so that this does not occur.

The scaling of gain levels in the Allison system is based upon the first 100 states being valued at 0.5 dB and the remaining 25 states at 2 dB. Thus:

$$100 \times 0.5 = 50 \text{ dB}$$
$$25 \times 2 = \underline{50} \text{ dB}$$
$$100 \text{ dB} \quad \text{Total range}$$

This approach is based upon the relative insensitivity of the ear to gain changes at low levels and provides maximum resolution in the range when the ear is most sensitive.

A degree of signal conditioning is required to maintain accuracy as data are shuttled back and forth between tracks. The level of the decoded output is maintained approximately one-half step higher than the corresponding encoding threshold. This amounts to a kind of bias which ensures that normal record and playback gain errors will not cause level errors which could be cumulative in the repeated encode-decode processes. A secondary scanning rate of 5 kHz is also available in the Allison system for special applications.

For the most part, the system is used for gain control, but other functions which can be controlled by DC voltage levels can also be incorporated in the system. Automated Processes, Incorporated, a company which has long been associated with the Allison process through the interface equipment which it manufactures, has introduced voltage-controlled equalizers along with standard voltage-controlled faders.

Details of the API automated fader module are shown in Figure 7-15. When Switch-1 is in the indicated position, the automatic functions are by-passed completely and the program is simply routed through the fader in the normal fashion. When the automatic functions are engaged, the program is fed through the VCA and its level is controlled by the DC output of the fader or by information from the data track.

In the *write* mode, DC from the fader controls the VCA and is also fed to the level encoding function. In the *read* mode the DC signal from the decoder operates the VCA. At the same time a meter on the module gives an approximate indication of the control signal. For making transitions between *read* and *write* modes a null indication is useful for level matching so that smooth transitions are maintained.

The *update* mode provides a simpler method of going from *read* to *write*. If the fader is set at its −15 dB position and Switch-2 set for *update*, DC from the decoder is fed back to the VCA through the fader, and alterations in level can be made up or down from that point. The operator must only remember to reset the fader at the −15 dB point before going back to the *read* mode if he wishes to maintain a smooth transition without a sudden shift in level.

In practice, the *update* mode is used for minor corrections in the level of a previously mixed track. It cannot be used to correct an improperly mixed track. For that function the *write* mode must be used.

The Quad-Eight "Compumix" System

The Compumix system can accommodate 63 8-bit functions, and the basic code is shown in Figure 7-16,a. A *sync word*, consisting of two complete cycles at 2.4 kHz, is located at the beginning of each sequence, or frame, and initiates the entire cycle. The 63 8-bit words follow the sync word serially. The time occupied by each word is .833 msec, and the time occupied by the entire frame is .0533 second, corresponding to a rate of 18.7 frames per second.

An 8-bit word provides 2^8, or 256 states, and the 8-bit words are in a biphase format as shown at Figure 7-16,b. In the biphase format a binary "0" is signified by one change of the wave form direction per clock period, while a binary "1" is

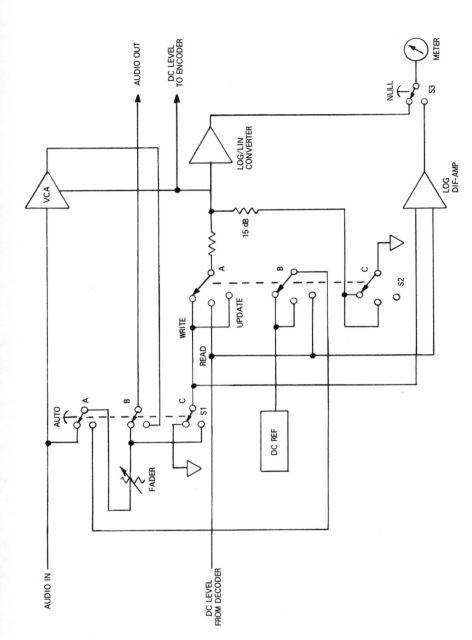

Figure 7-15. Details of the fader module manufactured by Automated Processes, Inc., interfacing with the Allison system. (*Courtesy Automated Processes, Inc.*)

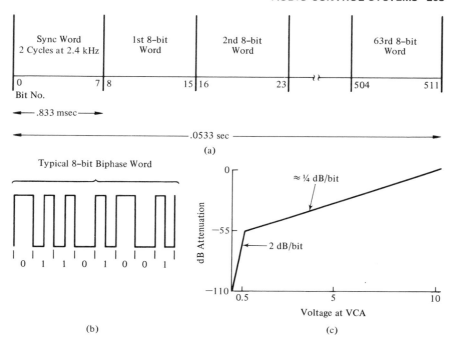

Figure 7-16. The Quad-Eight Compumix system. The basic biphase frame of 64 8-bit words is shown in (a). Principle of the biphase code is shown in (b). Attenuation vs. voltage at the Compumix VCA is shown in (c).

signified by two changes in direction per clock period. The frequency rate for the binary "1" indication is 9600 Hz, while that for the "0" is 4800 Hz.

The biphase code is basically very accurate because it is self-clocking, deals only with two states (positive and negative), and consists only of two frequencies an octave apart. It can be accurately detected even when recorded on a very noisy track. In the Compumix system, once an error is detected, all data are discarded until the next sync word, and previous positional information is maintained.

For gain control functions the resolution of the system is as shown in Figure 7-16,c. Approximately .25 dB per bit resolution is provided from 0 to −55 dB, with 2 dB per bit resolution from −55 dB to −110 dB. The DC voltages from the fader are linear with respect to fader position, and the scaling shown in Figure 7-16,c is formed by a linear taper generator in the Compumix system working in conjunction with the logarithmic gain of the VCA.

Figure 7-17 shows a functional diagram of the system. In the *write* mode (indicated by *W* in the diagram), DC positional information from all faders is fed to

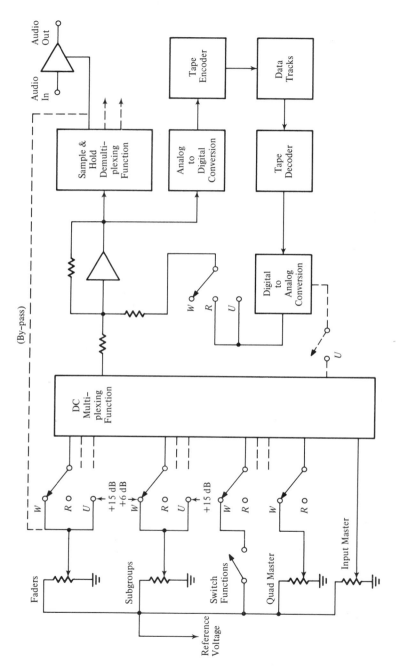

Figure 7-17. Functional diagram of the Compumix system.

a DC multiplexer, providing a sequence of DC voltages representing all fader positions. The output of this is fed to a DC amplifier and then to a sample-and-hold demultiplexer whose outputs are control voltages controlling each of the VCA's.

The subgroup function provides a means of grouping various faders to be controlled by a single fader. Separate information for the subgroup fader position is not stored; it is added directly to the information of those inputs assigned to it. A given fader may be assigned to any one of eight subgroups, selected by a thumbwheel at each input fader.

A "quad" master fader provides control of four-channel program output. It can be set in either *read* or *write* modes and normally affects a set of four VCA's located after the quad buss assignments.

An input master fader provides a means of controlling all input levels. It is a *write only* function.

In the *read* mode (indicated by *R* in the diagram), information from the data tracks is fed back through to the DC summing point and from there to the sample-and-hold demultiplexing function for control of the VCA's. At the same time, the faders are disabled.

In the *update* mode (indicated by *U* in the diagram) positional information from the faders is once again fed to the DC multiplexer for updating of only those faders which are in the update mode. In this mode, a 15-dB bias is added to the fader. Under this condition there will be an exact match with the level previously encoded when the fader is set at −15 dB. In the Compumix system, as in the Automated Processes approach, the *update* mode allows new positional information to be added to the information already present from the previous *write* mode operation.

In the *write* mode, information from both faders and subgroup faders is recorded. A 6-dB bias is applied to the subgroup fader so that a −6 dB setting of that fader results in unity gain, allowing further adjustments to be made both above and below.

If a subgroup fader is placed in the *update* mode, any input faders assigned to it are disabled, and only the subgroup fader is functional. In this mode a 15-dB bias is applied to the subgroup fader for proper matching of levels when the subgroup fader is set at −15 dB.

It is possible to by-pass the entire multiplex/demultiplex function by routing the DC information from the fader directly to the corresponding VCA's. This procedure would be used only in the case of system malfunction and is shown as a dashed path at the top of the diagram from the input fader to its corresponding VCA.

BIBLIOGRAPHY

1. *Motion Picture Sound Engineering* (prepared by the Research Council of the Academy of Motion Picture Arts and Sciences) (D. Van Nostrand, New York, 1938).

2. J. Frayne and H. Wolf, *Sound Recording* (John Wiley & Sons, New York, 1949).

3. W. Jung, *IC OP-AMP Cookbook* (Howard W. Sams, Indianapolis, 1974).

4. R. Rundstein, *Modern Recording Techniques* (Howard W. Sams, Indianapolis, 1974).

5. H. Tremaine, *Audio Cyclopedia* (Howard W. Sams, Indianapolis, 1969).

6. S. Walker and P. Buff, "A Practical Approach to Recording Studio Automation" (presented at 43rd Audio Engineering Society Convention, September 1972).

8
Magnetic Recording

INTRODUCTION

The magnetic medium has shaped the evolution of contemporary recording in such a fundamental way that it becomes difficult to think of the creative process apart from the essential benefits of multitrack capability and ease of editing. The principle of magnetic recording has been known since the turn of the century, but the problems of noise and distortion kept it from being anything more than a curiosity. High-frequency bias was discovered in the twenties, and with it the fundamental problems of distortion and noise were on their way to being solved. But the physical medium itself remained an intractable one. Earlier experiments used steel ribbon, with its excessive expense and handling difficulties. Later on, wire recorders solved some of the handling problems but offered only minimal improvements in quality.

It was not until the early forties that all the right ingredients came together. The Germans developed the *magnetophon*, a tape recorder embodying HF bias and excellent mechanical tape-handling characteristics. These early machines were brought back to the U.S. after the war and quickly convinced the recording and broadcasting interests that the "new medium" had substantial advantages over the direct-to-disc process of that day. Developments came quickly, and tape manufacture progressed

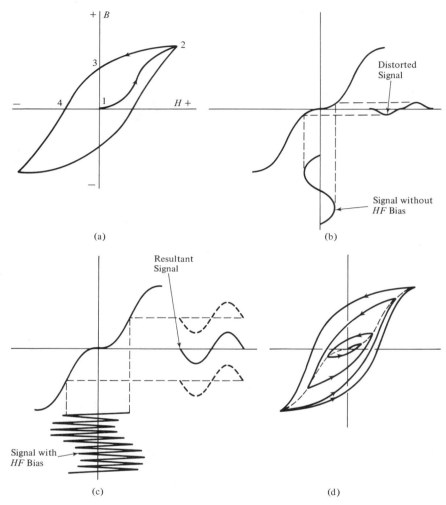

Figure 8-1. The role of HF bias. A *hysteresis* loop is shown in (a). An unmagnetized parti-cle, exposed to a magnetizing force H, will follow the nonlinear path from 1 to 2. When the force is turned off, the remnant flux, B, will be at 3. A negative value of H is required to bring the particle back to a zero flux level at 4. The process is symmetrical in the negative B and H directions. A distorted signal output is shown in (b) when an audio signal is applied directly to the magnetic medium. When HF bias is added to the audio signal, in (c), a more linear transfer is obtained. Erasure of a signal is accomplished, in (d), by exposing a mag-netized particle to a rapidly changing and diminishing bias field. The hysteresis loop be-comes smaller with each cycle of the bias wave form, finally ending at zero.

dramatically. By 1950 it had become established as the master recording medium for both the record and broadcast industries.

ELECTRICAL AND MAGNETIC CONSIDERATIONS

The role of HF bias in magnetic recording is not perfectly understood, but it has long been known that the addition of a super-sonic signal to the audio program results in a reduction of noise and distortion. A graphical representation of how distortion is reduced is illustrated in Figure 8-1. In a sense, the HF signal biases, or displaces, the audio components, resulting in their being recorded over more linear portions of the magnetization curve.

Once the magnetic tape medium has been "linearized" by HF bias, recording is a fairly straightforward procedure. (See Figure 8-2.) Tape is passed over an *erase head*, then to a *record head* where the signal is applied to the tape, and finally to the *playback head* where the signal is retrieved. The HF bias serves as well to erase remnant signals previously recorded on the tape, while the mixture of HF bias and audio results in recording of the audio.

The playback process is the result of *magnetic induction*. When a magnetic field rises and falls in the neighborhood of a coil of wire, a voltage is induced across the coil. Given a magnetic field, or *magnetic flux*, which is constant with frequency, the induced voltage is proportional to the frequency itself, as shown in Figure 8-2,c. The playback voltage rises 6 dB/octave up to the region where various losses become significant. One of these losses is wavelength-dependent and is called *scanning loss*. It depends upon the playback head gap width and reaches null points in response when the recorded wavelength is equal to the gap width or submultiples of it. Other losses which become significant at high frequencies are eddy current losses in the head core material and demagnetization losses. In a well-designed system these collective HF losses do not become significant over the operating bandwidth.

Trade-offs Between Distortion, Frequency Response, and Noise

The chief factor relating distortion, noise, and frequency response in a magnetic recording system is high-frequency bias. When bias is set too low there may be ample high frequency response, but distortion at longer wavelengths (low frequencies) will be too high. Adjusting the bias for peak output at long wavelengths corrects the distortion problem, but results in less recording sensitivity at higher frequencies. Thus, more boosting, or pre-emphasis, of high frequencies is necessary in order to maintain flat response. The curves of Figure 8-3 show the dependence of various wavelengths upon bias level.

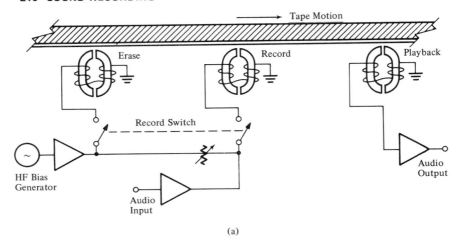

(a)

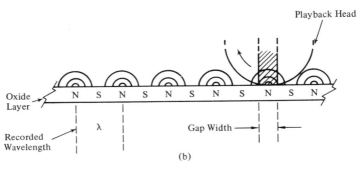

(b)

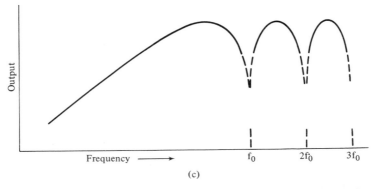

(c)

Figure 8-2. Basic principles of tape recording. The arrangement of *erase, record,* and *playback* heads is shown in (a). As a general rule, the bias frequency is at least *five times* the highest audio frequency to be recorded. Typical values are in the 100–150 kHz range. The playback process is shown in (b), and output of the playback head is shown in (c).

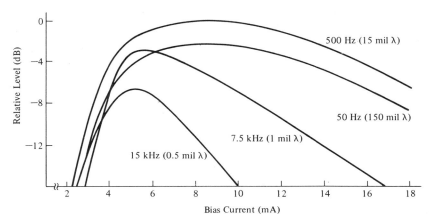

Figure 8-3. Tape output at several wavelengths as a function of bias current. Peak output at higher frequencies (shorter wavelengths) takes place at values of current around 5 milliamperes, while output at lower frequencies (longer wavelengths) takes place at a value around 9 or 10 milliamperes. The higher-value bias also corresponds to lowest distortion for long wavelengths, and it is customary to establish operating bias at the point which gives maximum output for long wavelengths. (*Data courtesy 3M.*)

Purity of the HF bias waveform is essential if low noise performance of the recording system is to be realized. Even harmonic components in the bias waveform have the effect of creating a DC offset in the record head, and the result is a dramatic increase in the ground noise level of the system.

Standard Playback Curves

In order for recordings to be compatible between machines and locations, playback response curves are rigorously defined, and standard test tapes are available as equalization references. If a tape is recorded with constant magnetic flux at all frequencies, then the output of a playback head will *rise* 6 dB/octave with frequency, since the induced voltage is proportional to the *rate of change* of the flux. The output of the head will be as shown in Figure 8-4, curve *a*; and playback equalization as shown at curve *b* must be applied if the response is to be maintained flat, as shown at curve *c*.

Standard playback curves are shown in Figure 8-5. Note that the curves shown in (a) exhibit a precise relation to tape speed; for each doubling of speed, the break point in the playback curve is raised an octave. This relationship maintains the lowest possible distortion for the entire range of tape speeds. The NAB curve, shown in (b), was established early for 15-ips use, and it was later determined that newer tapes could be "pushed" at $7\frac{1}{2}$-ips so that the same playback curve could be used. It should be obvious, however, that the NAB curve is not optimum for both speeds.

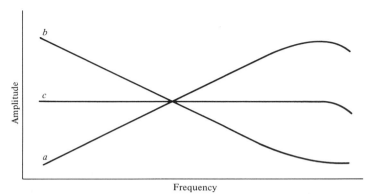

Figure 8-4. Basic playback equalization. The electrical output of the playback head rises with frequency for constant-flux recording, as shown at curve *a*; it must be equalized by a complementary curve (*b*) if response is to be flat (curve *c*).

Recording Equalization

There are no standard record curves. Recording equalization is a system variable which must be adjusted for the kind of tape which is used and, to a lesser extent, the individual character of the recording head. It is very instructive to review the varying equalization requirements for tape as it has evolved over the last 15 years. (See Figure 8-6.)

EVOLUTION OF MAGNETIC TAPE

The earliest tape used with the German *magnetophons* was a plastic material with iron oxide dispersed throughout it; one could record on either side of the tape. Later, a tape with an oxide coating on a plastic base was developed, and this tape resulted in greater signal strength because of the higher density of oxide next to the heads. In the U.S. things got off to a slow start, and some of the first tapes were composed of oxide on a paper base. The first plastic tapes used an acetate base, noted for its brittleness, affinity for moisture, and general mechanical instability. Polyester bases are universally used now for serious recording purposes and offer extremely stable mechanical characteristics and imperviousness to moisture.

The dramatic improvement in tape over the last 15 years is shown in Figure 8-7. The medium has been improved in both directions; the noise floor has been lowered and the upper limits, consistent with an established distortion level, have been raised as well.

The improvement in HF response, shown in Figure 8-6, has made possible a higher level of performance of tape recorders at lower speeds. Newer oxide formulations, those less susceptible to erasure by HF bias, result in better recording efficiency at high frequencies. Other factors in the improvement of tape are better control of oxide particle size and distribution, as well as the density of the oxide in the coating. Simply making the oxide coating thicker will, of course, increase the signal output at long wavelengths, but HF response will suffer by comparison. Therefore, tape manufacturers have sought more efficient binding methods so that more oxide can be contained in the oxide layer.

As tape has improved in its dynamic range, the phenomenon of *print-through* has become more of a problem. Print-through is the transfer of signal from one oxide layer to another and is related to the particle size distribution in the oxide layer. If the oxide-binder-plasticizer mixture was improperly milled, or mixed, there will be fine particles of oxide much smaller than desired dispersed throughout the mixture. These fine particles are very easily influenced by the magnetic fields present in adjacent tape layers and tend to pick up the signals present in those layers.

The oxide used in manufacturing tape is *gamma ferric oxide* (Fe_2O_3). "Gamma" refers to the particular crystalline formation. The particle shape is needle-like or *acicular*, and the desired particle length is about 20 to 30 μinch. Roughness in handling and milling tends to break off small pieces, resulting in lesser print-through and noise performance.

For special purposes, other materials are used for tape manufacture. Chromium dioxide (Cr_2O_3) is used in certain cassette tapes operating at $1\frac{7}{8}$ ips where relatively high output from a very thin oxide layer is essential. At $1\frac{7}{8}$ ips a 15-kHz signal produces a recorded wavelength of 125 millionths of an inch. By comparison, a 15-kHz signal recorded at 15 ips for professional application has a wavelength of one *mil*, or one-thousandth of an inch. Chromium dioxide exhibits well-controlled particle size distribution and thus has low noise as well as low print-through. Coating thicknesses for Cr_2O_3 tape can be as low as 80 μinch for short-wavelength recording. Typical oxide thickness for current mastering tape is on the order of 500 μinch. Cobalt *doping* of iron oxide has been used to create formulations of higher coercivity. In the doping process, trace amounts of cobalt are added to the oxide and take their place in the lattice structure of the oxide crystals. The technique is not without its problems, and such formulations are not normally used in professional audio recording.

Mechanical requirements placed upon tape call for long-term stability under a wide variety of storage conditions as well as smooth handling at high rewind speeds. In the last ten years, professional tape has been manufactured with a *matte* finish on the back side of the tape about 100 μinch thick. During fast rewind and forwarding of the tape the matte backing provides a higher coefficient of friction between the adjacent oxide layers, resulting in smoother winding.

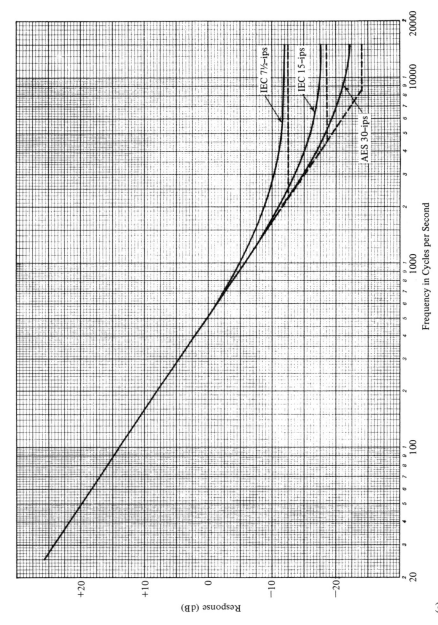

(a)

Frequency in Cycles per Second

Response (dB)

IEC 7½-ips

IEC 15-ips

AES 30-ips

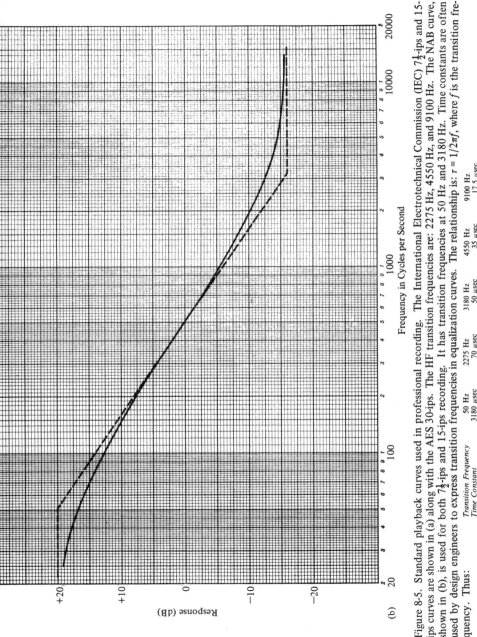

(b)

Figure 8-5. Standard playback curves used in professional recording. The International Electrotechnical Commission (IEC) $7\frac{1}{2}$-ips and 15-ips curves are shown in (a) along with the AES 30-ips. The HF transition frequencies are: 2275 Hz, 4550 Hz, and 9100 Hz. The NAB curve, shown in (b), is used for both $7\frac{1}{2}$-ips and 15-ips recording. It has transition frequencies at 50 Hz and 3180 Hz. Time constants are often used by design engineers to express transition frequencies in equalization curves. The relationship is: $\tau = 1/2\pi f$, where f is the transition frequency. Thus:

Transition Frequency	50 Hz	2275 Hz	3180 Hz	4550 Hz	9100 Hz
Time Constant	3180 μsec	70 μsec	50 μsec	35 μsec	17.5 μsec

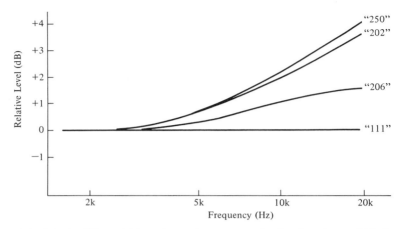

Figure 8-6. Relative HF sensitivity of several tapes normalized to Scotch type 111. In each case, long wavelength bias was adjusted for maximum output. Playback head gap width was 100 μ inches, and tape speed was 15 ips. Scotch 202 tape was characteristic of the first generation of low-noise tapes made by a number of manufacturers, and its flat output required far less pre-emphasis than type 111. Scotch 206 represented a trade-off of high-frequency sensitivity for greater long-wavelength capability, and thus produced somewhat higher output overall as compared with type 202 (see Figure 8-7). Scotch 250 restores high-frequency output sensitivity in excess of the previous tapes. (*Data courtesy 3M.*)

ELECTRICAL LINEARIZING TECHNIQUES

Disc cutting heads and amplifiers make use of inverse feedback to flatten their response and reduce distortion. In these systems the output signal is compared with the input signal, and any error detected is fed into the system out-of-phase so that the error is corrected. By comparison, with tape recording there is no feedback from the remnant signal on the tape into the system input for error-correcting.

It is characteristic of systems with inverse feedback to exhibit good linearity and low distortion up to some point at which fundamental limits of the medium or device are reached; beyond that point there is a rapid onset of clipping and gross distortion. The magnetic tape medium goes into distortion gradually; in the parlance of the art, it "overloads gently." In Figure 8-8,a we see a typical transfer characteristic for a magnetic medium. If a "predistorter" is placed in series with the recording function and carefully adjusted so that its input-output characteristics complement those of the tape itself, then the overall system transfer characteristic can be linearized. The process can be applied only to a limited degree, but the improvement can be significant at low frequencies.

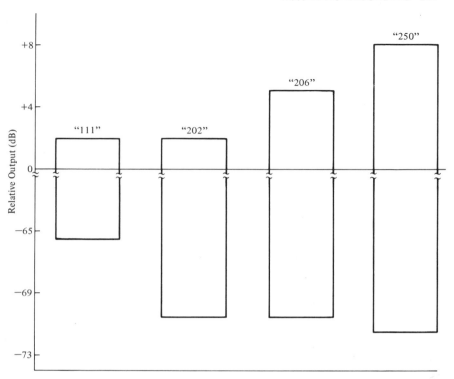

Figure 8-7. The dynamic range of various tapes. The tapes shown in the previous figure are compared in terms of overall dynamic ranges. Maximum signal level is defined as the 3% THD point for long wavelengths, while minimum usable level is defined as the noise floor measured through an NAB standard noise weighing network. Scotch 202 provided a dramatic decrease of 5 dB in ground noise level relative to 111. This response is characteristic of the many low-noise tapes introduced during the early sixties. In the second half of the sixties a new kind of high output–low noise tape was introduced by a number of manufacturers, and it is characterized by Scotch 206. Essentially, the noise floor remained the same as with low-noise tape, but the output capability increased 3 dB. Toward the mid-seventies, a newer generation of tape was introduced by several manufacturers, and that improvement is characterized by Scotch 250. An overall improvement in dynamic range of 4 dB was realized as an increase in operating level of 3 dB and a decrease of the noise floor by 1 dB. Thus, the basic tape medium has increased in dynamic range by about 12 dB in just about as many years. (*Data courtesy 3M.*)

Although the technique has been used in some professional recorders, it is not a part of the mainstream of current design practice. Chief difficulties are the delicate dependence of the process upon system gain and differences between batches of tape.

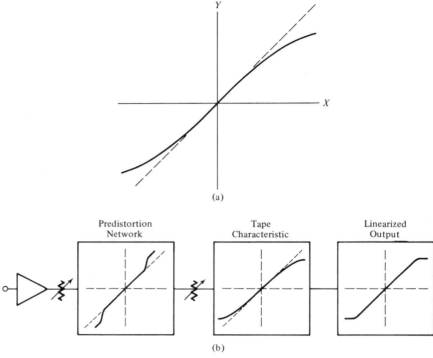

Figure 8-8. "Predistortion" in magnetic recording. The basic transfer characteristic of a tape recording system is linear over a wide range, as shown in (a). At the extremes, *tape saturation* results in significant nonlinearity. A "predistorter" can correct some of this non-linearity, as shown in (b), but cannot extend the fundamental limits of the system.

MECHANICAL CONSIDERATIONS

Basically, the function of the tape transport is to move tape at constant velocity during the record and playback processes and provide quick and easy access to any part of the recording through fast-forward and rewind modes. These goals are not easily achieved, and design considerations have changed over the years as tape widths have progressed from $\frac{1}{4}''$ through $\frac{1}{2}''$ and $1''$ up to $2''$.

Let us first consider some of the problems inherent in the narrower tape widths operating at speeds of $7\frac{1}{2}$ and 15 ips. Narrower tape, especially $\frac{1}{4}''$, does not present significant guidance problems on the transport; it bends, or warps, easily enough to conform to the tape path. The greatest problem is *flutter*, a rapid instability of tape motion that is due to many causes. Mechanical irregularities in the transport are the chief cause, but "violin bow" action of the tape as it passes over the heads may contribute "scrape flutter," which causes a graininess or coarseness in the quality of sound if it is excessive. To eliminate these problems there are numerous idlers, or rollers, in the tape path in intimate contact with the tape, and their purpose is to smooth out the irregularities in the motion. Because of the low mass of $\frac{1}{4}''$ tape reels, the acceleration demands of the spooling motors in the fast-forward and rewind modes are fairly minimal.

A typical layout for a tape transport is shown in Figure 8-9. The supply reel is shown at the left, and it is supplied with *reverse torque*, or hold-back, during the record and playback processes. The tape passes around the idler at *a*, which serves to smooth out gross irregularities in tape motion as the tape comes off the reel. As the tape passes the erase, record, and playback head stack at *b*, it is essential that the tape motion be as smooth as possible. Often, small idlers are placed between the heads to filter out what little scrape flutter may develop as the tape passes each head. Obviously, the nature of the finish of the oxide layer and the finish of the head surface play an important role in determining the character of any motion irregularities developed during contact, and considerable attention is given to this matter in the manufacture of tape.

As the tape passes the head stack it goes through the *capstan/pressure roller* assembly at *c* and *d*. The capstan turns at constant velocity, and the smoothness of its motion determines in many ways the basic integrity of the transport.

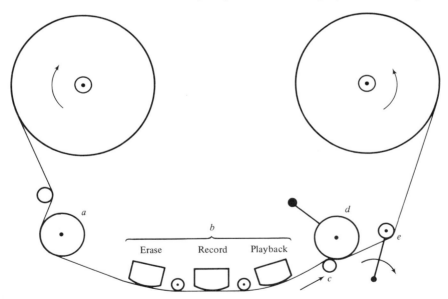

Figure 8-9. A typical layout for an open-loop tape transport.

Usually capstans are directly driven, extensions of the motor shaft itself; in other designs they may be extensions of large flywheels which are belt-driven. The pressure roller holds the tape against the capstan so that capstan motion is transferred to the tape. It is invariably made of synthetic rubber, smoothly surfaced on a precision bearing.

As the tape passes through the capstan drive, it loops over a spring-loaded guidance arm, shown at *e*, whose function is to ensure even stacking of the tape as it winds onto the take-up reel and to detect tape breakage and avoid tape spill.

Another approach to transport design is shown in Figure 8-10. This design is referred to as *closed loop* because the loop of tape passing over the heads is effectively isolated from the spooling motors by the dual capstan nature of the tape drive. The transport shown in Figure 8-9 is known as an *open loop* system. Given proper attention to all design parameters both approaches yield equal performance; however, tape editing and splicing is generally easier on open loop transports.

Today's tape transports have progressed far beyond their predecessors in ease of operation. They are virtually foolproof; an operator may go from *fast-forward* to *record* mode confident that the machine will slow down, come to a halt, and then go into the record mode. Sophisticated logic and motion sensing are part of any good professional transport and make it nearly impossible to spill or break tape, no matter what the operating mode. These functions have become all the more important with the increase in usage of 1" and 2" tape.

The mechanics of handling the wider tapes are quite different from the requirements of the narrower widths. An obvious difference is the greater mass of the tape reel and the consequent need for bigger spooling motors so that fast-forward and rewind functions can be handled efficiently. Likewise, the capstan drive must be capable of accelerating a greater load. Tape guidance is a major problem. The wide tapes will not warp; so all tape guides must be extremely precise and stable so that motion is at all times at right angles to the reference plane of the transport's top-plate.

Another reason for maintaining precise guidance has to do with *azimuth* relationships between tracks. Azimuth refers to the angular relationship between tape motion and the record and playback head gaps. The desired angle is, of course 90 degrees, and that represents *zero azimuth error*. If the tape should skew as it goes over the heads, then a momentary azimuth error exists which can cause losses at high frequencies. The effect is especially bad with wider tapes, because the greater distance between outside tracks maximizes the time displacement caused by the angular error. The delicate nature of even slight azimuth error with the wide tapes is shown in Figure 8-11.

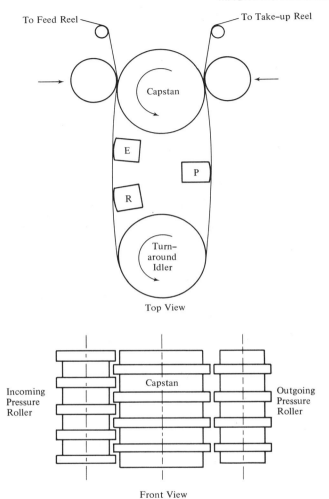

Figure 8-10. A closed-loop transport. A single capstan controls tape motion at the heads and provides isolation from the spooling motors. The capstan has *two* effective diameters. The incoming pressure roller engages the smaller diameter, and the outgoing pressure roller engages the larger diameter. As a result, the tape loop around the heads and turn-around idler is maintained under a constant tension. In the 3M Mincom design using this arrangement, the outer diameter of the capstan is 1.9088″ ± .001″ and the inner diameter is .003″ ± .001″ smaller.

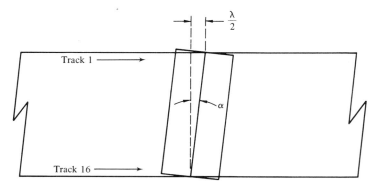

Figure 8-11. Effect of azimuth error. If a common signal is present on both tracks 1 and 16 of a 2-inch tape, then an azimuth error of $\alpha = 0.014°$ will result in total cancellation of a 15-kHz signal if the tape is recorded at 15 ips. By contrast, an azimuth error of 0.23° is required to generate the same loss between the two tracks of a 15-ips $\frac{1}{4}$-inch recording. The difference is roughly 16-to-1.

Flutter is far less a problem with the wider tapes. The greater mass and the higher speeds of 15- and 30-ips result in significantly higher momentum, and this seems to filter out irregularities in the motion of the tape. As a consequence idlers tend to be smaller, and there are fewer of them on the transports designed to handle wider tapes.

TAPE SYNCHRONIZING AND INDEXING TECHNIQUES

As we have stated before, one of the great benefits of the magnetic medium is the ease with which tracks can be added to a recording at different times. This involves a number of techniques, ranging from the simplest demands of recording new tracks in synchronization with those already on the tape, automatic indexing of tape, and the more complex demands of electronic editing.

Sel-Sync

Under the trade name *Sel-Sync* (*Sel*ective *Sync*hronization) Ampex introduced a means of recording new tracks in synchronism with previously recorded ones by using the *record heads* for playback. In this way the normal time gap between record and playback heads could effectively be reduced to zero. The method is shown in Figure 8-12. Note that the input to the playback amplifiers can be switched to either the playback or record head. In the synchronization mode those tracks previously recorded (tracks 1, 2, and 3) would be played back over their respective record heads, while track 4 would be energized for recording in the normal way. The performer normally would monitor tracks 1, 2, and 3 via headphones.

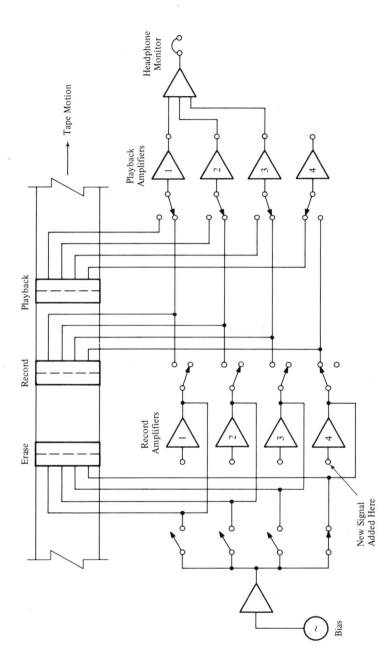

Figure 8-12. Basic flow diagram for Sel-Sync technique. A new signal is added on track 4 in synchronism with the previously recorded tracks 1, 2, and 3.

In the early days of this technique, the frequency response of the record heads in their roles as playback heads left much to be desired; it was sufficient for monitoring purposes only. Later improvements resulted in playback in the synchronization mode virtually identical to the playback head itself in terms of noise and frequency response. Thus, it became possible to combine and shift tracks on a multichannel master tape as desired.

Insert Recording

A very important feature of a tape recorder used in synchronization work is its ability to go in and out of the record mode without producing annoying clicks or thumps on the tape. In order to do this, the bias, both at the erase and record heads, has to be turned on and off very smoothly.

As a tape recorder normally goes into the record mode, bias is switched to the erase and record heads simultaneously. Because of the spacing between the two heads, the segment of tape between them will not be properly erased. Furthermore, when the bias is turned off, there will be a corresponding gap in the tape. At higher tape speeds these gaps are quite short, perhaps no more than 0.1 second, and they are often ignored.

The problem is solved by energizing the erase head *before* the record head by an amount equal to the time gap between them. Likewise, when going out of the insert record mode, the erase head is deactivated before the record head by the same amount of time. Figure 8-13 shows details of the insert recording process.

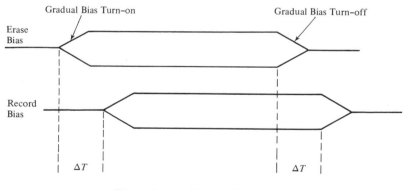

$$\Delta T = \frac{\text{Distance between Erase and Record Heads (inches)}}{\text{Tape Speed (inches per second)}}$$

Figure 8-13. Basic principles of insert recording. Proper insert recording requires that there be a gradual HF bias turn-on and turn-off in order to prevent the audibility of the transitions in and out of the record mode. It is also customary in more sophisticated machine designs to delay the turn-on and turn-off of record bias relative to erase bias in order to avoid gaps or overrecording on the tape.

Automatic Indexing

In the process of adding tracks it is necessary for the performer to "rehearse," as it were, with the tracks already recorded. One of the nuisances in this phase of the creative process has always been the drudgery of shuttling the tape back and forth between the starting and stopping points. Many tape recorder manufacturers now offer some form of automatic cueing or indexing, which frees the engineer from the task of doing it manually. In reality, these automatic cueing systems are little more than sophisticated embellishments on the familiar tape counter found on most machines. As shown in Figure 8-14, positional information from the tape counting idler is fed to a comparator, where the instantaneous tape position is compared to a *preset* position, corresponding to the beginning of the repeated musical segment. There is no code on the tape itself; the positional information is derived solely from the rotation of the tape counting idler.

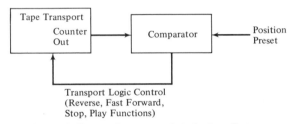

Figure 8-14. Block diagram for automatic indexing of a tape recorder.

Address Codes and Electronic Editing

Going a large step beyond the fairly simple technique we have just described, the development of address codes allows tape to become a truly synchronous medium. With it, two or more tape machines can be operated in near perfect synchronism, and predetermined switching between machine outputs, *electronic editing,* can be performed to timing accuracies of $\frac{1}{30}$ second.

The most widely used address code was developed by the Society of Motion Picture and Television Engineers for the special demands of video tape recorders, but its benefits for audio applications are obvious—especially as we move into creative areas which involve visual and aural aspects on an equal basis. The address code established by the SMPTE gives information, updated thirty times a second, concerning frame number, seconds, minutes, and hours. The code format is *binary coded decimal* (BCD) recorded in biphase fashion. Figure 8-15 outlines the fundamentals of the system. Binary values of "0" and "1" are arranged in groups of four to represent the decimal numbers 0 through 9. A typical 8-bit binary "word" is shown in (b) along with its waveform. Zero is represented by a shift in the waveform once per clock period, while two shifts per period represent the binary value of one. The SMPTE code uses 80 bits to identify each frame, and at 30 frames/second the bit rate is 2400/second. The code is shown in (c). Of interest is the fact that there are 32 spare bits which can be assigned by the user for other data.

In audio use, the code can be used to interlock two or more tape recorders at a cost of one track each for synchronizing. One machine functions as a "master," and the other "slave" machines will automatically search their recorded code via the comparator, reducing the error to zero and establishing syn-

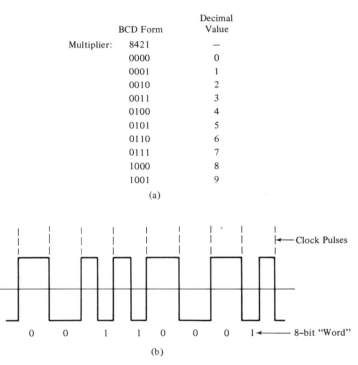

	BCD Form	Decimal Value
Multiplier:	8 4 2 1	—
	0000	0
	0001	1
	0010	2
	0011	3
	0100	4
	0101	5
	0110	6
	0111	7
	1000	8
	1001	9

(a)

(b)

Figure 8-15. The SMPTE address code. Decimal values from 0 to 9 can be encoded in a 4-bit binary form as shown in (a). For example, the decimal number 7 is coded as 0111. The equivalent multiples are 1, 2, and 4, yielding 1 + 2 + 4 = 7. The biphase waveform is shown in (b), and the complete 80-bit code is shown in (c). The bit allocation is: 16 for synchronizing, 27 for address assignment, 32 undefined spare bits, 2 fixed zeros, and 3 unassigned zero bits.

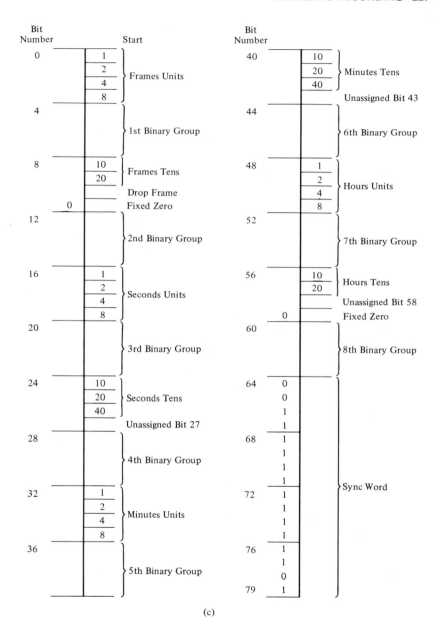

(c)

Figure 8-15. (*Continued*)

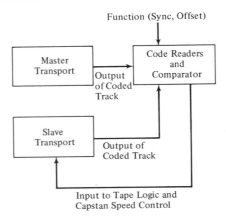

Figure 8-16. Synchronizing two tape transports with an address code. Two or more slave transports can be run in synchronism with a master transport within 1/30 second. A time offset can also be established between transports for special effects.

chronism between transports. A block diagram of this function is shown in Figure 8-16.

If the aim is only to synchronize two tape machines, then the complexity of the SMPTE code is not necessary. The code does *two* things; it provides a synchronizing pulse as well as the address information. For synchronizing purposes, it is necessary only to record a repetitive waveform, 60 Hz for example, on spare tracks of the recorders and compare them upon playback. Other synchronizing codes have been devised and optimized for certain applications, and the range of application runs the gamut from simple synchronizing of two tape recorders up to sophisticated command of many machines, audio as well as video, in advanced multimedia production.

ALIGNMENT TAPES AND STANDARDS

Alignment tapes are normally used for the following three functions:

1. Playback equalization
2. Establishing proper azimuth
3. Establishing reference level

Alignment tapes are difficult to make and are accordingly rather expensive. Many an engineer has tried to make his own when faced with the high cost of a 2" alignment tape and found out just how difficult it can be. There is, of course, no substitute for a proper alignment tape, and with reasonable care a tape can last for a long time. Some precautions are obvious. The tape should never be used on a machine which has not been thoroughly demagnetized or checked out mechanically. It is equally important to store the tape with an even wind and under the recommended storage conditions.

Reference Levels

In the early days of magnetic recording, reference level was established as the 1% third harmonic distortion point at 1 kHz with a given type of tape. This was not a very rigorous standard and was difficult to duplicate. Later, when accurate flux measuring devices became available, it was determined that the *flux density* per unit tape width at reference level was about 185 *nanoWebers per meter.* Currently, alignment tapes in the U.S. are produced at levels of 185, 200, and 250 nanoWebers/meter, a range of 2.7 dB. Fussy engineers will, of course, want to standardize on one level or the other. In Europe the DIN standard is 320 nanoWebers/meter, some 4.7 dB higher than the 185 nanoWeber/meter standard.

Operating Levels

Operating level and reference levels are not the same. The reference flux level is used to establish a zero reading on the tape recorder's VU meters. Because of the vast improvements in tapes in recent years, the distortion level associated with the reference flux level is considerably lower than 1%, closer to 0.3%. Accordingly, engineers have tended to record at higher levels, and some of the newer tape formulations allow as much as 3-dB offset in recorder alignment settings because of the increased output capability.

Because of the dependence of most noise-reduction systems on precise line reference levels, casual readjustment of tape reference levels is to be *avoided*. In any well-run recording complex, standards must be rigorously established and all operating personnel must understand them. Under no conditions should an engineer be allowed to tamper with reference settings because he thinks he can make a "better recording that way."

Equalization Standards

In the U.S. it is common to use the NAB standard at 15 and $7\frac{1}{2}$ ips and the AES standard at 30 ips. European tapes are usually made with the IEC standard, and many of them find their way to the U.S. for record production purposes. Alignment tapes are available for all of these standards, and a well-run recording complex will either have these tapes on hand or know what the proper corrections are when using other reference tapes.

When full track alignment tapes are played over multitrack heads, the phenomenon of *fringing* will cause erroneous reading. Many producers of alignment tapes provide correction tables so that these errors can be correlated. The effects of fringing are most significant in the region below 100 Hz.

Track Width Standards

Current track width standards for professional recording formats are shown in Figure 8-17.

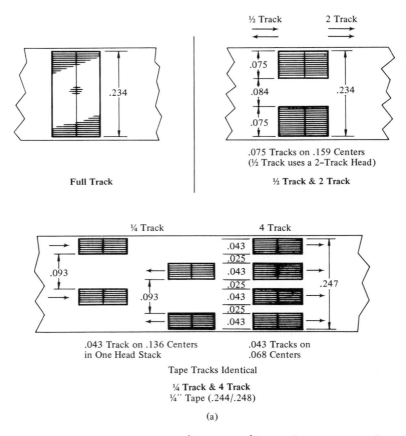

(a)

Figure 8-17. Track width standards for $\frac{1}{4}''$ tape (a), $\frac{1}{2}''$ and 1″ tape (b), and 2″ tape (c). Typical gap widths for professional tape recorders are 175–250 μinch for playback heads and 500–1000 μinch for record heads. For machines designed for $7\frac{1}{2}$ ips, typical playback head gap widths are 100–150 μinch and record head gap widths are about 500 μinch. (*Data courtesy Ampex.*)

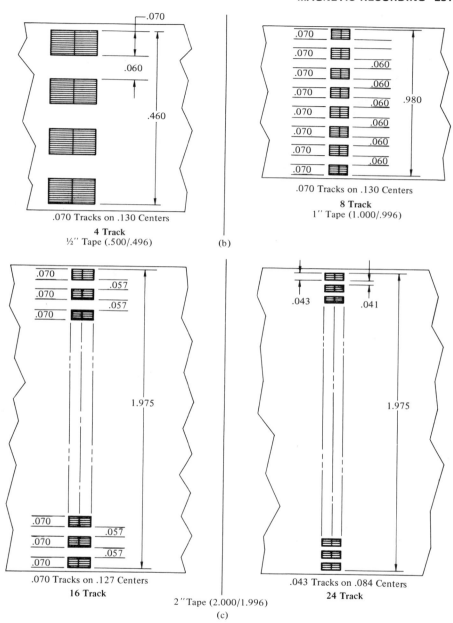

.070 Tracks on .130 Centers
4 Track
½″ Tape (.500/.496)

(b)

.070 Tracks on .130 Centers
8 Track
1″ Tape (1.000/.996)

.070 Tracks on .127 Centers
16 Track

.043 Tracks on .084 Centers
24 Track

2″ Tape (2.000/1.996)

(c)

Figure 8-17. (*Continued*)

TAPE RECORDER ALIGNMENT PROCEDURES

Tape recorders vary somewhat in their specific alignment requirements because of the different principles of design. However, the following sequence of procedures is fundamental to all tape machines, and any recording engineer should know how and why these procedures are performed.

A. Mechanical alignment and check out
   1. Before the engineer subjects an expensive alignment tape to a new transport, he must first make sure that the transport is in proper mechanical order. He should assure himself that take-up and hold-back tensions on the supply and take-up reels are within the range specified by the manufacturer.
   2. The capstan pressure roller thrust should also be within the range specified by the manufacturer.
   3. Using a roll of expendable tape, the engineer should assure himself that the machine operates properly in all of its transport modes and that tape travels over the head stack with a minimum of up and down motion or skew.
   4. The transport should be thoroughly cleaned with appropriate solvent recommended by the manufacturer.
B. Check-out of the playback function
   1. The machine must first be thoroughly demagnetized. Any remnant magnetism of heads or guides will increase the noise level and result in some degree of erasure of high frequencies in the alignment tape.
   2. The azimuth of the playback head must be set so that playback head output is maximized. If the head is considerably off azimuth, the engineer is advised to ensure that his azimuth setting is the proper one and not one of the smaller response peaks which are in evidence when the playback head is considerably off azimuth.
   3. Playback equalization is then set using that segment of the alignment tape provided for the purpose.
   4. The gain of the playback system is then set using full level tone provided on the alignment tape for this purpose. The engineer should be certain that only one reference level is used in a given studio complex. Current level standards vary by 2.7 dB on U.S.-made alignment tapes, and this is a sizeable range. Good engineering practice calls for a consistently applied standard.
C. Record electronic check-out
   1. The azimuth of the record head is checked by recording a short wavelength, for example, 15 kHz at 15 ips, and observing the output through the playback head as the azimuth of the record head is adjusted for peak

output. In this manner the playback head is used as a secondary azimuth standard in setting the record azimuth. An alternate method can be used on machines where there is provision for playback using the record head. In this case the engineer proceeds as he did with the playback head, using the alignment tape as the primary standard.

2. Setting record bias level is done by recording a medium-wavelength signal, such as 500 or 1,000 Hz, and adjusting bias until there is a peak in the output of that signal as measured at the playback head. The operating manual will specify a bias adjustment procedure, and it should be carefully read.

3. Some machines provide for an adjustment of the bias waveform purity, which influences the noise level of the recording. The procedure varies from machine to machine, so the operating manual should be checked. After the setting for minimum noise has been determined, it is wise to demagnetize the heads again as a precaution against inadvertent magnetization of the heads during the adjustment of the bias waveform.

4. Adjustment of record equalization is performed by inserting frequencies from an oscillator and setting the response for flattest possible playback.

D. Adjustment of erase bias current

1. Manufacturers' instructions should be carefully followed here. On some earlier machines, bias levels fluctuated somewhat depending upon the total number of record functions which were engaged at one time. On some older machines, setting of erase bias level *after* the record bias setting causes a slight shift in record bias level, resulting in small changes in sensitivity and equalization. It is always wise to recheck record equalization after setting erase bias level and adjusting the bias calibration, if the machine has one. Newer machines have better regulation of the bias supply, and this minimizes shifts in bias level between different operational modes.

BIBLIOGRAPHY

1. D. Greisinger, "Reducing Distortion in Analog Tape Recorders," *J. Audio Eng. Soc.*, vol. 23, no. 2 (1975).
2. S. Katz, J. McKnight, and R. Morrison, "Alignment," *Recording Engineer/Producer*, vol. 6, no. 1 (1975).
3. J. Kempler, "Making Tape," *Audio Magazine*, pp. 38–44 (April 1975).
4. C. Lowman, *Magnetic Recording* (McGraw-Hill, New York 1972).
5. D. R. Mills, "The New Generation of High Energy Recording Tape," *Recording Engineer/Producer*, vol. 5, no. 6 (1974).

9

Signal Processing Devices

INTRODUCTION

Signal processing is a term which applies to all devices used to modify signals during recording and transfer operations. Such processors as compressors, equalizers, and reverberation devices are intended to modify the sound of a recording, often to a profound degree. Other processors, such as HF limiters, noise reduction, and distortion correction devices, are intended to improve the quality of the transmission channel itself and not to alter basic musical values. For this reason these latter devices are often referred to as *signal conditioners*.

There is a temptation for beginning engineers to over use signal processors, especially equalizers. Typically, there is a tendency to correct faulty microphone placement through equalization when a far better solution would be a change of microphone or microphone location. Properly applied, the use of signal processors results in a superior product; improperly applied, a recording can be ruined beyond repair. Some processors, such as compression and equalization, are reversible to a degree, and some of the damage resulting from improper use may be undone. Excessive reverberation, on the other hand, cannot be removed from a recording.

We shall divide signal processors into a number of categories for our discussion in this chapter:

1. Equalizers and filters

2. Limiters and compressors
3. Noise gates
4. Noise reduction
5. Artificial reverberation
6. Digital time delay
7. Special effects: "phasing," voltage-controlled filters, envelope shaping and ring modulators

EQUALIZERS AND FILTERS

An equalizer is a device which alters the frequency response of a recording or monitoring channel. It is easy to lose sight of the original meaning and application of the term; the first equalizers were used in telephony and were for the purpose of making the output of a transmission line *equal* to its input. This basic function is shown in Figure 9-1.

Because of line losses the output of a telephone line is rolled off at high frequencies, and it is standard practice to introduce a complementary network restoring those attenuated frequencies so that the integrity of the signal is maintained. By extension, the term *equalizer* has been applied over the years to devices, both fixed and variable, which provide variations in frequency response.

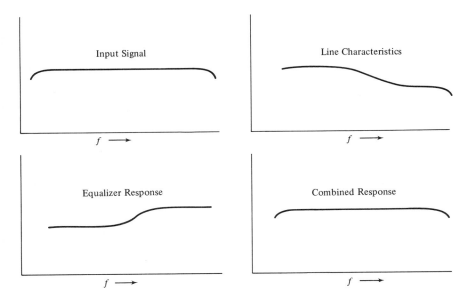

Figure 9-1. Basic function of a transmission line equalizer.

The earliest use of equalizers for recording was in the motion picture industry. The necessity of recording dialog at various distances from the actors dictated by the visual requirements of the scene meant that the recording engineer had to "equalize" the dialog tracks if speech intelligibility was to be consistent from scene to scene in the theater. A form of dialog equalizer was developed with curves as shown in Figure 9-2. The device had controls for LF, MF, and HF alteration, and the three sections interacted to make a composite curve.

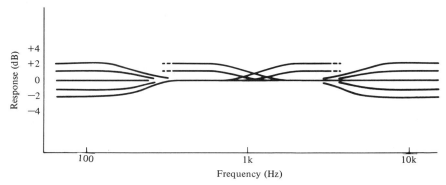

Figure 9-2. LF, MF and HF characteristic curve for a dialog equalizer used in motion picture sound recording.

More versatile *program equalizers* were developed during the fifties. These devices provided LF boost and attenuation, MF peaking functions with variable bandwidth, and HF boost and attenuation. Typical curves are shown in Figure 9-3.

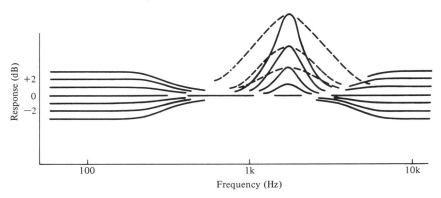

Figure 9-3. Family of curves for a program equalizer. Functions include HF and LF shelving actions for boost and attenuation. Variable peaking is available at selected mid-range frequencies, and bandwidth of the peaking action is variable.

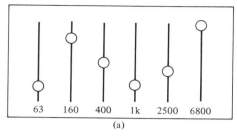

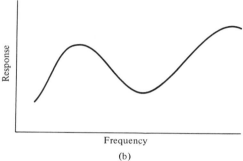

Figure 9-4. A graphic equalizer. For the control positions shown in (a), the frequency response curve shown in (b) takes on a form resembling the position of the controls.

Program equalizers found their main application in adjusting composite program information for the best overall effect in final transfer operations. "Presence" could be added by peaking the signal in the 1.5-kHz to 3-kHz range, while bass-treble relationships could be adjusted by means of the LF and HF controls.

A more general approach to equalization requirements was provided by *graphic equalizers* (see Figure 9-4). Graphic equalizers have vertical slide controls for both peaking and dipping functions, and the physical position of these controls provides a reasonable graphical representation of the equalization curve itself.

Perhaps the most versatile equalizers of all are the so-called *parametric equalizers*. The name derives from the fact that individual aspects, or parameters, of the equalization process may be varied without interaction between those functions. One section of a parametric equalizer provides for adjustment of frequency, the degree of peak or dip at that frequency, and the spread, or bandwidth, at that frequency. Characteristics of a parametric equalizer are shown in Figure 9-5. A typical parametric equalizer may have from three to eight sections, with adjacent sections overlapping for the broadest possible coverage.

Filters are ordinarily of two kinds, *high-* and *low-pass*. They provide sharp cut-

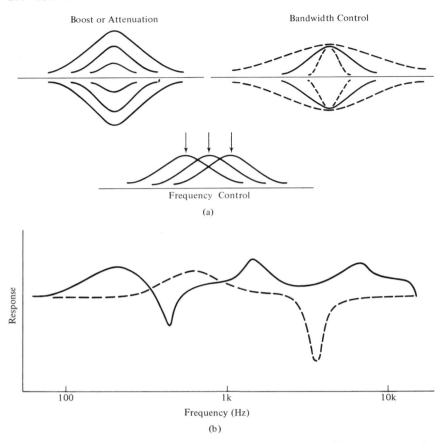

Figure 9-5. Characteristics of a parametric equalizer. Functions of boost or attenuation, bandwidth control, and frequency control are shown in (a). Typical composite equalization curves are shown in (b).

off above and below specified frequencies, as shown in Figure 9-6,a. The cut-off slope is normally 18 dB/octave for maximum effectiveness. *Notch filters*, shown in Figure 9-6,b, are usually variable in depth as well as frequency. Some parametric equalizers can provide fairly close approximations to notch filter response.

Applications of Equalizers and Filters

Equalizers and filters are used for two purposes: to correct certain problems which may have arisen during recording or transfer processes and to alter the

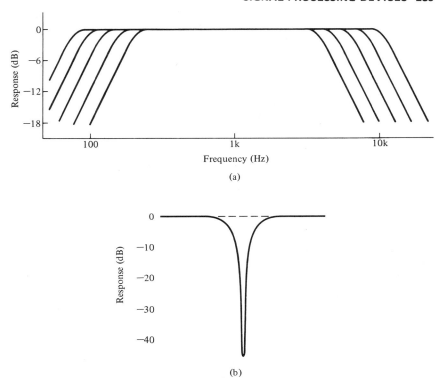

Figure 9-6. Filters used in recording. Typical response curves for high- and low-pass filters are shown in (a). A typical notch filter is shown in (b). Adjustment of the notch frequency as well as the depth of the notch is customary. Some notch filters can provide 50 to 60 dB of attenuation.

timbre of an instrument for purely musical or creative reasons. Some typical remedial applications are listed below:

1. In transferring old 78-RPM discs, it is customary to use a high-pass filter set at about 50 Hz and a low-pass filter set anywhere from 3 to 6 kHz, depending upon the vintage of the disc. Since the bandwidth of the early disc systems was limited, wide-band playback will be noisier than need be since considerable noise exists beyond the recorded bandwidth, especially at high frequencies (see Figure 9-7,a).

2. Older recordings and those made under less than ideal conditions can often be made usable by "shelving out" some of the lower frequencies and adding a broad HF peak in the 5- to 10-kHz range. This can add a degree of brilliance to an otherwise lackluster recording (see Figure 9-7,b).

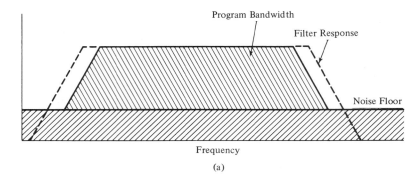

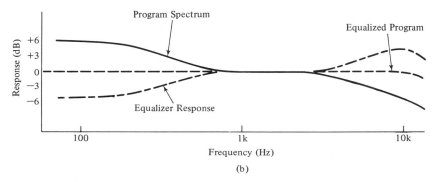

Figure 9-7. Some applications of equalizers. In (a) high- and low-pass filters are used to remove noise extending beyond the program bandwidth. In (b) equalizer response is roughly the inverse of the program spectrum, and this restores a degree of naturalness to the program.

3. If a recording has been marred by 60-Hz hum or other unwanted frequency, a carefully tuned notch filter may be used to remove the offending tone.

4. An engineer often has to "undo" some of the damage which has been inflicted on a recording by previous engineers. If the recording has been mixed down to a 4-, 2-, or single-track format, then little can be done. However, if the individual tracks of a multitrack recording have been overequalized, then the engineer has considerable latitude in applying reciprocal equalization curves to each track. He must determine this strictly by ear, and the most useful devices will be graphic and parametric equalizers.

It is recommended that the original tracks in a multitrack recording be left in as simple form as possible, with equalization being applied only during mixdown.

Creative Uses of Equalizers and Filters

In multichannel recording the selective use of equalization on individual tracks during the mixdown process affords the engineer and producer an extra creative dimension. We could not hope to catalog all of the effects here; rather, we shall describe some of the more useful ones.

1. *Fullness* may be added by boosting frequencies in the 100–300 Hz region. The effect is probably most useful on normally weak instruments, such as the acoustical guitar and the celesta. No more than 6–8 dB boost should be used.

2. A sound may be made to *project* more if a broad peak is added in the 800 Hz–2 kHz region. Again, 6–8 dB should be enough; any more boost would result in a disagreeable "sharpness" or "tinniness" of sound.

3. The *articulation transients* of many instruments may be heightened by emphasizing the appropriate frequency range. For example, an acoustical string bass will exhibit fundamentals in the 40–200 Hz region and significant overtones up to, say, 1 kHz. The sounds of the player's fingers on the strings are nonharmonically related to the actual tones produced, yet they are often equally important in defining the musical line. Adding a broad peak in the 1–2 kHz range will delineate them better. Similarly, the transients of fingers against the strings of an acoustical guitar can be heightened by boosting in the 2–4 kHz range.

4. *Crispness* in percussion instruments can be heightened by an HF shelving boost above 1 or 2 kHz. Bongo and snare drums often benefit from this. Again, the less equalization the better; 6 dB ought to suffice.

Several caveats are in order:

1. Boosting should be used sparingly, if at all, on metal-against-metal transients. The HF energy is already considerable, and adding more is simply courting tape saturation or overload in subsequent transfer processes.

2. *Never* use equalization as a substitute for better microphone placement. This is a habit which can easily grow out of laziness into sloppiness.

3. Do not boost too many tracks in the same frequency range. To do so makes for an unbalanced spectrum which is musically unsatisfactory. In pop-rock recording the goal should be a fairly flat energy spectrum from 50 Hz to 10 Hz during full ensemble passages.

As with the choice and location of microphones, the inquiring engineer will seek out his own special uses for equalizers, and it is an area where he will never cease to learn.

COMPRESSORS AND LIMITERS

Compressors and limiters are amplifiers whose gain can be automatically varied as a function of signal level; the *higher* the signal level is, the *lower* the gain. The significant features of a compressor are its *compression ratio, threshold, attack time*, and *release time*. These features are illustrated in Figure 9-8.

At low and medium input levels a compressor acts as a unity gain amplifier as shown in Figure 9-8,a; if the input is raised, say, 2 dB, the output is raised 2 dB. As the input is raised to the threshold region, which is adjustable over a fairly wide range, the device goes into gain reduction. For a 2-to-1 compression ratio, an input increase of 2 dB would result in an output increase of only 1 dB. For a 4-to-1 ratio, an input increase of 4 dB would only produce an output increase of 1 dB. The effect of attack and release time constants is shown in Figure 9-8,b. When there is a sudden change in the input level which puts the device into compression, there will be a slight degree of *overshoot* before the new gain requirements can be determined and put into effect. Attack times are usually very short, usually in the range of 100 μsec to 1 msec. Recovery times are usually adjustable from perhaps 0.1 second to as long as 2.5 or 3 seconds. The longer recovery times would be more applicable to slower, more sustained music, while faster recovery times would be more suited to faster programs. A very important design criterion is that the gain change *per se* should not be audible as distortion or undesirable modulation of the signal envelope. The most difficult aspect is the attack time; the rapid onset of gain reduction is likely to be audible as a "click" if insufficient attention has been given the design of the device. Piano recordings are among the most critical since there is little in the way of HF program material to mask these defects.

At the heart of a compressor is its level sensing, or detection, circuitry. In recent years RMS detection has been used in many compressor designs on the assumption that the RMS value of a signal is a better index of its loudness than either its peak or average value. A definite amount of time is required to determine the RMS level of a signal, and where the compressor must be used for

Figure 9-8. Characteristics of compressors. In (a) typical input-output curves for compressors are shown. The threshold of compression is the point where the input-output curve departs from its one-to-one relationship. A signal envelope is shown in (b). At t_1 the envelope increases into the region of compression. A slight degree of overshoot is shown (by the broken line) before the gain of the compressor can be reduced accordingly. At t_2 the program is restored to its original level, and again there is overshoot in the opposite direction (shown by the broken line) before the original gain is restored. A general diagram for a compressor is shown in (c). Normally, input and output levels can be adjusted independently, as can the threshold level. Metering is usually provided so that either output level or degree of gain reduction can be read.

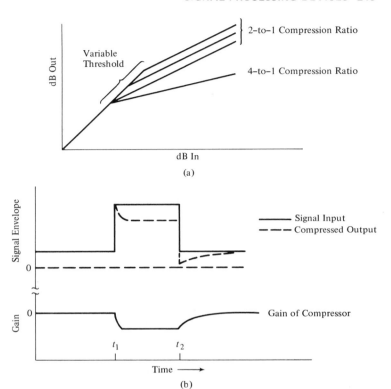

(a)

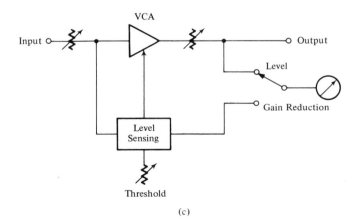

(b)

(c)

overload protection, then a combination of peak as well as RMS detection may be required.

Most compressors are single-band devices; that is, the gain control circuit operates on the entire audio spectrum at once. Multiband devices have been designed in which each frequency band is compressed independently of the others. Usually there are no more than two or three bands in these devices, and their major application is in tape duplicating or disc transfer operations where level requirements are critical. They are best used sparingly; otherwise the musical spectrum will be adversely affected.

A *limiter* is a special kind of compressor. Compression ratios of 10-to-1 or greater usually define a limiting action since output levels are effectively clamped to the threshold level. Fast attack times are essential for good limiting, and recovery times are customarily in the range of 0.1 to 1.0 second.

Applications of Compressors and Limiters

Compressors and limiters have been used for many years chiefly for automatically adjusting a wide-dynamic-range input signal to fit a transmission or storage medium of lesser dynamic range. The devices were probably first used extensively in broadcasting, where compressors made the relatively wide dynamic range of phonograph records compatible with the narrower requirements of AM radio transmission and of average home listening environments. At the same time limiters were used as a kind of "safety valve," preventing overload or overmodulation of the transmitter.

In recording, compressors have many uses; we present a few of them below.

1. A vocalist who tends to move toward and away from a microphone produces a signal with wide variations in level. A properly adjusted compressor can smooth out much of this variation, producing a recorded track which can be more easily processed later.

2. Variations in the output of an electric bass can easily be smoothed out by the application of gentle compression, thus providing an even and solid bass line. If the recovery time is *long* compared with the natural decay rate of the instrument, then the original character of the instrument will be maintained.

3. In the preceding example, if the recovery time of the compressor is fast compared with the natural decay rate, then the sound of the instrument will be transformed into an almost "organ-like" sound, exhbiting little of its natural decay characteristic (see Figure 9-9).

4. A similar effect can be obtained by applying *heavy limiting* with as short a recovery time as available to cymbals. Heavy limiting implies that the input signal is always above the limiting threshold, so the program appears at a fixed

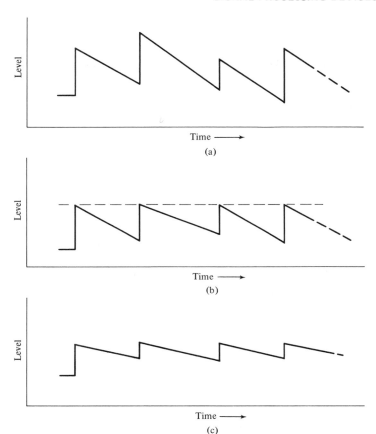

Figure 9-9. Typical compressor application. The envelope of a plucked bass is shown at (a). With a moderate degree of compression, the peaks of the signal can be clamped at a predetermined level as shown at (b). If the recovery time of the compressor is faster than the normal decay rate of the plucked bass, then the effect shown at (c) will be heard.

output level. The effect is bizarre and is reminiscent of cymbal tracks played backwards.

5. A special limiter known as a "de-esser" employs a pre-emphasis network ahead of the gain reduction function making the device especially sensitive to HF sounds in speech and vocal tracks. Thus, it provides a limiting action only on excessive sibilant sounds which may have resulted from either improper microphone choice or equalization during the original recording.

In general the most natural sounding compression of dynamic range can be accomplished manually by an engineer who knows the program at hand. However, where many tracks are involved or where there may be numerous unexpected changes, compressors are a necessary adjunct to the mixing process. Thus, there is often a need for compression capability which can be patched into the high-level inputs of a console for processing of selected individual tracks.

NOISE GATES AND EXPANDERS

In many kinds of multitrack recording the dynamic range of a given track may be fairly small, perhaps no more than 15 or 20 dB. Sounds picked up which are below this range may in a sense be regarded as noise and can only be considered a nuisance during the mix-down process. Ideally, we would like for the microphone to be open when program is present and effectively closed when the program is off. A device known as a *noise gate* can accomplish this.

Operation of a noise gate is shown in Figure 9-10. The input-output characteristics of a noise gate are shown in (a). The device acts as a unity gain amplifier at normal operating levels. As input level is lowered, the gating threshold is reached, and the gain of the amplifier is reduced, thus lowering the level of noise or other disturbances in the recording. Both the gating threshold and the degree of gain lowering are adjustable. Some units provide the added flexibility of adjustable slope over the gain-varying range, as well as adjustable attack and release times.

A noise gate is an *expander;* it is the inverse of a compressor since its output is always of greater dynamic range than its input. Some noise gates, notably the Allison Research Kepex unit, provide for *external* operation of the expansion function. In this way, a given program can be keyed on or off by another program, providing a variety of unusual effects.

NOISE REDUCTION SYSTEMS

The foregoing discussions of compression and expansion lead naturally to the subject of *noise reduction.* Basically, a noise reduction system provides for compression of a signal during the record mode followed by complementary expansion during the playback mode. In this way, the noise inherent in the recording process may be minimized. The basic principle is shown in Figure 9-11.

Noise reduction of this sort differs from the simple noise gate in that it involves *coding* as well as *decoding* of the program. If the action is to be inaudible as far as the program is concerned, then the respective thresholds of the compressor and expander must be precisely adjusted. Also, attack and release times must be such that the *dynamic tracking,* the matching of compression and expansion, yields a net result of zero dB gain with little overshoot.

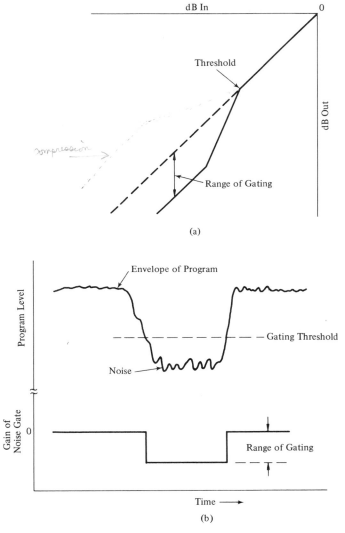

(a)

(b)

Figure 9-10. The noise gate. The input-output curve for a noise gate is shown in (a). When the signal level reaches an adjustable threshold, the output is reduced in gain relative to the input. In many noise gates the range of gating, or attenuation, can be adjusted, as can attack and release time constants. A typical application of a noise gate is shown in (b). The engineer establishes a gating threshold on the assumption that any signal below that threshold can be considered as noise to be eliminated in the recording. That noise will then be lowered by the gating range which the engineer has determined.

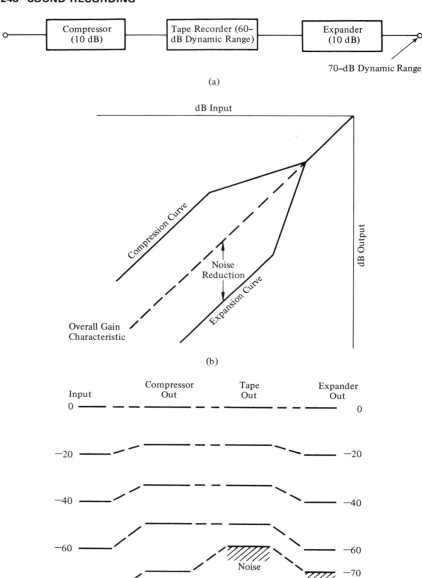

(a)

(b)

(c)

The Dolby Noise Reduction System

The Dolby noise reduction system is widely used in professional recording, and it has become a standard for international master tape exchange between record companies and their affiliates. Details of the Dolby "A-type" noise reduction system are shown in Figure 9-12.

The audio spectrum is divided into *four* bands, and separate compression-expansion is provided for each level. The lower three bands provide 10 dB of action, and the upper band provides 15 dB. The unique feature of the Dolby system lies in the fact that, at high program levels when there is no compression or expansion, the signal flow is straight through the system, by-passing the compressors. By simple switching of the location of the compressor in the circuit, a module may be converted from the compression (record) mode to the expansion (playback) mode. Thus maximum module flexibility is maintained for all operating conditions. Input-output tracking with the Dolby A-type system is maintained to well within 1 dB in each band.

The B-type Dolby system is widely used in amateur tape recording and FM broadcasting. It is a single-band approach in which HF signals are boosted in the compression (record) mode and attenuated in the expansion (playback) mode. It is effective in reducing HF noise components in tape and FM systems. Both A- and B-type Dolby systems depend upon proper matching of compression and expansion thresholds; thus record and playback levels must be closely matched for ideal system performance.

The DBX Noise Reduction System

The DBX noise reduction system is shown in Figure 9-13. Unlike the Dolby system, it is a single-band system with its single compressor-expander pair operating over the entire spectrum.

Audible modulation of the noise floor of a transmission system is a fundamental problem with all noise reduction systems. The Dolby approach solves

Figure 9-11. Fundamentals of a noise reduction system. In a typical noise reduction system, the input program to a recorder is compressed while the output is expanded to the same degree. If proper attention is paid to the matching of compression and expansion curves as well as to attack and release time constants, then the output will exhibit a dynamic range increased by the amount of compression-expansion action, as shown in (a). Typical compression-expansion curves are shown in (b). Note that the curves complement each other to provide a linear overall input-output gain characteristic. Another view of noise reduction is shown in (c). Compressor output shows a dynamic range of 10 dB less than the input. The noise level at the output of the tape machine is at −60 dB. When the compressed signal is expanded by 10 dB, the effective noise floor of the machine is reduced to −70 dB.

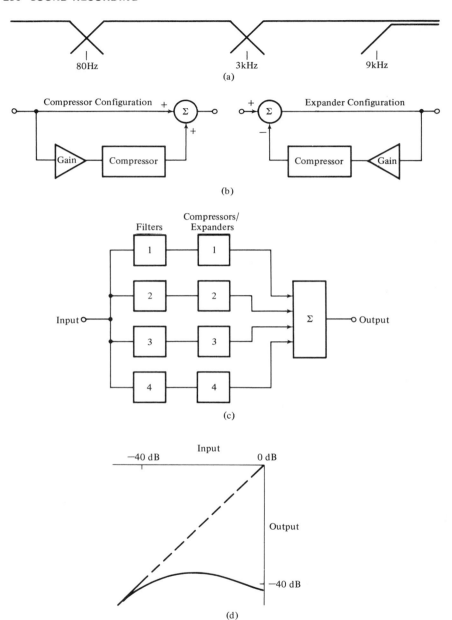

(a)

(b)

(c)

(d)

the problem by acting on the audio spectrum in several bands separately. The DBX system satisfies the same demand through a pre-emphasis/de-emphasis scheme.

The input signal is given an HF pre-emphasis as is the input to the level-sensing circuit. On playback, the audio channel has a complementary HF de-emphasis, while the gain-sensing circuit operates on the pre-emphasized signal. Level sensing in the DBX system is done with RMS detectors as opposed to peak or average detection. There is no reference level for playback-record alignment; input and output functions match each other over a wide range without the need for level adjustment.

The Burwen Noise Reduction System

The Burwen noise reduction system is similar to the DBX system. The input signal is pre-emphasized, and the output is given a complementary de-emphasis. The compression-expansion curve is such that a 3-dB change in the input results in a 1-dB change in the compressed signal. Characteristics of the Burwen system are shown in Figure 9-14.

Audibility of Noise Reduction Systems

On the surface, noise reduction systems seem to offer "something for nothing." Obviously there is a psychoacoustical factor working in favor of these systems, and it is the relative insensitivity of the ear to shifts in the noise floor *if the noise is already at a low level.* The inquisitive engineer may ask why noise reduction was not employed earlier in the evolution of the art. We have already suggested the answer: practical noise reduction was not possible until the recording art had progressed to a fairly refined point where shifting of the noise floor would be relatively inaudible. In other words, a noise reduction system might easily extend the effective dynamic range of a 65-dB recording system to 75 dB; it would have a difficult job, however, increasing the dynamic range of a 45-dB recording system to 55 dB because of relative audibility of the noise-floor shift.

Even the best of noise reduction systems can be heard in operation under the right conditions. Overshoot and errors in the dynamic tracking of the systems

---

Figure 9-12. The Dolby noise reduction system. Characteristics of filter responses are shown in (a), and the basic Dolby compressor-expander configurations are shown in (b). Note that the same elements are used for compression as well as expansion. Their positions are transposed, and signal subtraction is used in the expansion configuration. A block diagram of a complete Dolby processor is shown in (c), and typical compressor response is shown in (d).

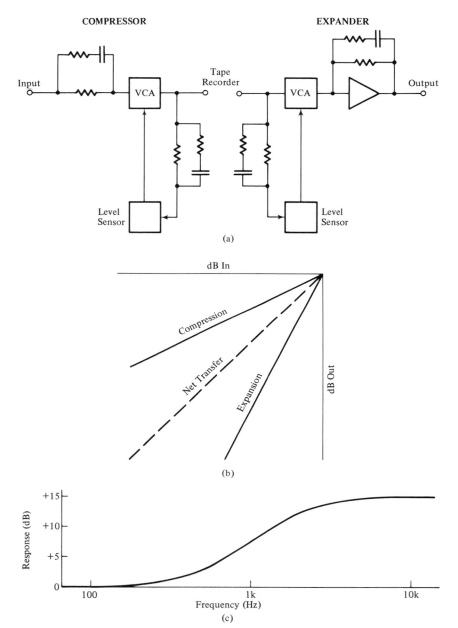

Figure 9-13. The DBX noise reduction system. The basic block diagram of the compression-expansion scheme is shown in (a). The input signal is given a high frequency pre-emphasis [shown in (c)], and that same pre-emphasis is used ahead of both record and playback level sensors. In the output network the inverse of the curve shown in (c) is applied to the program to restore overall flat system response. Compressor-expander characteristics are shown in (b). There is a 2-to-1 compression-expansion ratio over the entire range of the system.

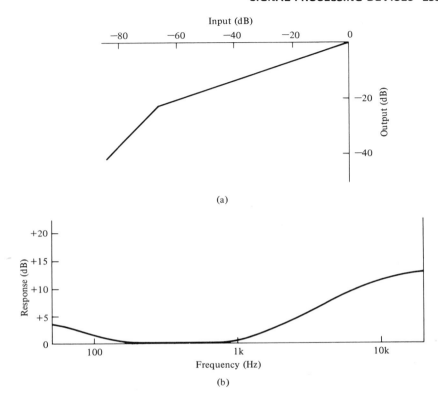

Figure 9-14. The Burwen noise reduction system. The Burwen system is similar to the DBX system except that its compressor characteristic has a 3-to-1 action down to a level of about 70 dB below normal input level, as shown in (a). The playback expander has the inverse curve. Record pre-emphasis is shown in (b), and playback pre-emphasis is the inverse of this curve.

are almost never in evidence; rather, subtle shifts in the noise floor are heard as modulation noise behind the program. The offending signals are usually a lightly stroked tympani, or any other exposed signal with little HF masking. Wide-range monitor systems operating at high levels make these defects more obvious.

In general, the *less* the degree of gain reduction, the less obvious will be its operation. This statement is especially true with composite program material, and it points to a natural advantage of the Dolby system with its 10-15 dB range. The DBX and Burwen systems, with their wider ranges, may be more au-dible in operation on composite program; but in the special case of multichannel recording, shifts in the noise floor tend to go unnoticed because of the ensemble of many tracks in operation at the same time.

The trade-off is inevitable; noise reduction is bought at the price of audibility a small fraction of the time. The fact that it cannot be heard under most condi-tions is its *raison d'etre*.

It may seem obvious to most engineers, but the neophyte needs to be reminded that noise reduction techniques can only be used with *flat storage or transmission* channels; signal output must be directly related to signal input. Any attempt to use noise reduction in and out of, say, a noisy reverberation device would not work inasmuch as the reverberation device is a generator of new sounds. The playback expander would have the general effect of shortening the reverberation time by lowering the signal during exposed reverberant decays. By the same token, a signal cannot be equalized while in the "compressed" mode; it must first be expanded, or decoded, before additional signal processing.

If a 16-track tape recorded with noise reduction techniques is being mixed down to stereo and subsequently re-encoded by the same noise reduction system, *18* processors will be required, 16 for playback and 2 more for re-encoding. Thus, the general implementation of noise reduction in a large studio complex can get into large numbers rather quickly.

ARTIFICIAL REVERBERATION

As we have discussed in previous chapters, the relations between direct sound, early reflections and the reverberant sound field are essential in conveying space information in a recording. When natural reverberation is not a part of the input signal to a recording system, the engineer must have recourse to a variety of reverberation devices to fill the need. Practical reverberation devices fall short of natural performance environments in two regards:

1. The initial time delay between the direct sound field and the onset of the reverberant sound field is too short.

2. The density of normal modes is too sparse to create a "colorless" reverberant field. As a result most artificial reverberation devices tend to sound "too small" and lend their own coloration to a processed track.

By way of illustration, let us consider a typical auditorium with characteristics:

$$V = 500,000 \text{ ft}^3$$

$$S = 50,000 \text{ ft}^2$$

$$\bar{\alpha} = 0.18 \text{ (at 500 Hz)}$$

Then T_{60} at mid-frequencies will be 2.5 seconds.

The initial time gap between the receipt of direct sound by a listener and the first reflection cannot be stated with any real accuracy, but it will be related to the *mean free path* (MFP) in the room. The MFP is the average uninterrupted path length sound travels between successive reflections. In rooms of "regular" proportions (where length, width, and height are considerably less than 2-to-1 ratios of each other), an approximation of the mean free path is given by: MFP (feet or meters) = $4V/S$, where V is the room volume (in cubic feet or meters) and S is the surface area (in square feet or meters).

For the room information given above, the equation gives a value of 40 feet for MFP, and this corresponds to a time delay of:

$$T = 40/1,130 = 35 \text{ msec}$$

Let us compare this with a typical acoustical reverberation chamber with the same reverberation time at mid-frequencies:

$$V = 2500 \text{ ft}^3$$

$$S = 1050 \text{ ft}^2$$

$$\bar{\alpha} = 0.05$$

In this case the MFP would be about 10 feet, corresponding to a delay of 9 msec.

If a loudspeaker is placed in the chamber, one or more microphones will pick up reverberant signals. The initial time delay will be so short that a sense of size and space will be poorly conveyed. Thus it is customary to use artifical reverberation in conjunction with time delay, usually of the order of 30–50 msec. (See Figure 9-15 for details of an acoustical reverberation chamber.)

Another significant difference between the small reverberation chamber and the auditorium is the density of normal modes. Let us assume that the longest dimension of the auditorium is 100 feet. Then the lowest room mode is about 5.5 Hz. Above 55 Hz the mode density would be sufficient to produce even response and relatively colorless reverberation. In the reverberation chamber the longest dimension is almost 17 feet, and the lowest normal mode is 33 Hz. This room could therefore not be expected to exhibit sufficient mode density below 330 Hz, and the result would likely be a tendency to "ring" at selected frequencies in the mid- and low-mid-frequency range.

Good reverberation chambers are fairly rare these days, and most of the good ones were built some years ago when there were no alternative methods of generating acceptable reverberation. They are expensive to build and take up a good bit of space. They are hard to isolate acoustically; as a result, they have been consigned to basement locations where excessive moisture usually takes its toll, causing flaking of plaster surfaces. Nevertheless, there are a number of principles regarding their implementation and use which the audio engineer should know.

In sound pickup in a reverberation chamber it is important to minimize the amount of direct signal components, and a ribbon microphone with its null plane aimed at the loudspeaker is recommended (Figure 9-16,a). If it is desired

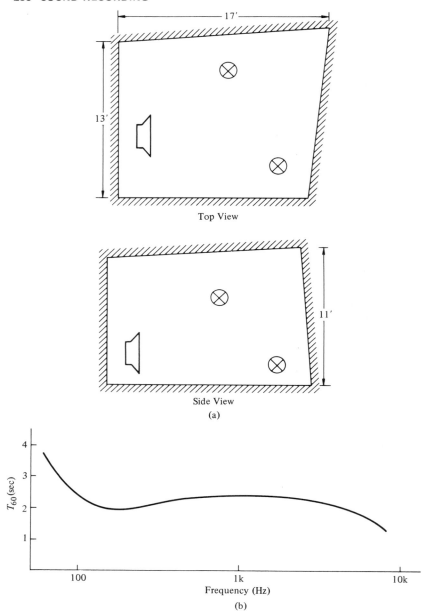

Top View

Side View

(a)

(b)

to use a coincident pair of microphones for stereophonic reverberation, Gerzon (8) suggests the use of a figure-eight loudspeaker with the microphone pair located along its null plane (Figure 9-16,b).

A variation on stereophonic pickup has been suggested by Davis (5), and it requires that a large reverberation chamber be divided in two sections by a large nonabsorptive barrier which does not quite block off the two sections. The arrangement is fed via stereophonic loudspeakers and the return signals arrayed stereophonically. The leakage from one side to the other gives a broad stereophonic spread to the reverberant signal.

Most reverberation chambers have a fixed reverberation time, but it is possible to make such a chamber variable by controlling the amount of effective absorption. The scheme shown in Figure 9-16,d, used by the Victor Company of Japan, provides variable absorption by exposing more or less fiber glass through remote control. The range of reverberation times is shown in Figure 9-16,e.

Mechanical Reverberation Devices

In the last 15 years mechanical reverberation devices have become standard in the recording industry. There are two types, vibrating metal plates and vibrating springs.

The EMT-140, the most popular current reverberation device, uses a steel plate approximately 1×2 meters in size tightly suspended in a metal frame. The plate is driven by a moving coil transducer, and two piezo-electric transducers are used for stereophonic pickup. The plate is energized into transverse vibrational modes with multiple reflections taking place at the boundaries of the plate. When properly tensioned the EMT-140 exhibits high mode density with especially good HF response. Reverberation time can be adjusted over a wide range by moving a porous damping membrane closer to or farther away from the steel plate (see Figure 9-17,a). The range of reverberation time control is shown in Figure 9-17,b.

Figure 9-15. Details of an acoustical reverberation chamber. Top and side views are shown in (a) and loudspeaker-microphone positions are suggested. The dimensions of a reverberation chamber are normally related to the cube root of 2, and this yields length, width, and height dimensions in the ratios of $1:1.25:1.6$ ($2^0:2^{1/3}:2^{2/3}$). The proportions provide for the most even distribution of normal room modes at low frequencies. Reverberation chambers are typically finished in concrete or hard plaster, properly sealed and painted. These materials provide an absorption coefficient at middle and high frequencies on the order of 0.02, enabling fairly long reverberation times to be developed in a small space. Typical reverberation times vs. frequency for this chamber are shown in (b). In reverberation chamber design, it is customary to angle the walls slightly so that there are no parallel surfaces. This prevents so-called flutter echoes between opposite walls and provides better diffusion of sound during the early part of the decay.

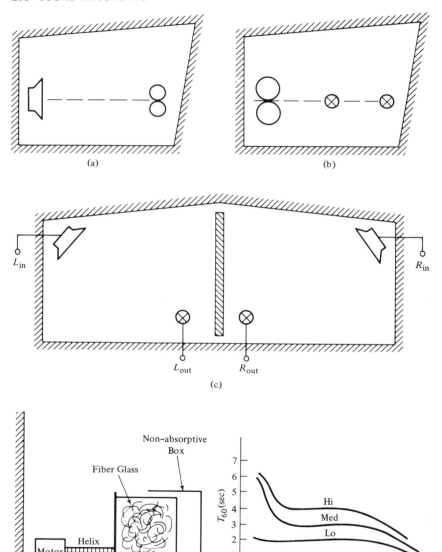

(a)

(b)

L_{in}

R_{in}

L_{out} R_{out}

(c)

Non−absorptive Box

Fiber Glass

Helix

Motor

(d)

Hi

Med

Lo

T_{60}(sec)

100 1k 10k

Frequency (Hz)

(e)

The EMT-140 has the virtue of being adjustable to very short reverberation times and can thus be used to add density and richness to musical textures without the confusion of musical detail which longer reverberation times might cause.

The EMT-140 is large and must be isolated acoustically. If not properly tensioned, there may be considerable variation in performance between units. These difficulties have been largely overcome with the new EMT-240, a device operating on similar principles but much smaller in size using a very thin gold alloy foil instead of a steel plate (see Figure 9-17,c).

Spring Reverberation Devices

For the most part spring reverberators have been used in conjunction with electrical or amplified musical instruments such as guitars or organs. The success of these devices as reverberation generators for recording has been decidedly limited because of coloration due to insufficient mode density. Most spring reverberators are low-priced units, and they are usually designed around mass-produced spring assemblies about 10 to 12 inches long which are driven in a *torsional,* or twisting, mode. The torsional wave is reflected back and forth along the spring, and the end opposite the driver has a magnetic receiver where the reverberation signal is picked up.

Many of the more expensive embodiments of spring reverberators, especially those with custom-designed spring units, provide a higher quality of performance and can be successfully used for limited recording applications. If these units are used in sufficient quantities, each one on a different track of a multitrack recording, the defects of one reverberator may be successfully masked by the remaining ensemble of reverberators.

A notable exception to these comments on spring reverberators is the AKG Model BX-20. The BX-20 provides the density of modes necessary for professional recording use by employing a long, randomly structured spring which is

---

Figure 9-16. Applications of reverberation chambers. In order to minimize direct sound pickup from the loudspeaker in a reverberation chamber, a figure-eight microphone pattern is often used with its null plane toward the loudspeaker (a). Where more than one microphone is used, a figure-eight loudspeaker pattern may be used with microphone locations along its null plane, as shown in (b). A large reverberation chamber may be partitioned as shown in (c) to allow leakage from one side to the other; this creates an interesting enhancement of stereophonic program material. Reverberation time can be made variable by providing adjustable absorption in the room. A scheme suggested by the Victor Company of Japan is shown in (d). A block of dense fiber glass is normally housed in a nonabsorptive box. A motor-driven helix exposes the fiber glass in varying degrees, and the resulting control of reverberation time is shown in (e).

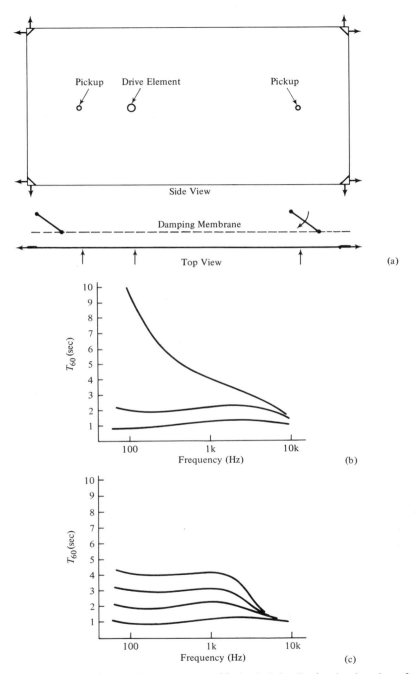

Figure 9-17. The EMT-140 reverberation plate. Mechanical details showing location of drive and pickup elements and damping membrane are shown in (a). The reverberation time vs. frequency can be adjusted over the range shown in (b). The EMT-240 uses a gold alloy foil as a reverberation element, and its reverberation time vs. frequency curves are shown in (c). The foil is 270 mm by 290 mm and is 18 microns thick. Note the relative flatness of the curve over a wide range of reverberation time settings.

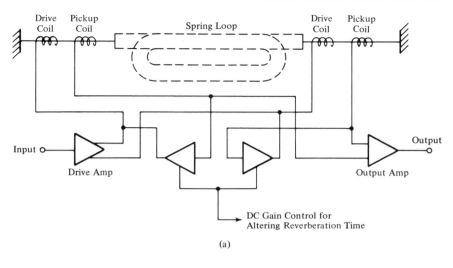

(a)

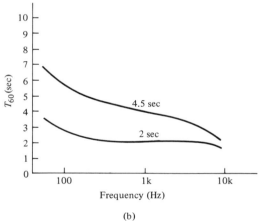

(b)

Figure 9-18. The AKG Model BX-20 reverberation unit. The drive and pickup circuitry are shown in (a). Note that there are both drive coils and pickup coils at each end of the spring loop. The adjustment in reverberation time is achieved by feeding a portion of the signal from each pickup coil back into their respective drive coils in the correct polarity to cause regeneration of the signal. The range of reverberation time adjustment is shown in (b).

folded to occupy a fairly small space, as shown in Figure 9-18,a. Two spring units are contained in one case, and the entire assembly can be easily transported without need for adjustment. The reverberation time is variable through electromechanical regeneration by means of the circuit shown in Figure 9-18,b.

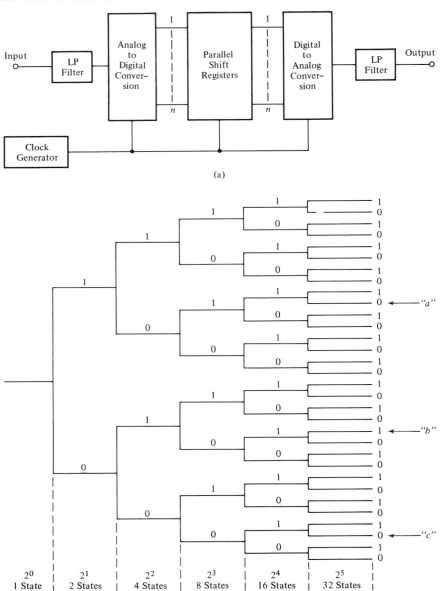

(a)

(b)

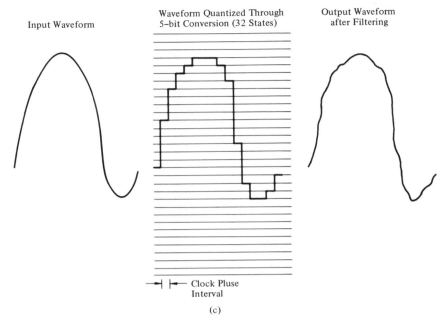

Figure 9-19. (*Continued*)

Digital Time Delay Devices

The development of *large-scale integrated circuit techniques* (LSI) in recent years has made possible economical processing of audio signals in the digital domain. The most useful of these applications has been generating time-delayed signals in the important range from 5 msec to 100 msec. The basic function is shown in Figure 9-19,a.

The signal to be delayed is filtered at the input to remove all frequency components above some cut-off point, usually 15 kHz. Then the signal is converted

---

Figure 9-19. Digital time delay. The basic layout of a digital delay unit is shown in (a). Quantizing of the input signal is done by the process shown in (b). For every increasing power of 2, the number of possible states of the signal is doubled, and any given state can be expressed as a binary number. For example, state "*a*" is represented by the binary number 10110; each successive digit indicates the next branch to be followed. State "*b*" is represented by the binary number 01011, and state "*c*" by the number 00010. In this manner, only "zeros" and "ones" are used to define a given input signal level at a given time. Typical waveforms are shown in (c). Here, an input waveform is quantized at every clock pulse into one of 2^5, or 32, values. In this form the signal is transmitted down the shift registers, each of the 5 bits moving in parallel. The digital-to-analog converter restores the signal, and the output filters remove the noise products resulting from the quantizing action.

from its normal *analog* form to *digital* form. In digital form the signal is fed to a set of shift registers. These are devices containing upwards of 1024 sections, each section capable of storing a binary bit ("0" or "1") and shifting that bit from one section to the next as initiated by the clock pulses. The shift registers constitute a digital delay line, and there are output taps at many positions along the line providing desired amounts of time delay. The delayed digital signals are fed to a digital-to-analog converter, and the output is filtered to reduce HF noise components resulting from the digitizing process.

Figure 9-19,b shows in detail how the input signal is converted to digital form. With progressive powers of 2 (2, 4, 8, 16, 32, –) more resolution is provided in digitizing, or *quantizing,* the input signal. The figure shows the extent of 2^6, or *64* quantizing levels, and this is referred to as 6-bit conversion. In typical digital delay systems 12 bits are used, resulting in 2^{12}, or 1024, quantized states. The greater the quantization, the greater the signal-to-noise ratio of the system. In general, the signal-to-noise ratio is equal to 6 dB-times-number-of-bits, typically 72 dB for a 12-bit system.

Figure 9-19,c shows the effect of quantizing of the analog waveform. Here, 5-bit conversion is used, and the discrete levels in the quantized signal are quite apparent. Low-pass filtering at the output reduces the noise level.

The process of input-output conversion and also shifting along the delay path are initiated by clock pulses. If frequency response is to be maintained out to 15 kHz, then the clock pulse rate should be in the neighborhood of 45 kHz. LSI shift registers are usually available in 1024-bit units with subdivisions at 256 bits. The equation relating delay time, clock rate, and bit capacity is:

$$\text{clock rate} = \frac{\text{bit capacity}}{\text{delay time}}$$

Thus, for 1024-bit registers, a clock rate of 51.2 kHz will produce a delay time of 20 msec. With subdivisions at 256 bits, delay times in increments of 5 msec can be realized. For most recording applications, 5-msec resolution of delayed signals is quite adequate.

Digital devices are expensive, especially for longer values of time delay. Over the years, electromechanical systems such as tape transports and tape loops have been used, but they are subject to variability of response and tape wear and need constant maintenance. Acoustical delay lines have been only moderately successful, although they can exhibit excellent noise and frequency response characteristics for values of delay up to about 30 msec.

SPECIAL EFFECTS

One of the most popular special effects is known as *phasing,* an outgrowth of studio practice of the mid-sixties. When two tape recorders are fed the same signal and their delayed outputs recombined, then any varying differences in the delay time between the two machines, such as would result from small differences in speed between them, will produce comb filter response which shifts back and forth in a random fashion.

The basic phasing scheme is shown in Figure 9-20. In (a), the term T represents the fixed delay of each tape recorder, the time gap between record and playback heads. The term Δt represents the *difference* in delay between the two machines and is the net value of delay which causes the comb filter response. (Refer to the discussion of comb filters in Chapter 3.)

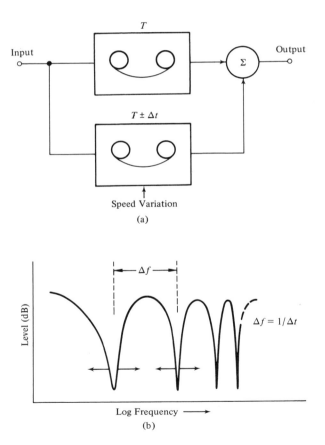

Figure 9-20. Principles of "phasing." Using two tape recorders, as shown in (a), a speed variation is introduced into one machine, and their outputs are combined to yield variable comb filter response shown in (b).

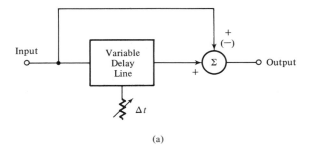

(a)

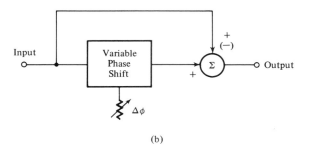

(b)

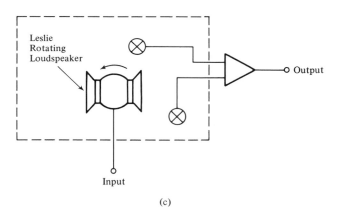

(c)

Figure 9-21. Alternate methods for phasing. In (a), a variable delay line is used in place of the two tape machines shown in the previous figure. In (b) time delay has been replaced by variable phase shift. In (c), microphones are placed close to a Leslie rotating speaker assembly, and the combined output of the two microphones yields a random and constantly shifting pattern of peaks and cancellations.

The value of Δt can be varied electrically by driving one tape machine with an external AC power source whose frequency can be shifted around 60 Hz. Another method of varying Δt is for the operator to place his thumb on the flange of the feed reel, thus slowing it down. This practice has given rise to the term "flanging," and it is synonymous with *phasing*.

The above technique for phasing is cumbersome and introduces a fixed time offset, T, into the program being phased. So-called *instant* phasing is possible through the use of a delay line whose total delay can be varied in small steps over a wide range or through the use of a variable phase shift network. These methods are shown in Figure 9-21,a and b.

A similar effect can be produced with the Leslie rotating loudspeaker assembly which is commonly used with electronic organs (Figure 9-21,c). A pair of microphones placed close to the rotating speakers will produce varying cancellations and reinforcements as a result of the rotation.

The sound of phasing is hard to describe. It is most effective on broad band signals such as cymbals and snare drums. It produces a bizarre "swishing" sound as the peaks and dips move up and down the spectrum. On vocal tracks the effect is often a "disembodied and ghostlike" quality; and the rotating loudspeaker arrangement of Figure 9-21,c has been used extensively for this effect.

Many special effects are a direct outgrowth of the interface between electronic music synthesis and standard recording practice. The more useful of these techniques are: *voltage-controlled filters, voltage-controlled envelope shapers,* and *ring modulators.*

Voltage-controlled filters take a number of forms, but one of the most common is a low-pass filter, as shown in Figure 9-22. The cut-off frequency is controlled at one input and is variable over a large range. Another voltage input controls regeneration, or positive feedback, around the filter, enabling a response peak to be developed at the cut-off frequency. Voltage-controlled filters were developed to add musical inflection to noise sources, oscillators, and other static ingredients of electronic music. Their careful use with instrumental timbres can result in unusual and interesting musical effects.

An *envelope shaper* is basically a voltage-controlled amplifier, as shown in Figure 9-23,a. A more useful form is shown in Figure 9-23,b. Here there is a detector circuit ahead of the DC control point, and this enables the envelope of one instrument to be superimposed on another instrument, as shown in (c). A sustained tone is applied at the input and percussive signals at the control input. The detector produces a control voltage proportional to the envelope of the percussive sounds, and the sustained input is then modulated by the resulting envelope.

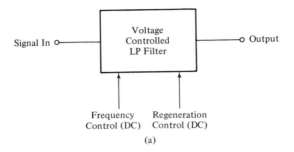

Signal In o———————[Voltage Controlled LP Filter]———————o Output

Frequency Control (DC)   Regeneration Control (DC)

(a)

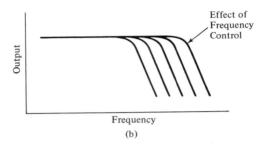

(b)

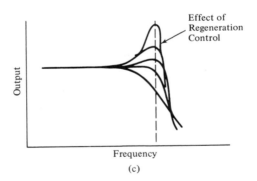

(c)

Figure 9-22. A voltage-controlled low-pass filter. The basic scheme is shown in (a). The effect of frequency control (with fixed regeneration) is shown in (b). The effect of regeneration control (with fixed frequency) is shown in (c).

A *ring modulator* is simply a signal multiplier; its output is the instantaneous product of the two input signals. The name derives from the earliest form of

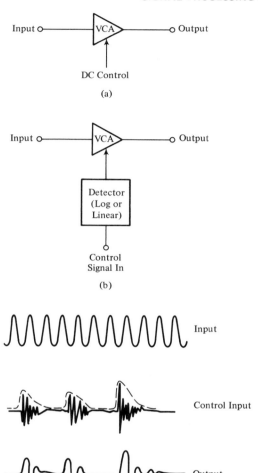

(a)

(b)

(c)

Figure 9-23. An envelope shaper. A basic VCA is shown in (a); with the addition of the detector ahead of the DC control input, the VCA becomes an envelope shaper, as shown in (b). Typical application of the device is shown in (c). In this example the input is a steady state signal, and the control input is a percussive signal whose envelope is shown as a dotted line. The envelope is fed to the VCA, and the output signal is the steady state signal modulated by the envelope of the control input signal. The technique can be used to provide novel percussive effects from instruments which are not capable acoustically of such response.

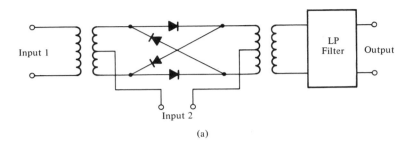

(a)

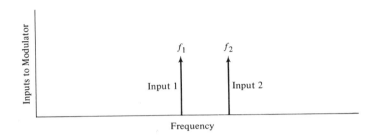

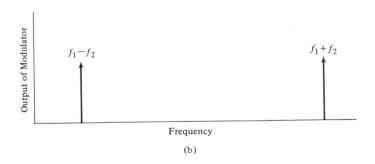

(b)

Figure 9-24. The ring modulator. The basic form is shown in (a). This type of modulator has been replaced by standard operational circuit components for most electronic music and recording applications. Typical input and output relations are shown in (b). If Input 1 consists of f_1 and Input 2 of another frequency, f_2, then the output will contain neither of those frequencies; instead the sum and difference of the frequencies will be present.

the device, as shown in Figure 9-24,a. When two signals are multiplied, the product does not contain either frequency; rather, the *sum* and *difference* of the two frequencies are present, as shown in (b). With complex waveforms at both inputs of a ring modulator the output can be counted upon to be nonharmonically related to either input. Typically, if one input is in a normal musical pitch range and the other input in a very low frequency range (5-20 Hz), then the output will retain some of the character of the first input with a severe "growl" to it.

With random inputs, the output bears no relation to either of the inputs. The effect is often reminiscent of shortwave radio reception, when many signals, voice-modulated as well as coded, intermodulate one another.

CONCLUSION

From the point of view of new product introduction, the signal processing area is one the most active. Hardly an issue of a recording trade journal goes by without an introduction of a new device, and the imagination is staggered by future possibilities. The impact of electronic music synthesis is obvious and undeniable, but the serious recording engineer must at all times keep his frame of reference firmly grounded in the live creation of music in the studio.

BIBLIOGRAPHY

1. B. Bartlett, "A Scientific Explanation of Phasing," *J. Audio Eng. Soc.,* vol. 18, no. 6 (1970).
2. D. Blackmer, "A Wide Dynamic Range Noise Reduction System," *db, The Sound Engineering Magazine,* vol. 6, no. 8 (1972).
3. B. Blesser and F. Lee, "An Audio Delay System Using Digital Technology," *J. Audio Eng. Soc.,* vol. 19, no. 5 (1971).
4. R. Burwen, "Design of a Noise Elimination System," *J. Audio Eng. Soc.,* vol. 19, no. 11 (1971).
5. John Davis, "Practical Stereo Reverberation for Studio Recording," *J. Audio Eng. Soc.,* vol. 10, no. 2 (1962).
6. R. Dolby, "An Audio Noise Reduction System," *J. Audio Eng. Soc.,* vol. 15, no. 4 (1967).
7. J. M. Eargle, "The Record Industry in Japan," *Recording Engineer/Producer,* vol. 5, no. 2 (1974).
8. M. Gerzon, "Stabilizing Stereo Images," *Studio Sound,* vol. 16, no. 12 (1974).
9. H. Meinema *et al.,* "A New Reverberation Device for High Fidelity Systems," *J. Audio Eng. Soc.,* vol. 9, no. 4 (1961).
10. M. Rettinger, "Reverberation Chambers for Broadcasting and Recording Studios," *J. Audio Eng. Soc.,* vol. 5, no. 1 (1957).

11. M. Schroeder and B. Logan, "'Colorless' Artificial Reverberation," *J. Audio Eng. Soc.,* vol. 9, no. 3 (1961).
12. T. Wells and E. Vogel, *The Techniques of Electronic Music* (University Stores, Inc., Austin, Texas, 1974).

10
Disc Recording and Reproduction

A BRIEF HISTORY

After more than three-quarters of a century the disc record remains the most accessible form of recorded music. It is a descendent of the Edison cylinder, the earliest form of mechanical recording. The history of the phonograph record is a richly varied and occasionally stormy one; those readers who are interested in it should refer to the superb historical account *From Tin-Foil to Stereo*, by Read and Welch (8).

Until the mid-twenties recordings were made using available acoustical energy. Performers were placed in front of an assemblage of horns whose throats were all connected to a vibrating diaphragm which actuated a cutting stylus. It was a brute-force system capable of only a few subtleties. Replication techniques were crude, and the finished product was quite noisy. The playback process was acoustical as well, and it is amazing that music could pass through the acoustical-to-mechanical transformation and back again without electrical gain and still be listenable.

Electrical recording was pursued in the mid-twenties because of its obvious benefits of greater bandwidth and higher level. Maxfield and Harrison of Western Electric developed the first practical electrical recording system, and with it the door was opened, at least partially, to that creative world of electronics which we are still exploring today. The broadening of fre-

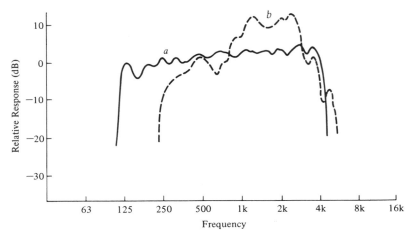

Figure 10-1. Typical acoustical phonograph response with electrical recordings (curve *a*) and acoustical recordings (curve *b*). (Data after Maxfield and Harrison)

quency response of the Western Electric system over a typical acoustical system is shown in Figure 10-1.

The improvements afforded by the Western Electric process soon caught the fancy of record-producing companies worldwide, and Western Electric made their system available to the industry on a license-with-royalty basis. On the playback side, acoustical "wind-up" phonographs continued to dominate the scene even as late as the mid-thirties. These devices did not disappear altogether until the micro-groove long-playing record was introduced in 1947.

Because Western Electric demanded payments for the use of their recording system, EMI (Electrical and Musical Industries) of England set about to develop their own method. Alan Blumlein, a name we discussed earlier in the chapter on stereophonic sound, developed a moving coil cutting system which circumvented the Western Electric patents and allowed EMI to pursue its own important directions in electrical recording.

During the late thirties and the war years the disc art progressed as best it could under the restrictions of noise and limited playing time which plagued the 78-RPM disc. The desire for a *long-playing* medium had fascinated the industry for many years, and $33\frac{1}{3}$-RPM discs had been known from the early days of motion picture sound. As is so often the case with industrial progress, significant steps forward seemed to be related to how well a number of individual improvements could be brought together in a single embodiment. Such was the case with the Columbia LP (long-playing) record in which Peter Goldmark combined the playing time benefits of $33\frac{1}{3}$-RPM with a quiet vinyl chloride compound and the high-frequency capabilities of stylus/groove dimensions significantly smaller than those used for 78-RPM records. The LP spelled final doom for acoustical playback devices (well on their way out already as a result of natural attrition), and provided the way for important developments in phonograph cartridge and cutter head design.

The LP was introduced in 1948, and 10 years later the stereo LP followed. Actually, the first stereo disc was cut by Blumlein in 1931, but the process was felt to be either too far ahead of its time or simply too complex for commerical exploitation, so it lay in the EMI archives for many years.

In the early days of the stereo disc there was a brief skirmish between British Decca (who had opted for channel assignments as *vertical* and *lateral* motion of the groove) and Westrex in the U.S. (who, like Blumlein, had made the channel assignments as a 45° pair). Westrex won out quickly because logic was on their side. Through the decade of the sixties many refinements came about both in stereo cutting and playback technology, and the medium became one of outstanding dynamic range and frequency response. A well-produced stereo disc contains significant information on the order of *microinches* of amplitude, some 60 dB below normal maximum levels.

Progress in disc technology has continued through the first half of the seventies and has brought with it the feasibility for *quadraphonic* discs in which a pair of 30-kHz carriers are cut into the two groove walls along with the normal stereo program.

All things considered, with this last development the LP has probably reached its logical limit in information density. On the horizon are various video-disc formats with vastly increased storage capability over the four-channel LP, and it is logical to assume that any future disc format offering either more channels or longer playing time will make use of the video-disc principle. Meanwhile, the LP as we know it today, with its quad, stereo, and monophonic capability, will be current for many years to come.

BASIC GROOVE GEOMETRY

Basic Stylus Motion for Monophonic and Stereophonic Recording

In monophonic, the stylus moves in the lateral plane at right angles to the direction of groove motion. Stylus velocity is the rate at which this side-to-side motion takes place, and it is usually expressed in centimeters per second (cm/sec). A cross section of a monophonic groove is shown in Figure 10-2,a. Stereo groove motion consists of separate modulation of each groove wall as shown in Figure 10-2,b and c. When both channels are equal and in phase the motion is lateral, the same as for monophonic (Figure 10-2,a). When the signals are equal

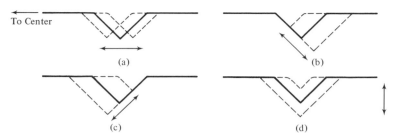

Figure 10-2. Basic groove motions shown in cross section. Lateral (monophonic) motion in (a); stereo right-channel only in (b); stereo left-channel only in (c); vertical motion in (d).

Figure 10-3. Scanning electron microscope photograph of stereo record grooves (100× magnification). Note the independent modulation of each groove wall. (*Courtesy Victor Company of Japan*)

and out-of-phase, the motion is vertical (Figure 10-2,d). The convention of having in-phase signals produce lateral motion results in monophonic compatibility.

Nominal groove width is 2.5 to 3 mils, depending on the program level, and the radius of the groove bottom is 0.2 mil or less. A photomicrograph of typical stereophonic grooves is shown in Figure 10-3.

Groove Displacement, Velocity, and Acceleration

If a disc were to be cut with constant displacement as shown in Figure 10-4,a, then the groove velocity would rise 6 dB/octave with frequency. At a reference

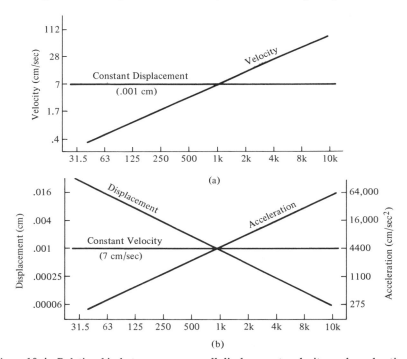

Figure 10-4. Relationship between groove wall displacement, velocity, and acceleration. If a groove is cut with constant displacement over the frequency range of 31.5 Hz to 16 kHz, as shown in (a), the velocity covers a 56-dB range, 512-to-one. This range of velocity is difficult to accommodate because of the electrical demands it makes on the cutting head. Constant-velocity recording, as shown in (b), results in LF space demands which are inefficient, so recording curves have developed as a compromise between constant displacement and constant velocity requirements. The relationships between peak velocity, displacement, and acceleration are:

Peak displacement = Peak velocity/$2\pi f$,

Peak acceleration = ($2\pi f$) Peak velocity

peak velocity of 7 cm/sec at 1 kHz, velocity requirements at 10 kHz would be 20 dB greater, or 70 cm/sec. This represents an electrical toll on the cutting device which would be intolerable.

Alternatively, if velocity is held constant with frequency, as shown in Figure 10-4,b, then the displacement rolls off 6 dB/octave with frequency, representing a waste of valuable recording space in the disc. (Note that stylus *acceleration* rises 6 dB/octave when velocity is held constant.)

Standard Recording Characteristics

Obviously, a compromise between constant-velocity and constant-displacement recording is called for. Figure 10-5 shows curves used in the early days of electrical disc recording. Curve *a* represents constant velocity above 500 Hz and constant displacement below. This curve helped in space saving, but constant velocity at higher frequencies made for a rather noisy transfer. Later the curve was modified by raising the velocity somewhat at high frequencies, thus allowing the signal to ride over the noise level. Playback curves were the *inverse* of the record curves so that the net response was flat.

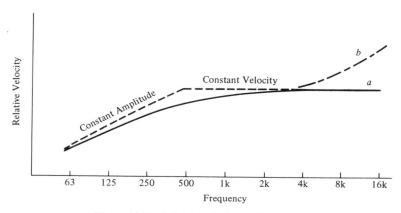

Figure 10-5. Early electrical recording curves.

As the LP record developed in the early fifties, a number of record curves were used, and they are shown in Figure 10-6. These curves were all superseded by the RIAA curve shown in Figure 10-7. This curve, first proposed by RCA, was soon adopted by the record industry worldwide.

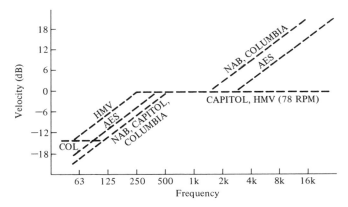

Figure 10-6. Recording characteristics of the early fifties. The transition frequencies for a number of recording curves common during the early LP era are shown. A transition between constant velocity and displacement occurred between 250 and 500 Hz, and a second transition to constant displacement occurred above the 1600–2000 Hz range. Only the Columbia LP curve provided for a constant-velocity boost below 100 Hz. The flat velocity curve above 2 kHz was for HMV and Capitol 78-RPM product only.

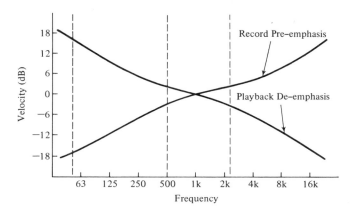

Figure 10-7. The RIAA recording and playback characteristics. These curves are a universally accepted compromise between the geometric demands of constant-velocity recording and the physical cutter head demands of constant displacement at high frequencies. The transition frequencies are 50 Hz, 500 Hz, and 2120 Hz. Time constants are 3180 μsec, 318 μsec, and 75 μsec.

OVERLOAD IN PHONOGRAPH SYSTEMS

There are three kinds of geometrical overload to be avoided in phonograph records: displacement overload, or overcut, as it is called; slope overload; and curvature overload.

Displacement Overload   low f

Overcut is usually the result of operator carelessness during the cutting of the master disc or an improper trade-off between playing time and recorded level. It results when a groove cuts into the space occupied by an adjacent groove. It can lead to improper tracking of the playback stylus if it is severe enough. In moderate degrees it may cause "groove echo," the transfer of signal from one groove to another. Worst of all, record processing is made difficult by overcut in that the separation of metal parts (masters, mothers, and stampers) can result in tearing of metal instead of a smooth parting of surfaces. For the most part overcut is eliminated by the newer disc transfer systems with their careful automatic attention to groove depth and pitch (grooves per inch).

15 min/side
max for 3hr
pay period

Slope Overload

Slope overload occurs when the sidewise stylus velocity is equal to the velocity in the direction of groove travel. This condition represents the maximum velocity, or slope, which can be tolerated, as shown in Figure 10-8,b. Slope overload is a function of diameter; the less the diameter, the more likely it is to occur, and modern disc transfer systems pay close attention to the groove slope in their signal conditioning stages. For a given groove velocity, slope is directly related to stylus velocity, as shown in Figure 10-8,c and d.

Curvature Overload

Curvature overload results when the curvature of the groove wall becomes greater than the curvature of the playback stylus as seen in the direction of groove motion (see Figure 10-9). Curvature overload is related to the *acceleration* of the cutting and playback styli, and avoidance of it is essential if distortion and record wear are to be minimized. Curvature overload is controlled by careful attention to overall transfer levels, suitable HF limiting, and tracing simulation. This last technique will be discussed in a later section.

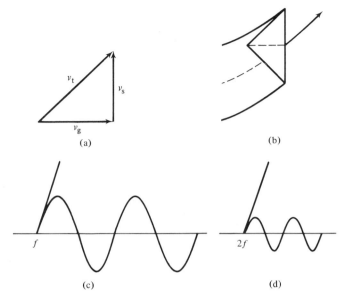

Figure 10-8. Slope overload. Slope overload occurs when (a) the lateral velocity of the recording stylus, v_s, is equal to the groove velocity, v_g. Under this condition the motion of the stylus is at an angle of 45° to the direction of groove travel, and the back facet of the stylus, as shown in (b), will interfere with the freshly cut groove wall. If signals are cut at the same velocity and diameter, the maximum slope of the waveforms will be the same, regardless of frequency, as shown in (c) and (d).

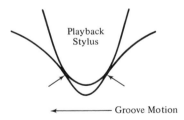

Figure 10-9. Curvature overload. Curvature overload occurs when the curvature of the groove is equal to or greater than that of the playback stylus. When the latter condition exists, the playback stylus contacts the groove wall at two points.

General Overload Limits

We have illustrated three kinds of geometrical overload in the record groove, and each one presents a limit over a certain portion of the recorded spectrum; over-

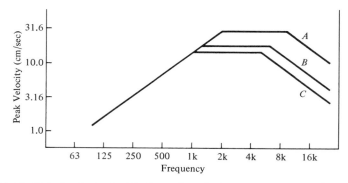

Figure 10-10. Velocity limits for LP discs. These limits are established for RIAA minimum ending diameters with a playback stylus radius of 0.0005″ for 78-RPM (*A*), 45-RPM (*B*), and 33⅓-RPM (*C*). The limit at low frequencies is determined by overcutting; the limit at high frequencies is determined by curvature overload.

cut at low frequencies, slope overload at mid-frequencies, and curvature overload at high frequencies. Typical limits are shown in Figure 10-10.

CUTTING HEADS

Basic Types

Stereo cutting heads used today are universally of the moving coil type with motional feedback. There are two basic designs, both described by Blumlein in his monumental 1931 patent. They are shown in Figure 10-11. In the "V-drive"

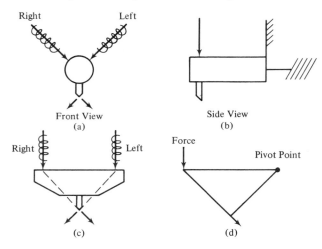

Figure 10-11. Basic stereophonic cutter mechanisms.

structure, which is typical of current Westrex, Neumann, and HAECO designs, forces are applied at 45° angles to the disc surface and are transferred by the stylus assembly in the same directions (Figure 10-11,a and b). The Ortofon designs use the "isosceles T-bar" design (Figure 10-11,c and d). Here, the two forces are applied in parallel to two corners of an isosceles right triangle. Each driving point acts as a pivot point for the other, and motions are resolved at angles of 45°. Thus, for the motion shown at Figure 10-11,d, the force applied at the left pivot point is resolved at an angle 45° to the right.

Each method has its virtues. The V-drive system allows for a larger magnet structure, and this usually means greater sensitivity and power-handling capability. The T-bar structure on the other hand provides smoother and better-balanced HF response. For normal stereo applications, however, the two approaches can be considered equal in performance.

Principle of Motional Feedback

The moving systems shown in Figure 10-11 are usually made with low mechanical losses and will tend to "ring" at resonance. In earlier days mechanical damping was added to these system to remove the resonant peak, a procedure wasteful of energy. Toward the late thirties, Bell Laboratories developed the principle of motional feedback in which a small coil located near the stylus sensed the motion of the stylus tip and fed a voltage back to the input at the amplifier out-of-phase. The resulting negative feedback tended to correct any errors in the output velocity of the cutter. The principle is shown in Figure 10-12.

The location of feedback coils is critical; in order for the stylus motion to be monitored as accurately as possible the coils should be as close to the stylus tip as possible. Figure 10-13 shows typical locations of drive and feedback coils for both types of structures.

Because of the proximity of drive and feedback windings, great care is taken to ensure that there is no transformer action between them. This can take the form of shielding, as in the case of Westrex and Neumann, or dual windings in opposition to cancel transformer action, as in the case of Ortofon.

A Variation on Motional Feedback

Feedback is greatest at the resonant frequency of the systems, and this frequency has been chosen over the years to be at the *geometric mean* of the bandwidth of the system (between 1 kHz and 2 kHz). Choosing the system resonance in this way causes an even distribution of feedback control over the useful frequency range of the device. For example, the geometric mean between 50 Hz and 20

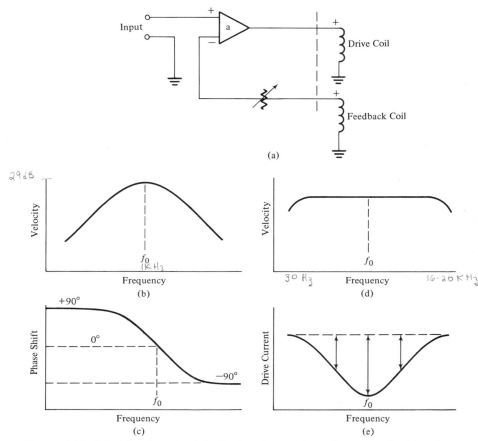

Figure 10-12. Principle of motional feedback. Cutter drive coils are usually driven by a constant current signal over the frequency band, resulting in an increase in velocity in the region of mechanical resonance (f_0). A feedback coil is located close to the cutting stylus and senses this increase in velocity as an *error signal*, a departure from the flat input signal. The error signal is fed back into the amplifier input in reverse polarity [shown in (a)], and it is adjusted so that the velocity peak is canceled. The output of the feedback coil has the same shape as the velocity curve shown in (b), and its phase response is as shown in (c). When the amount of feedback is properly adjusted, the resulting stylus velocity is flattened as shown in (d), and the corresponding drive current is reduced in the region of resonance, as shown in (e). The total feedback is greatest at resonance and less at frequencies above and below resonance, as indicated by the arrows in (e). Typical resonant frequencies for Neumann, Westrex, and HAECO cutters are in the 1-kHz range, while the Ortofon resonance is at 2 kHz. As with any system of negative feedback, distortion arising in either the cutter or electronics is reduced to a degree proportional to the feedback.

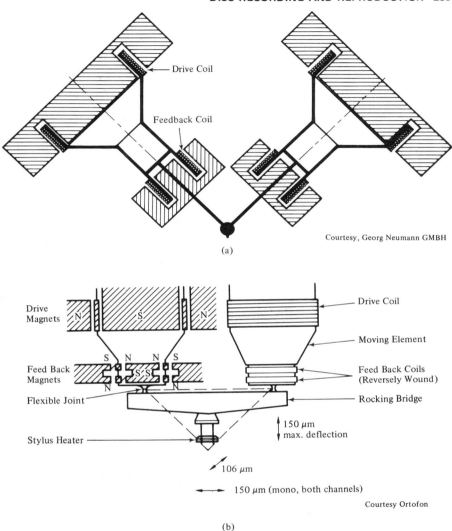

Courtesy, Georg Neumann GMBH

(a)

Courtesy Ortofon

(b)

Figure 10-13. Location of feedback coils. It is important that feedback coils be located close to the cutting stylus so that they may monitor its motion accurately. The detail in (a) shows drive coil, feedback coil, and stylus relationships for the current Neumann designs. Westrex and HAECO designs are similar. The detail in (b) shows the relationships for the Ortofon design. The reversely wound feedback coils reduce the susceptibility of the feedback coils to signals induced by the nearby drive coils. [(a) *Courtesy Georg Neumann GMBH*. (b) *Courtesy Ortofon*]

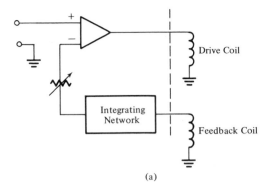

(a)

Figure 10-14. A variation on motional feedback. Current Ortofon designs add an *integrating network* in series with the feedback coil, as shown in (a), and this produces a family of feedback curves as shown in (b). The integrating network provides a bass boost over a portion of the low-frequency range, and the feedback signal in that range is proportional to the stylus *position* rather than its velocity. The action results in greater stylus control at low frequencies and improves overall system linearity. [(b) *Courtesy Ortofon.*]

kHz is:

$$\text{Geometric mean} = \sqrt{50 \times 20{,}000} = 1 \text{ kHz}$$

The resonances for current Neumann, Westrex, and HAECO cutters are about 1 kHz, while the resonance of Ortofon cutters is about 2 kHz.

Feedback control diminishes at the frequency extremes, and Ortofon has devised a method for increasing its control at low frequencies. The motional, or *velocity*, feedback is modified at low frequencies by introducing an *integrating network* in the feedback circuit which modifies the feedback signal in the 50 Hz to 1 kHz range so that feedback is proportional to stylus *displacement* instead of velocity. The technique gives much greater control at low frequencies than simple feedback, typically 13 dB at 100 Hz instead of 1 or 2 dB without the integrating network. Details of the process are shown in Figure 10-14.

Structural Details of Current Cutter Designs

Figure 10-15 shows details of current Westrex, Neumann, and Ortofon stereo cutting head designs. Note that the Westrex head rides on an *advance ball*, a smooth sapphire bearing which is in contact with the recording blank. The cutter head is counter-balanced so that only a small force is exerted on the advance ball—only enough to index the relatively massive head at a fixed distance above the master disc.

The similarity between the Neumann and Westrex structures is quite evident.

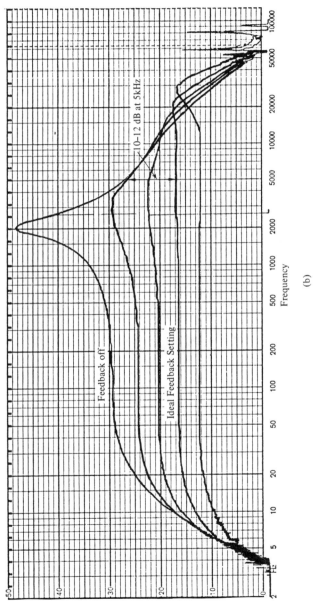

Figure 10-14. (*Continued*)

The linear dimensions of the Neumann head are about half those of the Westrex, and it does not ride on an advance ball.

The isosceles T-bar, or *bridge*, as it is often called, is obvious in the Ortofon design. This head does not use an advance ball; both it and the Neumann design are "floated," carefully counter-balanced by a spring and dash pot assembly which allows the heads to follow accurately the normal variations in thickness of master recording blanks.

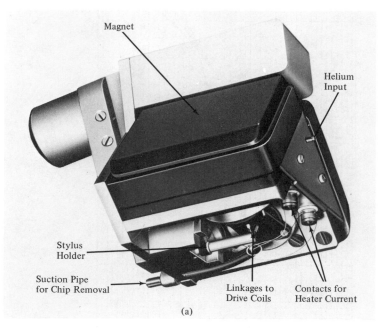

(a)

Figure 10-15. Mechanical details of typical stereo cutters. The Neumann SX-74 stereo cutter is shown in (a). The stylus holder is obvious, as are the mechanical linkages between it and the drive coils. The wires leading from the stylus carry the current for heating the stylus. The two magnet structures, located at angles of ±45° to the disc surface, form the upper structure of the cutter. The suction tube located next to the stylus provides for removal of the "chip," the lacquer material thrown off by the cutting stylus. The small opening at the front of the cutter is for helium gas cooling of the drive coils. The current Westrex 3-D cutter is shown in (b). It is similar to the Neumann but larger in size. While the Neumann has two magnets, one for each drive coil, the Westrex has a single magnet which serves both drive coils. The Ortofon DSS-731 cutter is shown in (c). The stylus holder–T-bar assembly is shown at the center of the device, and its ends are the drive points. The leaf springs which maintain the neutral position of the T-bar are visible. Not shown here is the suction pipe for chip removal. [(a) *Courtesy Georg Neumann GMBH*. (b) *Courtesy Westrex*. (c) *Courtesy Ortofon*.]

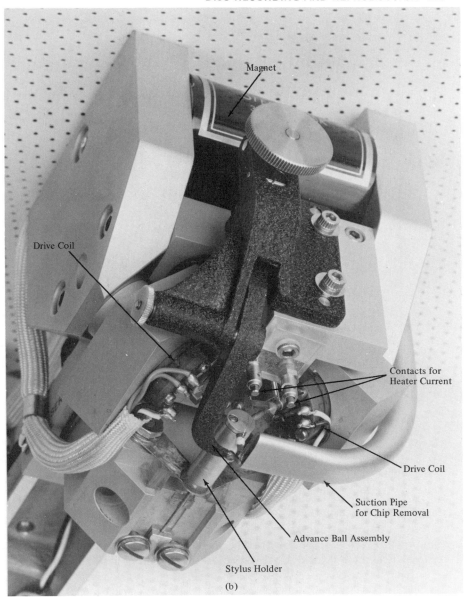

Figure 10-15. (*Continued*)

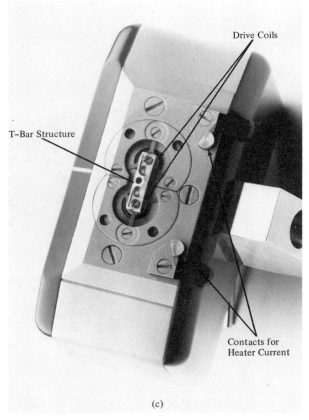

Figure 10-15. (*Continued*)

Controlling the Vertical Cutting Angle

In the early sixties a discrepancy was noted between the effective vertical cutting angle of typical cutters and the effective vertical tracking angle of playback cartridges. Most cartridges were inclined forward anywhere from 10° to 45°, while cutter heads were generally tilted anywhere between 0° and about 25°. To make matters more difficult, the geometrical tilt of a cutter head did not always agree with its measured forward cutting angle, in large part because of certain complicated effects arising out of the "spring-back" or elasticity of the lacquer recording material.

Gross mismatch between cutting and playback vertical angles caused distortion, especially at inner recorded diameters, and the industry was quick to standardize on forward angles in the range of 15° to 20°. Figure 10-16 shows the relationship of typical cartridge tilt with that of the three cutting heads we have discussed.

SPECIAL SIGNAL CONDITIONING TECHNIQUES

In recent years the demands for high-level disc transfer and freedom from distortion have resulted in improved cutting heads and increased drive amplifier power capability. The result is a generation of cutting head–amplifier combinations which are capable of easily inflicting slope and curvature overload on high-level program material if not properly monitored. This is as it should be; the medium should be first to distort—not the electromechanical system. Automatic or manual controls should be employed to whatever degree necessary to guarantee distortionless transfers; only in this way can disc performance be maximized. We shall now discuss four kinds of signal conditioning essential to state-of-the-art disc transfer: thermal protection of the cutter head, curvature limiting, tracing simulation, and LF vertical limiting.

Thermal Protection of the Cutter Head

Operator carelessness has burnt out many a cutter head and brought with it a repair bill in the five-hundred-dollar range. The drive coils are invariably fused or provided with some kind of circuit breaker, but sudden bursts of HF energy can inflict permanent damage before the protection mechanism has a chance to operate. More sophisticated systems provide some kind of thermal sensing, a monitoring of the temperature of the drive coils, providing a limiting of signal level, or a signal cut-out altogether, if the temperature approaches the failure point. It is rare that these limits are reached in normal practice, and they may be regarded as failsafe protection from system abuse.

Helium cooling raises the thermal overload capacity of cutter heads by a significant margin. It is a better conductor of heat than air, and the capacity of a cutting head can be increased as much as 5 dB through its use. It is important to note that helium is not "forced through" the drive coil gap in an effort to cool the system by brute force. Rather, a helium atmosphere is quietly maintained in the gap, thus enabling heat to be transferred more efficiently by conduction to the outer structure of the cutter head.

Curvature Limiting

At small cutting diameters, curvature overload can be reached long before the cutter thermal cut-out point. Thus, there is a need for special HF limiting to

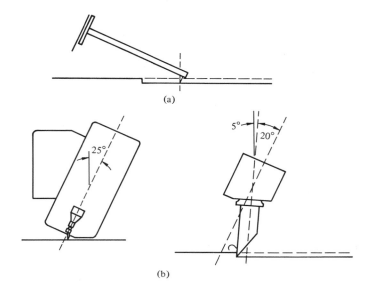

(a)

(b)

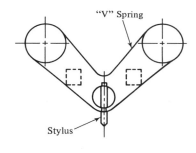

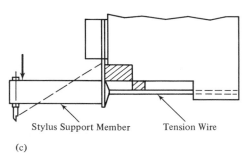

"V" Spring

Stylus

Stylus Support Member   Tension Wire

(c)

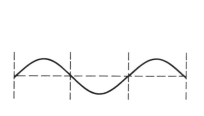

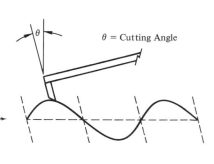

θ = Cutting Angle

(d)

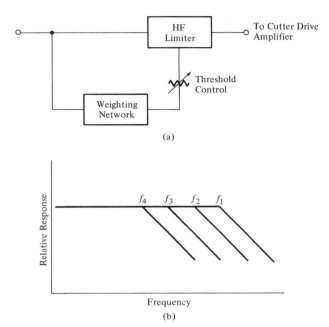

(a)

(b)

Figure 10-17. High-frequency overload protection. Incoming program is sampled via a pre-emphasis network which weights the program according to the cutter's characteristics, or predetermined curvature or slope limits. The weighted signal then is fed to a limiting circuit which provides rapid on-and-off attenuation of troublesome high frequencies. For minor problem signals the roll-off would commence at some f_1, usually above 10–12 kHz. Greater inputs would result in progressive lowering of the transition frequency, f_2 through f_4, down perhaps as low as 5 kHz.

prevent its occurence. Figure 10-17 shows details of an HF limiter adapted to the purpose.

The attack and recovery times of the HF limiter are purposely made quite short so that the audibility of the limiting action is held to a minimum. The result of the action is a groove of less curvature and greater trackability.

Figure 10-16. Control of the vertical tracking angle. The moving elements of current playback cartridges are tilted about 20° forward with respect to the disc surface because of structural demands, as shown in (a). Details of the Ortofon cutter and its tilt angle are shown in (b). Note that the angle is 25°. Lacquer springback accounts for about 5°, thus making the cutting angle effectively 20°. In the Neumann and Westrex designs, the required tilt in cutting action is achieved by designing the hinge angle for the stylus holder substantially less than 90°, as shown in (c). Because of the cutting angle of the cutter head, the waveform in the disc is skewed with respect to the input signal, as shown in (d). When the skewed signal is played back with a cartridge with the same angle, then the original wave form is traced properly.

Tracing Simulation

The cutting stylus is chisel-shaped, and the playback stylus is of circular cross section as it contacts the groove. As a result there is a tracing discrepancy between the two styli, as shown in Figure 10-18,a. The solid line represents a sine wave cut by the cutting stylus, and the dotted line represents the distorted waveform traced by a playback stylus whose radius in the scanning direction is r. Tracing simulation reverses this process; it acts on the waveform, producing an electrically distorted version of it, as shown in Figure 10-18,b, and introduc-

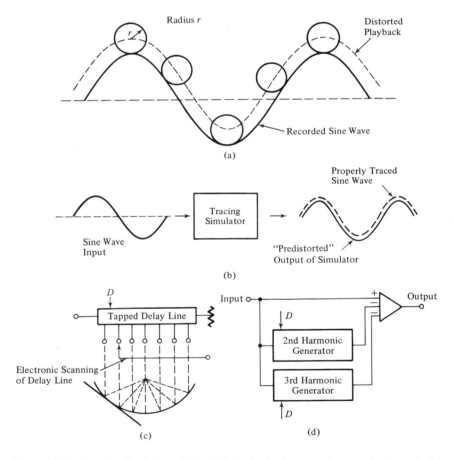

Figure 10-18. Tracing simulation. Distorted playback of a normal groove is shown in (a), and action of the tracing simulator is shown in (b). Two approaches to simulation are shown in (c) and (d).

ing that new waveform to the cutter head out-of-phase. As a result, the playback stylus traces back a *corrected* waveform resembling the input to the simulator.

Tracing simulators in use today work on two principles. The Neumann simulator generates individually the harmonics which correct the recorded waveform and adds them to the program signal out-of-phase. The simulators used by RCA, Victor Company of Japan, and Nippon Columbia generate, by to-and-fro scanning of the signal along a delay path, a direct analog of the distorted signal which is then fed to the cutter out-of-phase. Both systems are dependent on recorded diameter, as shown by D in the diagrams.

Low-Frequency Vertical Limiting

For a given amplitude, a low-frequency lateral signal requires less total distance between adjacent grooves than the same amplitude as a vertical signal, as shown in Figure 10-19,a. As a result, considerable space saving can be realized by reducing vertical excursions of the groove at low frequencies, as shown by circuits (b) and (c) of Figure 10-19. Properly applied below, say, 150 Hz, these circuits do not affect sound quality or phantom image localization; they have the added benefit of reducing the possibilities of *cutter lift*, the instantaneous lift of the cutting stylus out of the lacquer blank that is due to random large LF vertical signals.

SOME STYLUS-GROOVE RELATIONSHIPS

Stylus Contours

Cutting styli are shaped as shown in Figure 10-20,a. The function of the burnishing facet is to smooth the freshly cut groove and thus keep noise at a minimum. Since the burnishing facet is small by comparison with the playback stylus radius in the direction of scanning, we can easily simplify the picture and say that the cutting edge is "chisel-shaped" by comparison to the playback stylus.

Various configurations of playback styli have been used for stereo playback, beginning with the simple conical structure with a spherical tip. This tip does not align itself at all well with the groove wall and is used only in cheap playback units. The normal radius for such a stylus is 0.7 mil. The elliptical tip, introduced in the early sixties, provides a significant improvement with a horizontal, or *scanning*, radius of 0.3 mil and a vertical, or *bearing*, radius of about 0.7 mil. The contact area, however, is still small. (See Figure 10-20,b.)

In the early seventies, as a response to the particular needs of the CD-4 discrete quad disc, a new playback contour was introduced. It takes a number of forms, but it is known generally as the *Shibata* stylus (Figure 10-20,b). Its chief char-

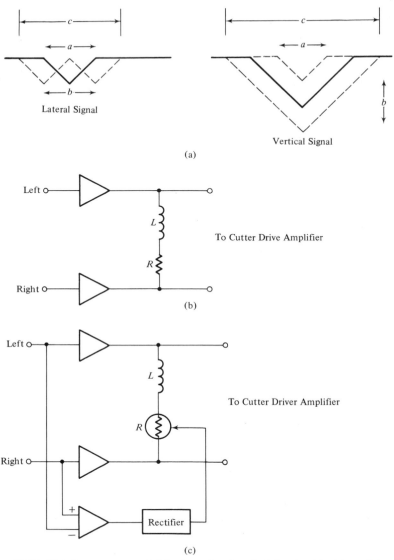

Figure 10-19. Relative space occupied by lateral and vertical signals. (a) A lateral signal of peak-to-peak amplitude b and minimum groove width a will occupy a total lateral space of $c = a + b$. If the same signal is present as vertical modulation of peak-to-peak value of b, and it is desired to maintain a minimum groove width of a, then the total lateral space occupied, c, will be equal to $a + 2b = c$. In (b), a resistor-inductor combination is in series with the left and right signals, and any differences at low frequencies (corresponding to vertical signals) will be shorted out. In (c), a differential amplifier senses the vertical components and converts that difference to a DC control signal to lower a variable resistance in a shunt path between channels.

acteristics are a small scanning radius and a large bearing radius. This combination ensures a large contact area (and less pressure on the groove walls for a given tracking force) consistent with a small scanning radius. The configuration is desirable for all forms of disc reproduction.

Forces at Work in the Record Groove

It is instructive, and even sobering, to analyze the forces at work in a stereo record groove under the dynamic conditions of playback. Given the peak stylus velocity in cm/sec we can compute both displacement in cm and the acceleration in cm/sec^2 as follows:

$$\text{Peak displacement} = \frac{1}{2\pi f} \text{ Peak velocity}$$

$$\text{Peak acceleration} = (2\pi f) \text{ Peak velocity}$$

In these two equations f represents frequency in Hz.

Let us assume that the instantaneous peak velocity at 10 kHz is 25 cm/sec, not an unreasonable number. Then the peak acceleration is:

$$(2\pi\, 10{,}000)\, 25 \text{ cm/sec}^2 = 15.7 \times 10^5 \text{ cm/sec}^2$$

The acceleration of gravity is 980 cm/sec^2; so the peak stylus acceleration is $15.7 \times 10^5/980 = 1{,}602$ times the acceleration of gravity (often stated as 1,602 "G's").

Force is equal to *mass times acceleration*; if we assume that the effective mass of the playback stylus is .0005 gram, then the force in *dynes* on the groove wall is:

$$F(\text{dynes}) = (.0005)\, 15.7 \times 10^5 = 785 \text{ dynes}$$

Expressed as grams-force, this is equal to $= 785/980 = 0.8$ grams-force. The force is quite small; however, it is *pressure*, or force per unit area, which causes groove damage. If we assume a conical playback contour with a contact area of 23.4×10^{-12} square meters, as shown in Figure 10-20,c, then the pressure on the groove wall is $0.8/23.4 \times 10^{-12} = 3.42 \times 10^{10}$ grams-force per square meter or, converted to pounds per square inch, this value becomes: 4.87×10^4 lbs/in^2! With the Shibata contour, the pressure due to inertial forces would be only half as great since the area of contact is roughly twice that of the conical tip. No wonder then that records do wear out!

In addition to those forces caused by inertia of the stylus, there is the fixed tracking force due to gravity. The gravitational force must at all times be greater than the inertial forces if groove wall contact is to be maintained under all playback conditions. Thus, in the case analyzed above, a tracking force of 1.13 grams

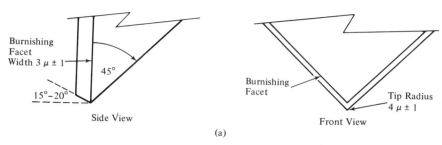

Figure 10-20. Cutting and playback stylus relationships Stereo cutting stylus details are shown in (a). The included angle of the tip is *less* than 90°, in the range of 88.5°, depending on the cutter tilt angle. When the stylus is tilted with respect to the disc, the resulting angle as viewed in the direction of groove motion is 90°. Playback stylus–groove relationships are shown in (b). *A* shows the contour of the cutting stylus. The contact points of a *Shibata*-type playback stylus are shown at *B*; note that the contact points closely match those of the cutting stylus. Contact points characteristics of elliptical and conical tips are shown at *C* and *D*. Further geometrical details of stylus-groove contact are shown in (c). Note that the Shibata stylus provides the largest contact area consistent with a small radius in the direction of groove travel. [(c) *Courtesy Audio Technica*]

would have to be maintained in the vertical plane if the components perpendicular to the groove walls were to be equal to the maximum inertial force: $(\sqrt{2}/2)$ $(1.13) = 0.8$ grams-force.

We can make the following observations:

1. The acceleration (and forces) due to gravity are always greater than the inertial acceleration (and forces) due to the back-and-forth movement of the stylus. The net force of the stylus must, of course, be *toward* the groove wall; otherwise mistracking and gross groove damage will be the result.

2. Pressures on the groove wall are always less if a large contact area is used. This is a strong argument for using Shibata stylus contours for all playback purposes.

MASTER LACQUERS

Lacquer recording blanks have been used for mastering since the late thirties, but it was not until the mid-forties that they completely replaced the various wax formulations which had been used for many years. The lacquer material is basically cellulose nitrate dissolved in a suitable solvent along with a plasticizer (usually castor oil), dyes, and various other ingredients. The material is flowed onto an aluminum blank and is slowly dried in a solvent-saturated atmosphere so that surface wrinkles will not develop.

Every engineer runs into lacquer problems at some time or other. He experiences difficulty in getting a quiet and smooth cut, and nothing he does seems

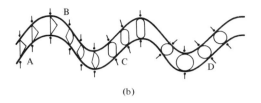

(b)

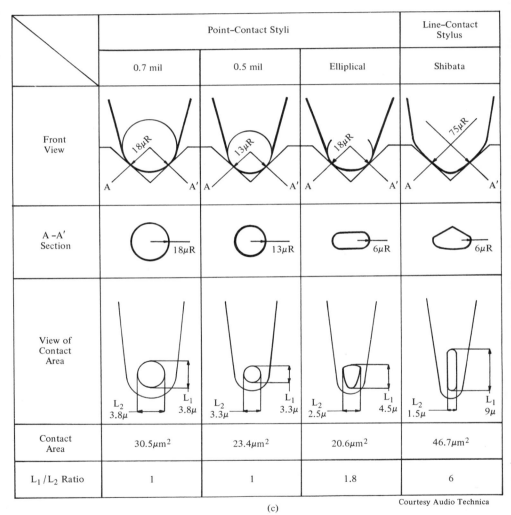

	Point–Contact Styli			Line–Contact Stylus
	0.7 mil	0.5 mil	Elliplical	Shibata
Front View	18μR	13μR	18μR	75μR
A–A′ Section	18μR	13μR	6μR	6μR
View of Contact Area	L₂ 3.8μ L₁ 3.8μ	L₂ 3.3μ L₁ 3.3μ	L₂ 2.5μ L₁ 4.5μ	L₂ 1.5μ L₁ 9μ
Contact Area	30.5μm²	23.4μm²	20.6μm²	46.7μm²
L₁/L₂ Ratio	1	1	1.8	6

Courtesy Audio Technica

(c)

Figure 10-20. (*Continued*)

to alter the situation substantially. These difficulties are usually batch-related, and it is a wise engineer who keeps several cartons of good lacquers on hand just for such emergencies.

The one variable the lacquer cutting engineer has control over is *stylus heat*, and adjusting it upward will often correct a noisy cut. The heat is applied to the stylus by several turns of wire around the sapphire shank through which current is passed. The exact amount of heat is hard to specify; it is that amount which results in a quiet cut without excessive formation of "horns," or ridges of lacquer material at the top of the groove. Horns are present to some degree at all times, but their excessive development can cause problems in processing.

The lacquer blank is a far from perfect medium; its wax precursor yielded a quieter and more accurate replica of the signal. In the final balance, however, the virtues of lacquer material far outweigh the problems. It is relatively cheap and easily transported from the studio to the processing plant. And of course the instantaneous playback capability of reference lacquers allows immediate verification of both esthetic and technical aspects of the transfer process. Reference lacquers can easily be played back 20 to 25 times without serious quality deterioration. A disadvantage is long-term instability. Properly stored, lacquer blanks can retain good cutting qualities for up to six to eight months. Beyond that time they dry out and tend to get noisy.

Lacquer cutting is a combination of shearing, embossing, and burnishing. The material is gelatin-like and "springy." As a result, the exact motion of the stylus is not transferred to the groove. For the most part these effects are of secondary importance, and they have not been completely analyzed.

Obviously, the advantages of lacquer greatly outweigh the disadvantages, and only a little effort has been spent in developing a substantially different cutting medium.

DISC TRANSFER SYSTEMS

Basic Requirements

A disc transfer system is a specialized audio control system whose main function is to transfer a master tape to disc with the required signal processing and conditioning. Ideally, a master tape which reaches this point has been carefully prepared and should not require extensive last-minute treatment. But such is not always the case, and a flexible disc transfer system must be able to provide the following functions.

A. Signal Processing
    1. Comprehensive equalization and filtering; all functions easily resettable
    2. Compression and limiting; all functions easily resettable

B. Signal Routing
   1. Stereo input to stereo disc transfer mode
   2. Stereo input to mono disc transfer mode
   3. Left or right input to mono disc transfer mode
   4. Patching facilities in and out of major blocks in the system
C. Monitoring and Metering Points
   1. Tape output
   2. Preview (advance head) output
   3. Signal processing output (cutter drive input)
   4. Cutter feedback
   5. Disc playback
D. Signal Conditioning
   1. Tracing simulation
   2. Slope and curvature limiting
   3. LF vertical limiting
E. Calibration Facilities
   1. Provision for flat velocity cutting and playback above 500 Hz
   2. Noise weighting filter and gain adjustment for reading low-level noise signals
F. Mechanical Functions
   1. Flexibility for accommodating various tape speeds, disc diameters, and disc speeds
   2. Comprehensive control of groove pitch and depth of cut (including duplication of signal processing elements in the preview system)

Typical System Layout

The block diagram for a typical disc transfer system is shown in Figure 10-21.

VARIABLE PITCH AND DEPTH CONTROL

Variable pitch and depth control optimize both playing time and level capability on longer discs through the efficient use of space on the disc. Essentially, grooves are made narrower and spaced close together when the level is low, and they are deepened and spaced farther apart as the signal level increases. It is no easy task to do this efficiently, and early methods of pitch and depth control were fairly coarse in their operation.

In recent years the Neumann VMS-70 lathe and variable pitch and depth system has developed this control to a high degree. In the Neumann system, the incoming program is previewed six-tenths of a revolution ahead of the groove being cut, and this information is further updated every quarter revolution.

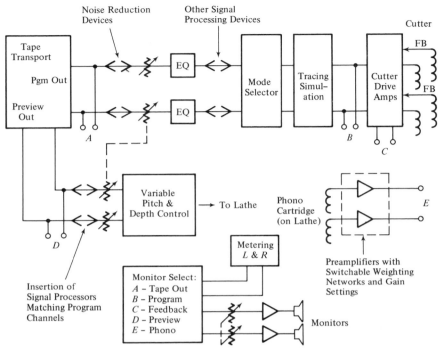

Figure 10-21. A typical lacquer transfer system. In an ideal system there would be duplicate equalizers, noise reduction devices, and other signal processing devices in the input to the variable pitch and depth system so that the maximum saving of space on the disc could be realized.

Groove depth requirements are determined by the vertical components of the program at hand. The information for this is picked up by the preview head and stored until it is needed half a revolution later.

Pitch requirements are determined by *three* factors:

1. Left groove wall requirements. The left channel program input determines this need, and the information is stored for one revolution so that the right wall of the following groove will not interfere.

2. Right groove wall requirements. The right preview signal determines this need.

3. Pitch change as a result of depth increase. The preview vertical component determines this need; the information is stored for one-half revolution until it is needed.

The above actions are indicated in Figure 10-22,a, and typical performance is shown in Figure 10-22,b.

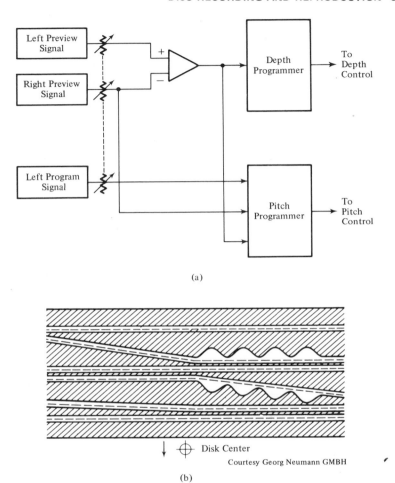

(a)

Disk Center

Courtesy Georg Neumann GMBH

(b)

Figure 10-22. Variable pitch and depth. In the Neumann VMS-70 system, three signals, as shown in (a), are used to determine the proper pitch and depth relationships. Typical action of the system is shown in (b). The right-channel modulation in groove 2 requires a decrease in pitch substantially ahead of the modulation so that there will be no overcut into groove 1. The decrease in pitch must be maintained one revolution so that groove 3 can be accommodated without overcut. Modulation on the left wall of groove 4 does not require a preview signal for proper pitch decrease; the signal controlling this is the left program input. Again, the decrease in pitch must be maintained one revolution in order to make room for groove 5. [(b) *Courtesy Georg Neumann GMBH*]

Relationships Between Playing Time, Pitch, and Groove Width

If a stereo LP record is maintained within dimensional limits established by the Record Industry Association of America (RIAA), its ending diameter for modulation will be no less than 4.75 inches. Starting diameter is 11.5 inches, and this arrangement gives an allowable 3.375 inches of recording space measured along a radius of the disc.

The equation relating average pitch (grooves per inch) and playing time, consistent with the stated dimensional restrictions is: Average pitch = Playing time × 9.87, where pitch is in lines per inch and playing time in minutes. For a 30-minute program, the average pitch will be 296 lines per inch; for a 25-minute program the pitch will be 246 lines per inch. Obviously, if the record ends at a larger diameter the average pitch will be proportionally greater.

Average groove width is determined by pitch as well as program level requirements. Rarely does the average unmodulated groove width become less than 2 mils since this invites both tracking and processing problems. In louder passages the average groove width may increase up to 3 or 3.5 mils as required. In the cutting of 45-RPM 7-inch singles, with their short playing times as well as high levels, average groove width may be as high as 5 mils.

FOUR-CHANNEL DISC TECHNOLOGY

Basic Principles

The four-channel disc is based on two additional *carrier* channels superimposed upon the normal stereo, or *baseband*, modulation. For the CD-4 system, the channel assignment, as shown in Figure 10-23,a, ensures stereo and monophonic compatibility by putting the sums of the front and back signals in the basebands and their *differences* in the carrier channels. When the carrier signals are demodulated, the four inputs are recovered through simple addition and subtraction:

$$\frac{(L_F + L_B) + (L_F - L_B)}{2} = L_F$$

$$\frac{(L_F + L_B) - (L_F - L_B)}{2} = L_B$$

Figure 10-23. Principles of the CD-4 quadraphonic disc system. Bandwidth allocations are shown in (a). The carrier portions occupy the frequency region from 20 kHz to 45 kHz. The basic recording system is shown in (b), and the playback system in (c). The modulator portion of the recording system is shown in (d). A phase-locked loop is used to maintain the center frequency f_0, of the system at 15 kHz (for half-speed cutting), while the modulating input directly varies the frequency of the voltage-controlled oscillator (VCO). N is established as 16, so the reference frequency 15 kHz/16, is 937.5 Hz.

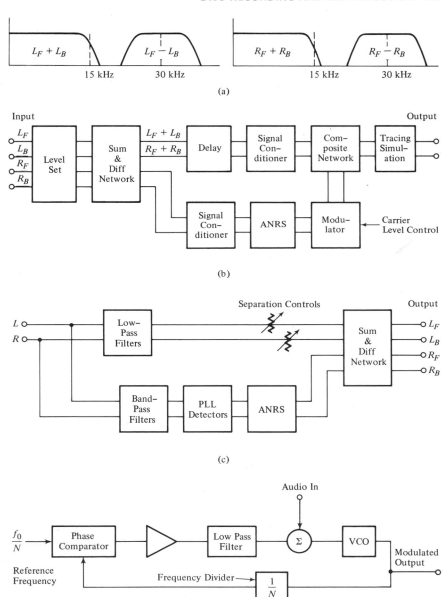

(a)

(b)

(c)

(d)

$$\frac{(R_F + R_B) + (R_F - R_B)}{2} = R_F$$

$$\frac{(R_F + R_B) - (R_F - R_B)}{2} = R_B$$

The carrier frequency is 30 kHz, and the modulation system is a combination of frequency and phase modulation. A basic block diagram of the modulation system is shown in Figure 10-23,b. The baseband signal is band-limited to 15 kHz, delayed 40 μsec, and then combined with the modulated signal. The difference signals are processed by a noise reduction compressor, pre-emphasized, and fed to the modulator. The combined baseband and modulated signals are then processed by a tracing simulator and then fed to the cutting system.

The playback process, shown in Figure 10-23,c, is essentially the inverse of recording. The baseband signal is separated by a low-pass filter, and the carrier signal by a 20–45 kHz band pass filter. Demodulation of the signal is by means of a phase-locked loop detector, after which it is equalized and fed to the complementary noise reduction system (ANRS). The recovered carrier signals are then combined with the baseband signals to obtain the four system inputs. The purpose of the 40-μsec delay in the baseband of the recording function is to adjust total delays through the recording and playback functions so that all signal components will arrive at the output of the demodulator with identical transit time delays.

The principle of modulation is shown in Figure 10-23,d.

Considerable care must be taken in cutting four-channel discs to avoid slope and curvature overload, since such overload may cause momentary carrier loss. The newer demodulators, however, minimize the effect of this loss through the use of high-speed muting of the carrier recovery system during times of carrier loss.

The tracing simulator used in the CD-4 disc process is a wide-band device because it must operate on baseband and carrier signals alike. At present, CD-4 discs are cut at half-speed, where cutter requirements in frequency response go up to 22.5 kHz.

Channel separation is important both in cutting and playback. The effect of cross-talk in the carrier region produces FM beat distortion, and total system cross-talk, through the cutting and playback processes alike, should be held to the 20–25 dB range.

Many benefits have resulted from the technology of the CD-4 disc, and none has been more dramatic than the general improvement in phonograph cartridge response, in terms of both increased bandwidth and channel separation. Figure 10-24,a shows a comparison between a typical stereo phonograph cartridge and

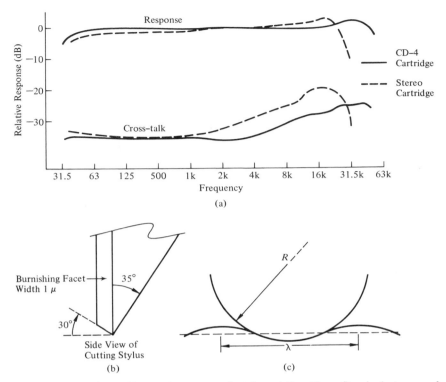

Figure 10-24. CD-4 cartridge performance and stylus relationships. Standard stereo and CD-4 cartridge performance is shown in (a). Note the extended response to 50 kHz and maintenance of 25 dB cross-talk with the CD-4 cartridge. The cutting stylus contour for CD-4 is shown in (b). Playback stylus-groove relationships are shown in (c). The carrier wavelength is 5.8 μ and its amplitude is 0.125 μ, corresponding to a signal of 45 kHz at a diameter of 6 inches (about 15 cm). This represents the most difficult tracing requirement for the system. The playback radius R is 7 μ.

one specifically developed for CD-4 playback. The extreme linearity of the CD-4 cartridge yields obvious benefits for stereo playback as well.

Cutting styli have been modified in order to cut a more accurate and higher level carrier signal on the groove wall, as shown in Figure 10-24,b. The nature of carrier amplitude and wavelength at inner diameters is shown at 10-24,c. Note that the carrier amplitude is quite small (0.125 μ) and that the radius of the playback stylus is approximately equal to the recorded wavelength. This case represents the most difficult tracking requirements of the system.

A scanning electron photomicrograph of CD-4 grooves is shown in Figure 10-25 along with normal stereo grooves for comparison. The CD-4 groove is compatible

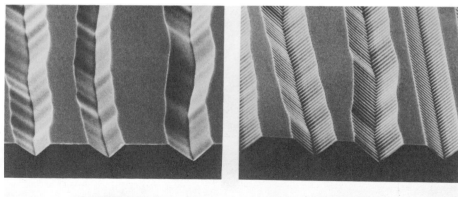

STEREO   **CD·4**

Figure 10-25. Scanning electron photomicrographs of stereo and CD-4 grooves, ×200. (*Courtesy Victor Company of Japan*)

with stereo cartridges, but wear of the carrier at the point of stylus contact is certain to take place with a stereo cartridge. However, replay of such worn records with a Shibata stylus will result in contact with new portions of the groove wall previously unplayed, and adequate quad performance can be expected.

The response of the noise reduction compressor is shown in Figure 10-26,a, and the carrier channel pre-emphasis curve is shown in Figure 10-26,b. The inverses of these curves are employed in the playback function. Reference deviation is ± 2.2 kHz at 1 kHz for a baseband peak velocity (per channel) of 3.9 cm/sec.

The UD-4 system is quite similar to the CD-4 system in its utilization of a pair of 30-kHz carriers for the additional channel capability. It is significantly different in that signal assignments are by way of a phasor matrix arrangement, 4-2-4 on the baseband pair, progressing up through 4-3-4 and finally to 4-4-4.

CALIBRATION OF DISC TRANSFER SYSTEMS

For day-to-day assurance of transfer accuracy, disc cutting systems are best maintained by using a reference disc and comparing test cuts with it by means of a high-quality playback cartridge. The playback of a reference lacquer closely approximates that of a vinyl pressing (especially at outer diameters), so that the comparison is a valid one. Figure 10-27 shows the relative frequency response characteristics of the master lacquer, metal mold (an interim step in the pressing operation), and finished pressing. The losses which occur at high frequencies

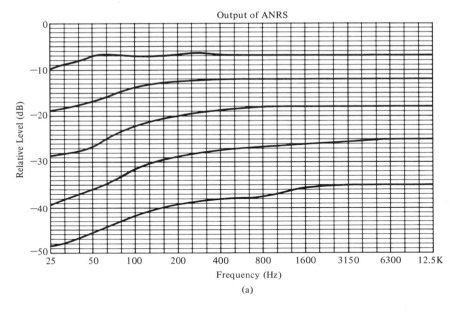

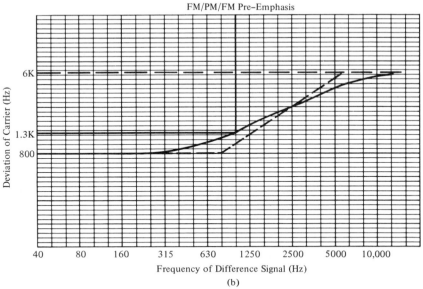

Figure 10-26. Automatic noise reduction system (ANRS) recording compression curves (a). Pre-emphasis curve for carrier signal (b). The curve is designated FM/PM/FM because its upper and lower portions correspond to constant frequency deviation, or FM, while the mid-portion corresponds to constant phase modulation, or PM.

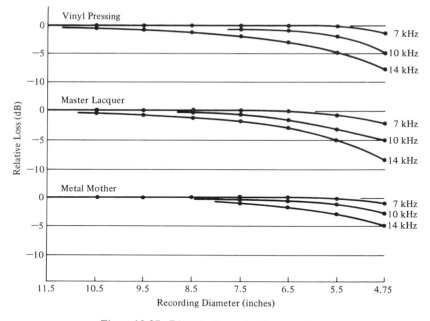

Figure 10-27. Diameter losses in disc recording.

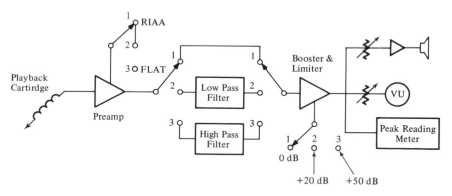

Figure 10-28. Block Diagram of a disc noise measurement system. Position 1 is used for normal audio checking and frequency response measurements. Position 2 inserts a 10–500 Hz band pass filter and increases the gain so that LF noise and rumble can be measured. Position 3 provides for flat velocity response, a 500 Hz–15 kHz band pass filter, and a 50-dB increase in gain so that HF noise can be assessed. In positions 2 and 3 a limiter protects the metering and monitoring circuits from overload. The system shown here is one channel of a stereo pair.

at inner diameters are called *scanning losses*, and deformation of the disc material contributes to them.

In earlier days there was some attempt made to boost high frequencies at inner diameters to compensate for these losses, usually at the expense of increased distortion. Today, no attempt is made to do this, and it is customary to calibrate the transfer system at outer diameters, allowing the response at inner diameters to roll-off as it will.

A block diagram of a typical disc measurement system is shown in Figure 10-28.

More elaborate calibration methods for disc systems include various optical methods, including the Buchman-Meyer technique and optical interferometry techniques. Neither of these techniques is suitable for routine system calibration. Interferometry techniques are expensive and are used only in analysis and design of stereo cutting heads.

RECORD PROCESSING

The processing of a master lacquer disc through the various metal-to-metal replication operations and finally to the vinyl pressing is a very intricate one involving many disciplines. The basic operations in the *three-step* process are shown in Figure 10-29.

Treatment of the Master Lacquer

The master lacquer is carefully inspected for any damage sustained in shipment. A common defect is the bleed-out of oils in the lacquer to the freshly cut surface; it can occur if the lacquer master was exposed to excessive heat during shipment. If the lacquer passes incoming inspection it is cleaned with a detergent, sensitized, and silvered. The silvering operation consists of precipitating metallic silver onto its surface by reduction of *silver nitrate*. If silvering is not properly done, the result can be "gritty" or "swishy" surface noise in the finished pressings.

The lacquer is then *preplated* at a low current density to build up a thin nickel surface on the silvered lacquer which is an accurate negative representation of the lacquer. Then the current density is increased to build up a substantial backing of nickel. The metal negative produced is called the *metal master*, and it is carefully separated from the lacquer.

Further Electroplating Processes

The metal master is cleaned and treated so that the next replication, the *metal mother*, can be grown by electroplating and separated from it. The metal

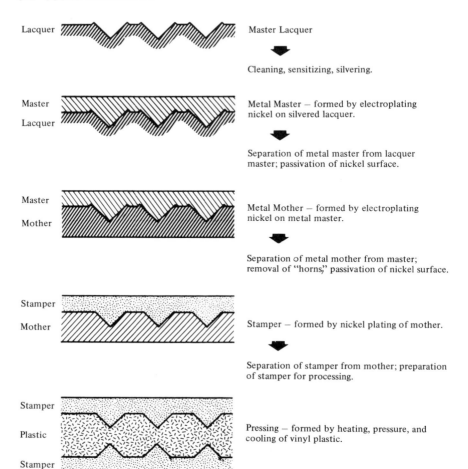

Figure 10-29. Representation of the three-step disc replication process.

mother is usually played throughout as the first verification of the audio quality of the transfer (master lacquers should never be played). If the mother is free of defects, *stampers* are electroplated from it in the same manner as before.

Preparation of Stampers and the Pressing Cycle

Stampers are ground on the back so that they will fit snugly against the press mold. The edges are crimped and the part carefully centered. They are then mounted into the press. The pressing cycle begins by placing a charge of hot

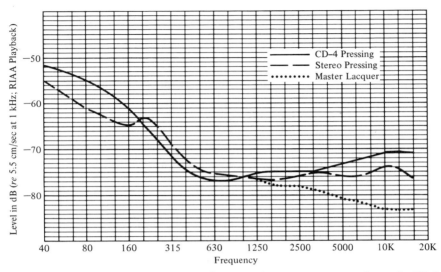

Figure 10-30. Third-octave noise spectra of a master lacquer, a stereo pressing, and a CD-4 pressing.

vinyl plastic between the stampers in the press along with the labels. Pressure and heat are then applied and the plastic is molded to conform to the stampers. When molding is completed, cold water is run through channels in the press mold, cooling the record so that it can be removed from the press without warping. The remaining plastic around the edge of the disc, referred to as "flash," is then trimmed off, and the process is finished.

The manufacturing process inevitably results in an increase in noise in the pressed record as compared to the lacquer original, as shown in Figure 10-30.

BIBLIOGRAPHY

1. D. Braschoss, "Disk Cutting Machine–Computer Controlled," *Radio Mentor* (October 1966).
2. J. M. Eargle, "Record Defects," *Stereo Review* (June 1971).
3. J. M. Eargle, "Performance Characteristics of the Commercial Stereo Disc," *J. Audio Eng. Soc.*, vol. 17, no. 4 (1969).
4. E. C. Fox and J. G. Woodward, "Tracing Distortion–Its Cause and Correction in Stereo Disc Recording," *J. Audio Eng. Soc.*, vol. 11, no. 4 (1963).
5. T. Inoue, "A Discrete Four-Channel Disc and Its Reproducing System," *J. Audio Eng. Soc.*, vol. 19, no. 7 (1971).
6. R. Narma and N. Anderson, "A New Stereo Feedback Cutterhead System," *J. Audio Eng. Soc.*, vol. 7, no. 4 (1959).

7. C. S. Nelson and J. W. Stafford, "The Westrex 3D Stereo Disk System," *J. Audio Eng. Soc.*, vol. 12, no. 3 (1964).

8. O. Read and W. Welch, *From Tin-Foil to Stereo* (Howard W. Sams, Indianapolis, 1958).

9. J. W. Stafford, "Maximum Peak Velocity Capabilities of the Disc Record," *J. Audio Eng. Soc.*, vol. 8, no. 3 (1960).

10. J. G. Woodward and E. C. Fox, "A Study of Program-Level Overloading in Phonograph Recording," *J. Audio Eng. Soc.*, vol. 11, no. 1 (1963).

APPENDIX I
Useful Equations and Mathematical Relationships

A. INEQUALITIES

$a > b$	a greater than b
$a \geqslant b$	a equal to or greater than b
$a >> b$	a much larger than b
$a < b$	a less than b
$a \leqslant b$	a equal to or less than b
$a << b$	a much less than b
$a \approx b$	a approximately equal to b
$a \neq b$	a not equal to b

B. ALGEBRAIC RELATIONSHIPS

$$a^x a^y = a^{(x+y)}$$

$$\frac{a^x}{a^y} = a^{(x-y)}$$

$$(ab)^x = a^x b^x$$

$$\left(\frac{a}{b}\right)^x = \frac{a^x}{b^x}$$

$$\sqrt[x]{\frac{a}{b}} = \frac{\sqrt[x]{a}}{\sqrt[x]{b}}$$

$$a^{-x} = \frac{1}{a^x}$$

$$(a^x)^y = a^{xy}$$

$$\sqrt[x]{\sqrt[y]{a}} = \sqrt[xy]{a}$$

$$\sqrt[x]{ab} = \sqrt[x]{a}\ \sqrt[x]{b}$$

$$a^{x/y} = \sqrt[y]{a^x}$$

$$a^{1/x} = \sqrt[x]{a}$$

$$a^0 = 1$$

Quadratic equations in the form

$$ax^2 + bx + c = 0$$

may be solved as follows:

$$x = \frac{-b \pm \sqrt{b^2 - 4ac}}{2a}$$

C. LOGARITHMS

Definition. If $a^x = y$, then x is the logarithm of y to the *base* a; or:

$$\log_a y = x$$

This also implies:

$$\text{antilog}_a x = a^x = y$$

The term "log" implies $a = 10$, the base of the *common* log system, and the term "ln" implies $a = e$, the base of the *natural* log system. ($e = 2.718281828 \cdots$.)
Properties:

$$\log xy = \log x + \log y$$

$$\log x/y = \log x - \log y$$

$$\log x^y = y \log x$$

$$\log \sqrt[y]{x} = (1/y) \log x$$

D. DECIBEL VALUES FOR VOLTAGE, CURRENT, SPL, AND POWER RATIOS

dB	Voltage, Current, or SPL Ratio	Power Ratio
0	1.000	1.000
0.1	1.012	1.023
0.2	1.023	1.047
0.3	1.035	1.072
0.4	1.047	1.096
0.5	1.059	1.122
0.6	1.072	1.148
0.7	1.084	1.175
0.8	1.096	1.202

dB	Voltage, Current, or SPL Ratio	Power Ratio
0.9	1.109	1.230
1.0	1.122	1.259
1.5	1.189	1.413
2.0	1.259	1.585
2.5	1.334	1.778
3.0	1.413	1.995
3.5	1.496	2.239
4.0	1.585	2.512
4.5	1.679	2.818
5.0	1.778	3.162
5.5	1.884	3.548
6.0	1.995	3.981
6.5	2.113	4.467
7.0	2.239	5.012
7.5	2.371	5.623
8.0	2.512	6.310
8.5	2.661	7.079
9.0	2.818	7.943
9.5	2.985	8.913
10	3.162	10.00
11	3.55	12.6
12	3.98	15.9
13	4.47	20.0
14	5.01	25.1
15	5.62	31.6
16	6.31	39.8
17	7.08	50.1
18	7.94	63.1
19	8.91	79.4
20	10.00	100.0
30	3.16×10	10^3
40	10^2	10^4
50	3.16×10^2	10^5
60	10^3	10^6
70	3.16×10^3	10^7
80	10^4	10^8
90	3.16×10^4	10^9
100	10^5	10^{10}
110	3.16×10^5	10^{11}
120	10^6	10^{12}

E. TRIGONOMETRIC RELATIONSHIPS

Definition of the functions:

sine a $(\sin a) = y/r$

cosine a $(\cos a) = x/r$

tangent a $(\tan a) = y/x$

cosecant a $(\csc a) = 1/\sin a$

secant a $(\sec a) = 1/\cos a$

cotangent a $(\cot a) = 1/\tan a$

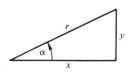

For any angles a and b:

$\sin^2 a + \cos^2 a = 1$

$\tan a = \sin a/\cos a$

$\sin (a \pm b) = \sin a \cos b \pm \cos a \sin b$

$\sin 2a = 2 \sin a \cos a$

$\cos 2a = \cos^2 a - \sin^2 a$

$\sin a \cos b = \frac{1}{2} [\sin (a + b) + \sin (a - b)]$

F. OHM'S LAW

$$E = \sqrt{WR}, \quad E = \frac{W}{I}, \quad E = IR$$

$$W = \frac{E^2}{R}, \quad W = I^2 R, \quad W = EI$$

$$I = \frac{E}{R}, \quad I = \frac{W}{E}, \quad I = \sqrt{\frac{W}{R}}$$

$$R = \frac{E}{I}, \quad R = \frac{E^2}{W}, \quad R = \frac{W}{I^2}$$

G. ELECTRICAL COMPONENTS IN SERIES AND PARALLEL

For two resistors in parallel:

$$R_T = \frac{R_1 \cdot R_2}{R_1 + R_2}$$

$$R_2 = \frac{R_1 \cdot R_T}{R_1 - R_T}$$

For n resistors in parallel, the total resistance, R_P, is:

$$R_P = \frac{1}{\dfrac{1}{R_1} + \dfrac{1}{R_2} + \dfrac{1}{R_3} \cdots + \dfrac{1}{R_n}}$$

For n resistors in series, the total resistance, R_s, is:

$$R_s = R_1 + R_2 + R_3 \cdots + R_n$$

For n capacitors in series, the total capacitance, C_s, is:

$$C_s = \frac{1}{\dfrac{1}{C_1} + \dfrac{1}{C_2} + \dfrac{1}{C_3} \cdots + \dfrac{1}{C_n}}$$

For n capacitors in parallel, the total capacitance, C_p, is:

$$C_p = C_1 + C_2 + C_3 \cdots + C_n$$

For n inductors in series the total inductance, L_s, is:

$$L_s = L_1 + L_2 + L_3 \cdots + L_n$$

For n inductors in parallel the total inductance, L_p, is:

$$L_p = \frac{1}{\dfrac{1}{L_1} + \dfrac{1}{L_2} + \dfrac{1}{L_3} \cdots + \dfrac{1}{L_n}}$$

H. FACTORS, UNIT PREFIX, AND SYMBOLS

10^{12}	tera	T
10^{9}	giga	G
10^{6}	mega	M
10^{3}	kilo	k
10^{2}	hecto	h
10^{1}	deka	da
10^{-1}	deci	d
10^{-2}	centi	c
10^{-3}	milli	m
10^{-6}	micro	μ
10^{-9}	nano	n
10^{-12}	pico	p
10^{-15}	femto	f
10^{-18}	atto	a

Examples:

$$10^2 = 100$$
$$10^3 = 1000$$
$$10^4 = 10,000$$

etc.

$$10^{-1} = 0.1$$
$$10^{-2} = 0.01$$
$$10^{-3} = 0.001$$
$$10^{-4} = 0.0001$$

etc.

J. USEFUL CONVERSIONS

1 millimeter (mm) = 10^{-3} meter

1 micron (μ) = 10^{-6} meter

.001 inch (mil) = 25 μ

$$1 \ \mu = 40 \times 10^{-6} \ \text{inch} \ (\mu \text{inch})$$

APPENDIX II
Absorption Coefficients for Common Materials

SOUND ABSORPTION COEFFICIENTS OF GENERAL BUILDING MATERIALS AND FURNISHINGS

Complete tables of coefficients of the various materials that normally constitute the interior finish of rooms may be found in the various books on architectural acoustics. The following short list will be useful in making simple calculations of the reverberation in rooms.

Materials	Coefficients					
	125 Hz	250 Hz	500 Hz	1000 Hz	2000 Hz	4000 Hz
Brick, unglazed	0.03	0.03	0.03	0.04	0.05	0.07
Brick, unglazed, painted	0.01	0.01	0.02	0.02	0.02	0.03
Carpet, heavy, on concrete	0.02	0.06	0.14	0.37	0.60	0.65
Same, on 40 oz. hairfelt or foam rubber	0.08	0.24	0.57	0.69	0.71	0.73
Same, with impermeable latex backing on 40 oz. hairfelt or foam rubber	0.08	0.27	0.39	0.34	0.48	0.63
Concrete block, coarse	0.36	0.44	0.31	0.29	0.39	0.25
Concrete block, painted	0.10	0.05	0.06	0.07	0.09	0.08
Fabrics Light velour, 10 oz. per sq. yd., hung straight, in contact with wall	0.03	0.04	0.11	0.17	0.24	0.35
Medium velour, 14 oz. per sq. yd., draped to half area	0.07	0.31	0.49	0.75	0.70	0.60
Heavy velour, 18 oz. per sq. yd., draped to half area	0.14	0.35	0.55	0.72	0.70	0.65

Materials	Coefficients					
	125 Hz	250 Hz	500 Hz	1000 Hz	2000 Hz	4000 Hz
Floors						
Concrete or terrazzo	0.01	0.01	0.015	0.02	0.02	0.02
Linoleum, asphalt, rubber or cork tile on concrete	0.02	0.03	0.03	0.03	0.03	0.02
Wood	0.15	0.11	0.10	0.07	0.06	0.07
Wood parquet in asphalt on concrete	0.04	0.04	0.07	0.06	0.06	0.07
Glass						
Large panes of heavy plate glass	0.18	0.06	0.04	0.03	0.02	0.02
Ordinary window glass	0.35	0.25	0.18	0.12	0.07	0.04
Gypsum board, $\frac{1}{2}''$ nailed to 2 × 4's 16″ o.c.	0.29	0.10	0.05	0.04	0.07	0.09
Marble or glazed tile	0.01	0.01	0.01	0.01	0.02	0.02
Openings						
Stage, depending on furnishings	–	–	0.25–0.75		–	–
Deep balcony, upholstered seats	–	–	0.50–1.00		–	–
Grills, ventilating	–	–	0.15–0.50		–	–
Plaster, gypsum or lime, smooth finish on tile or brick	0.013	0.015	0.02	0.03	0.04	0.05
Plaster, gypsum or lime, rough finish on lath	0.02	0.03	0.04	0.05	0.04	0.03
Same, with smooth finish	0.02	0.02	0.03	0.04	0.04	0.03
Plywood paneling, $\frac{3}{8}''$ thick	0.28	0.22	0.17	0.09	0.10	0.11
Water surface, as in a swimming pool	0.008	0.008	0.013	0.015	0.020	0.025

ABSORPTION OF SEATS AND AUDIENCE
(Values given in sabins per person or unit of seating)

	125 Hz	250 Hz	500 Hz	1000 Hz	2000 Hz	400 Hz
Audience, seated, depending on spacing and upholstery of seats	2.5–4.0	3.5–5.0	4.0–5.5	4.5–6.5	5.0–7.0	4.5–7.0
Seats, heavily upholstered with fabric	1.5–3.5	3.5–4.5	4.0–5.0	4.0–5.5	3.5–5.5	3.5–4.5
Seats, heavily upholstered with leather, plastic, etc.	2.5–3.5	3.0–4.5	3.0–4.0	2.0–4.0	1.5–3.5	1.0–3.0
Seats, lightly upholstered with leather, plastic, etc.	–	–	1.5–2.0	–	–	–
Seats, wood veneer, no upholstery	0.15	0.20	0.25	0.30	0.50	0.50
Wood pews, no cushions, per 18″ length	–	–	0.40	–	–	–
Wood pews, cushioned, per 18″ length	–	–	1.8–2.3	–	–	–

In the Sabine reverberation time equation, the term $S\bar{\alpha}$ in the numerator represents total boundary absorption in an enclosure. The unit is the *sabin*, equal to one square foot (or meter) of totally absorptive area. In the Norris-Eyring equation the corresponding term is $-S \ln(1 - \bar{\alpha})$. The term $\bar{\alpha}$ is arrived at by using the expression given in Chapter 1, and absorption coefficients are taken from tables such as the ones given above.

The additional absorption due to people present in the enclosure is not determined from absorption coefficients but rather from tables indicating sabins per person.

EXAMPLE:

For a room of $V = 500,000$ ft^3, $S = 50,000$ ft^2, and $\bar{\alpha} = .25$ @ 500 Hz, using the Norris–Eyring equation:

$$T_{60} = \frac{(.05)(500,000)}{-(50,000)\ln(1 - .25)} = 1.75 \text{ seconds}$$

The additional effect of 100 persons in the room is calculated:

$$100 \times 5 \text{ sabins per person} = 500$$

The additional 500 *sabins* of absorption is added in the numerator:

$$T_{60} = \frac{(.05)(500,000)}{-(50,000)\ln(1 - .25) + 500} = 1.68 \text{ seconds}$$

Index